EGON SCHIELE
THE RADICAL NUDE

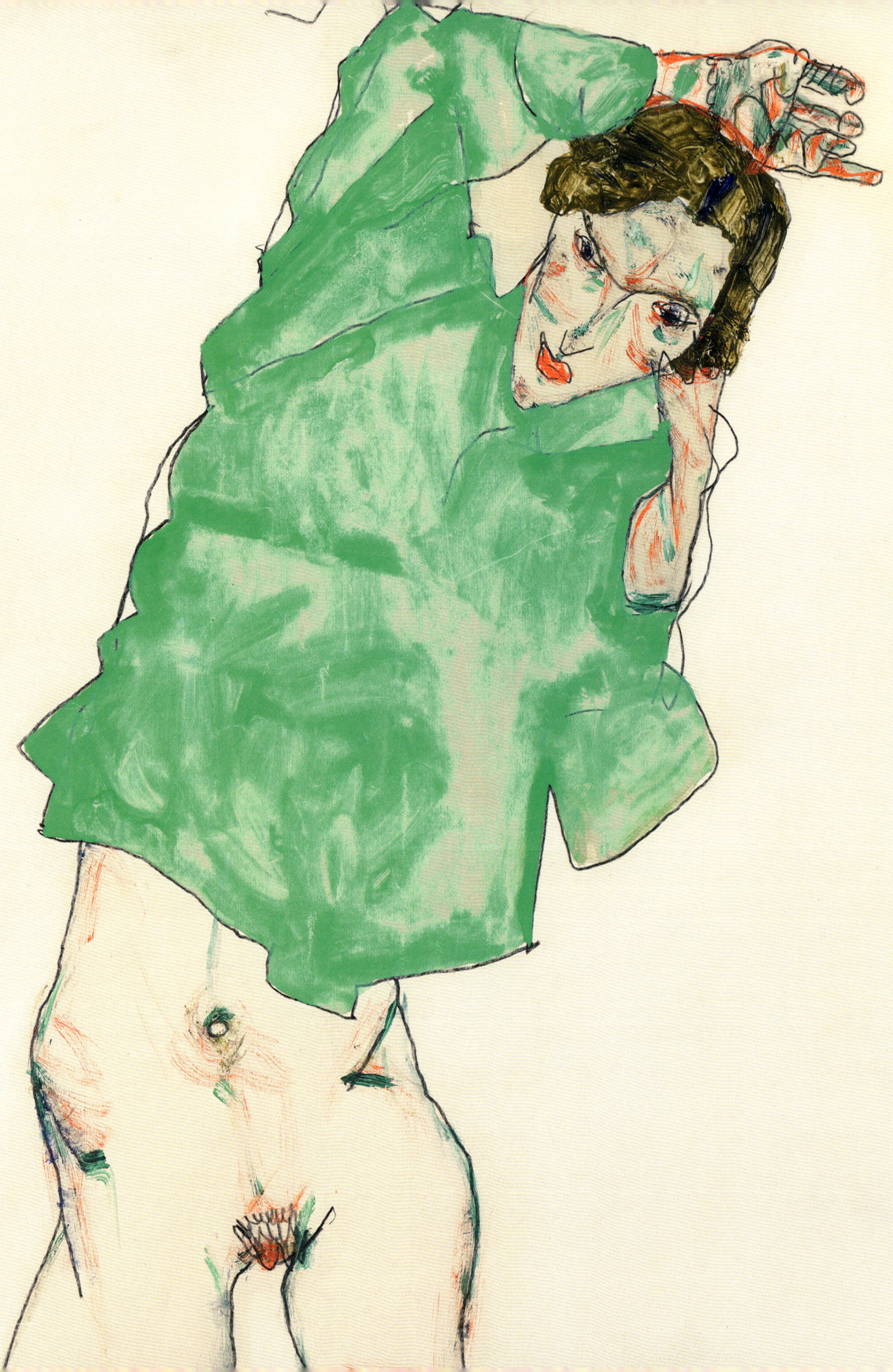

EDITED BY
Peter Vergo
Barnaby Wright

ESSAYS BY
Peter Vergo
Gemma Blackshaw
Kathryn Simpson

CATALOGUE BY
Peter Vergo

EGON SCHIELE
THE RADICAL NUDE

THE COURTAULD GALLERY
IN ASSOCIATION WITH
PAUL HOLBERTON PUBLISHING
LONDON

First published to accompany the exhibition

EGON SCHIELE
THE RADICAL NUDE

The Courtauld Gallery, London
23 October 2014 – 18 January 2015

The Courtauld Gallery is supported by the Higher Education Funding Council for England (HEFCE)

HIGHER EDUCATION hefce FUNDING COUNCIL FOR ENGLAND

ISBN 978 1 907372 69 8

British Library Cataloguing in Publication Data

A catalogue record for this book is available from the British Library

Produced by Paul Holberton publishing
89 Borough High Street, London SE1 1NL, UK
www.paul-holberton.net

Designed by Laura Parker
www.parkerinc.co.uk

Origination and printing by
E-graphic, Verona, Italy

Front cover: Egon Schiele, *Standing Nude with Stockings*, 1914 (cat. 29), detail
Back cover: Egon Schiele, *Erwin Dominik Osen*, 1910 (cat. 13)
Frontispiece: Egon Schiele, *Before the Mirror*, 1913 (cat. 28), detail
Page 12: Egon Schiele, *Nude Self-portrait in Grey with Open Mouth*, 1910 (cat. 16), detail
Page 30: Egon Schiele, *Standing Nude in Red Jacket*, 1913 (cat. 24), detail
Page 50: Egon Schiele, *Kneeling Male Nude with Raised Hand (Self-portrait)*, 1910 (cat. 10), detail
Pages 66–67: Egon Schiele, *Reclining Female Torso, Nude*, 1910 (cat. 20), detail

CONTENTS

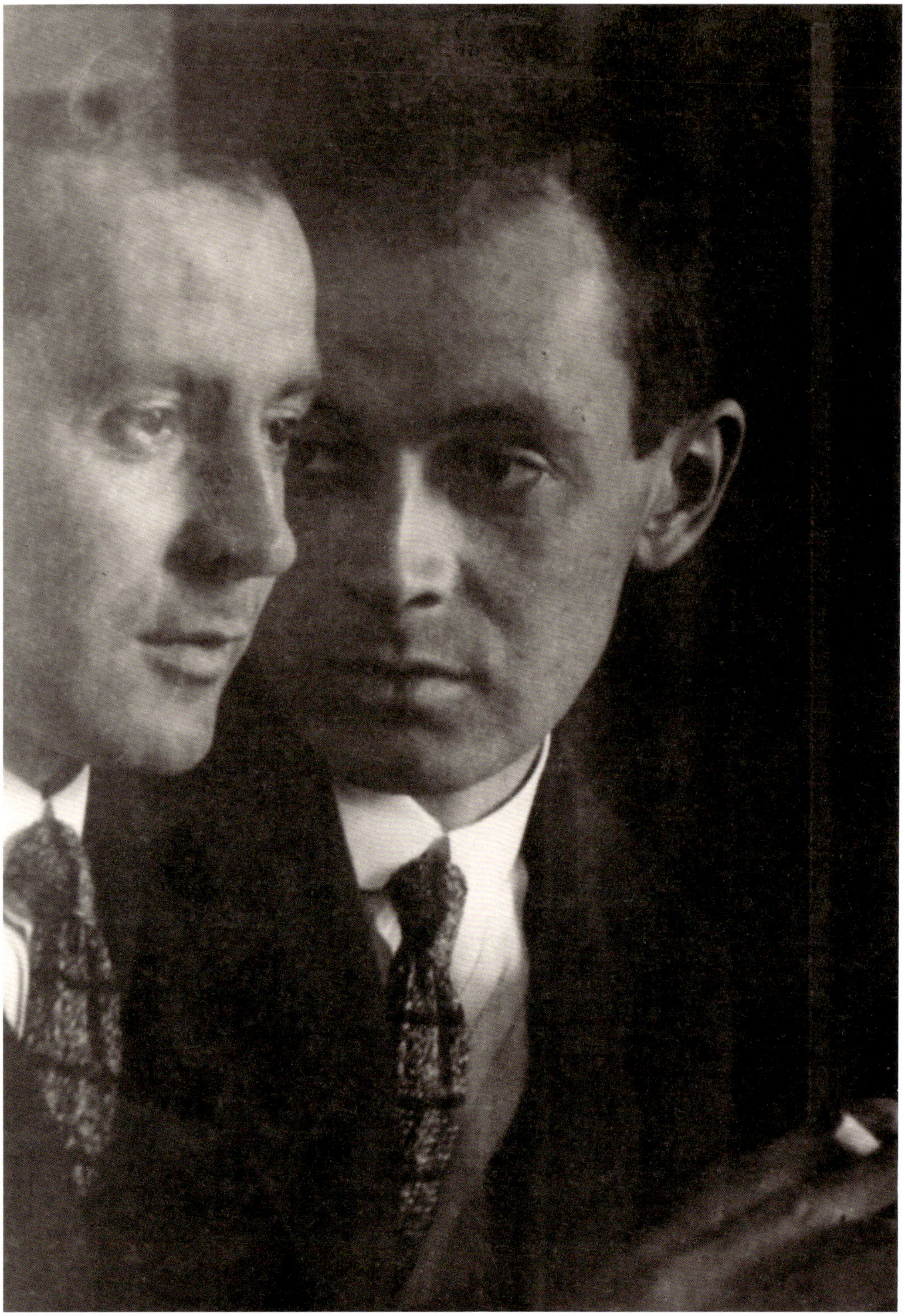

Egon Schiele in front of a mirror
(double self-portrait), c. 1914, photograph
Egon Schiele Archive, Albertina Museum, Vienna

FOREWORD

EGON SCHIELE is one of a small number of twentieth-century artists whose work, although self-evidently born of particular circumstances, has the power fully to transcend the constraints of period and style. Its impact and urgency is undimmed by the passage of a century. Viewers today perhaps respond most readily to the unflinching and apparently unmediated nature of Schiele's approach, an authenticity of psychological experience heightened by youth and precocious ability. Such an appreciation of Schiele's works as direct and profoundly self-expressive is in no way diminished by our simultaneous awareness of their self-conscious artistry and performative qualities.

It is remarkable to note that no public institution in the United Kingdom has devoted a monographic exhibition to Egon Schiele for over twenty years. Yet more striking is the fact that Schiele is almost entirely absent from our public collections. For The Courtauld Gallery to seek to address the former omission, and to permit itself the ambition of contemplating the latter, is not as strange as it may seem; The Courtauld has deep roots in Vienna, where Schiele's art was born. One of its very greatest benefactors, Count Antoine Seilern (1901–1978), lived in Vienna until 1939. He would later form a friendship with Schiele's contemporary Oskar Kokoschka, acquiring amongst other things the artist's first important graphic work, *The Dreaming Youths*, published in 1908. As well as a singular event, this exhibition is also a statement of our ongoing institutional commitment to this field.

Many individuals and institutions have helped us realise our ambition to organise this exhibition. First amongst them is undoubtedly The Leopold Museum in Vienna, which has contributed such an important group of loans. The encouragement of Elisabeth Leopold, in particular, has been essential and it is right that she should be the first in this honour roll. She recognised how this exhibition in London would continue the legacy of her husband, the late Rudolf Leopold, who played such a central role in the revival of interest in Schiele's work. Special thanks must also go to other good friends in Vienna: Tobias Natter, former director of The Leopold Museum; Franz Smola, current acting director, and Paul Asenbaum. I wish to extend my warm thanks to the other lenders, museums, but also the private owners who proved so willing to share their treasures with the wider public.

It is with no less gratitude that The Courtauld acknowledges the essential role of those who supported the exhibition in other ways. Martin Halusa not only helped nurture the original idea but was the decisive early benefactor of the project, setting it securely on its path. Richard Nagy's contribution was also vital. For many years his gallery has more or less been the sole home in London for Viennese art of around 1900. He gave the project his full support and helped to facilitate many important loans. We are enormously grateful to the AKO Foundation for its support and we are delighted to acknowledge the generosity of Marie and Joe Donnelly, Florian Härb and The Rothschild Foundation. Our thanks also go to Jane Kallir, author of numerous important publications on Schiele, and the Austrian Cultural Forum, London. The Friends of The Courtauld once again contributed generously.

It is a particular pleasure to acknowledge the two major sponsors of the exhibition: Lexington Partners and Swarovski, the famed producer of crystals whose Austrian heritage and commitment to creativity and design offered such an appealing point of contact. Both Lexington Partners and Swarovski were fundamental to making the exhibition possible. Our special thanks are due in particular to Marshall Parke and Nadja Swarovski.

Finally, my thanks go to the exhibition team and the authors of this handsome catalogue. Julia Blanks and George Mogg, the Gallery's registrars, navigated the complexities of administration and logistics with *sang-froid*. As curator of the exhibition Barnaby Wright, our Daniel Katz Curator of 20th Century Art, has added to an eye-catching list of projects which has been central to the success of the Gallery's exhibition programme. Eva Nijhof was a tireless advocate for the exhibition amongst our supporters, and Karin Kyburz organised the large quantities of images with her customary efficiency. I reserve my final thanks for Peter Vergo, who has contributed so substantially to the exhibition and catalogue. Professor Vergo has for many years been a leading scholar of early twentieth-century Austrian and German art and this project has benefitted enormously from his expertise and commitment.

Ernst Vegelin van Claerbergen
Head of The Courtauld Gallery

EXHIBITION SUPPORTERS

With grateful thanks to the following donors for their generous support

Sponsors

Lexington Partners SWAROVSKI

Benefactor

Martin Halusa

Supporters

AKO Foundation
Friends of The Courtauld
Marie and Joe Donnelly
Florian Härb
Jane Kallir (Co-Director, Galerie St. Etienne, New York)
Richard Nagy Ltd, London
The Rothschild Foundation
and those donors who wish to remain anonymous

ACKNOWLEDGEMENTS

THIS EXHIBITION has only been made possible by loans of exceptional works by Egon Schiele from the public institutions and private collections that have supported this project. The Courtauld Gallery would firstly like to thank The Leopold Museum, Vienna, for lending so generously to the exhibition. We extend our gratitude for other major loans to the Museum of Fine Arts, Budapest, The Museum of Modern Art, New York, the Wien Museum, Vienna, the Staatliche Graphische Sammlung, Munich, and the Germanisches Nationalmuseum, Nuremberg. Of equal importance to the exhibition are the works which have been lent by private owners and we offer our sincere thanks to each of them. We are most grateful to Richard Nagy for his support of the exhibition from an early stage and for helping to arrange many of the loans from private collections. Our thanks are also due to Patrick Legant for his assistance with additional loans for the exhibition.

The Courtauld Gallery wishes to record its sincere thanks to Peter Vergo for his extensive and invaluable work on this project, and to the other contributors to this publication, Gemma Blackshaw and Kathryn Simpson. We would also thank Barnaby Wright, Daniel Katz Curator of 20th Century Art at The Courtauld Gallery, for leading the curating of the exhibition and we extend our profound gratitude to Daniel Katz for his continued generous support of this position.

Many people have generously given advice and support at various stages in the development of this exhibition and publication. In particular, we would like to offer our warm thanks to Johann Thomas Ambrózy, Paul Asenbaum, László Baán, Szilvia Bodnár, Kathy Curry, Yasmin Doosry, Wolfgang and Ute Fischer, Andrea Glatz, Ulrich G. Großmann, Nina Hartl, Robert Holzbauer, Jane Kallir, Elisabeth Kögler, Johanne Lisewski, Glenn D. Lowry, Daniella Luxembourg, Nicola Mayr, Tobias Natter, Else Pruenster, Katrin Schmidt, Michael Semff, Franz Smola, Ursula Storch, Andreas Strobl and Anastasia Tennant.

Many people at The Courtauld have helped to bring this exhibition to fruition and particular thanks go to Graeme Barraclough, Louise Birrell, Julia Blanks, Sue Bond and her team, Stephanie Buck, Alice Clifford, Pierre Coulouma, Emma Davidson, Kate Edmondson, Alexandra Gerstein, Meghan Goodeve, Sarah Green, Henrietta Hine, the team at Kallaway (in particular, Tori Dance and Fiona Russell), Jack Kettlewell, Kate Knight, Karin Kyburz, Helen Martin Leake, Chloe Le Tissier, Caireen McGinn and her team, Eva Nijhof, Alice Odin, Anne Puetz, Karen Serres, Rachel Sloan, Jackie Sullivan, Deborah Swallow, Hannah Talbot, Lisa Tomlinson and Ernst Vegelin van Claerbergen. For their work on the production of this publication we would like to offer our thanks to Paul Holberton and Laura Parker.

This exhibition has been made possible by the provision of insurance through the Government Indemnity Scheme. The Courtauld Gallery would like to thank HM Government for providing indemnity and extends its thanks to the Department for Culture Media and Sport, and Arts Council England for administering the scheme.

SAMUEL COURTAULD SOCIETY

DIRECTOR'S CIRCLE

Anonymous
Andrew and Maya Adcock
Farah Asemi & Hassan Alaghband
Elke and Michael von Brentano
David G Broadhurst
Eva Bezelianskaia
I C Carr
Christie's
Mark and Cathy Corbett
Nicholas and Jane Ferguson
Mr Sam Fogg
The Garcia Family Foundation (U.K.) Limited
Sir Nicholas and Lady Goodison
Dr Martin Halusa
Mrs. Dana Høegh
Nick Hoffman
James Hughes-Hallett
Eugenia and Thomas Korossy
Daniella Luxembourg, London
Mr and Mrs Marks
The Honourable Christopher McLaren
John A. McLaren / AkzoNobel
Richard Nagy
Derek and Inks Raphael
Paul and Jill Ruddock
Sotheby's
Nicolai and Katja Tangen
John Watson and Betsy Blackwell
Niklas and Catherine Zennström

PATRONS' CIRCLE

Anonymous
Agnew's
Giancarla and Michael Alen-Buckley
Felix Appelbe
Mr Sandy Arbuthnot
Jean-Luc Baroni Ltd
John G. Bernasconi
Douglas Blausten
Julia Boadle
The Lord Browne of Madingley
James and Jennifer Butler
David and Jane Butter
John Byford
Julian and Jenny Cazalet
Mary Ellen Cetra
Mr Colin Clark
Robert Compton Jones
Daniel Katz Ltd
Samantha Darell
Amanda Deitsch and James Hochman
Roger and Rebecca Emery
Eykyn Maclean Ltd
David Gibbons
Richard Green (Fine Paintings)
Lucía V. Halpern and John Davies
Paula and Schuyler Henderson
Lady Heseltine
Joanna Hewitt
Jennifer Hicks
Andrew Hochhauser QC
Mike and Caroline Howes
David & Una Hudd
Philip Hudson
Monica Ishola
Nicholas Jones
Norman A. Kurland and Deborah A. David
Helen Lee and David Warren
Lefevre Fine Art
Professor Gerald Libby
Stuart Lochhead and Sophie Richard
Mark and Liza Loveday
Dr Chris Mallinson
Janet Martin
Mr Jay Massey
Clare Maurice
The Honourable Christopher McLaren
Norma and Selwyn Midgen
Edgar Miller
John and Jenny Murray
Mr Morton Neal CBE and Mrs Neal
Elizabeth Nicholson
John Nicoll and Laurence Colchester
Mr Michael Palin
Simon and Midge Palley
Lord and Lady Phillimore
Bridget Pinchbeck
Marie-Christine Poulain and Read Gomm
Leslie Powell
Tineke Pugh
Jacqueline Ranawake
Charles Rose
Lady Jennifer Rose
Sarah and Patrick Ryan
Mrs Janice Sacher
Dame Theresa Sackler
Philip Searl
Richard and Susan Shoylekov
Michael Smith, Barts Charity
William Slee and Dr Heidi Bürklin-Slee
Marjorie Stimmel
Sir Angus Stirling
Carlo Maria Suriano
Henry Tinsley
Johnny Van Haeften
Erik and Kimie Vynckier
The Rt. Hon. Nicholas & Lavinia Wallop
Richard West
George and Patricia White
Lynne Woolfson
Anita and Poju Zabludowicz

ASSOCIATES

Anonymous
Georgina Adam
Mrs Kate Agius
Lord Jeffrey Archer
Persephone Books
Mrs James Beery
Sarah Boardman
Henry and Maria Cobbe
Mr Oliver Colman
Elizabeth Courtenay-Stamp
Prisca and Andrew Cox
Camilla Davidson
Simon C. Dickinson Ltd.
Nova Dobb
Mr Andrew P Duffy
Ben Elwes Fine Art
David and Diane Frank
Mr Paul Green, Halcyon Gallery
Christopher J Gridley
Mrs Kathryn Gyngell
Edward Harley
Michael and Morven Heller
Mary G Herms
Cordula von Keller
Mr Timothy D Llewellyn
Raymond and Penelope Locke
Sophie Mallinckrodt
James McDonaugh
Virginia Morck
Philip Mould Ltd
Jim Moyes
Richard Oldfield
Desmond Page
Serena Prest
Geraldine Ramphal
The Lady Ridley of Liddesdale
Kristina Rogge
Eira Rojas
Mr Adrian Sassoon
Anna Somers Cocks
Rex De Lisle Stanbridge
Mr Robert Stoppenbach
Professor Deborah Swallow
Dr John Sweetman
Yvonne Tan Bunzl
Diana and John Uff
The Ulrich Family
The Weiss Gallery
Susan and Charles Whiddington
Hugh Wilson

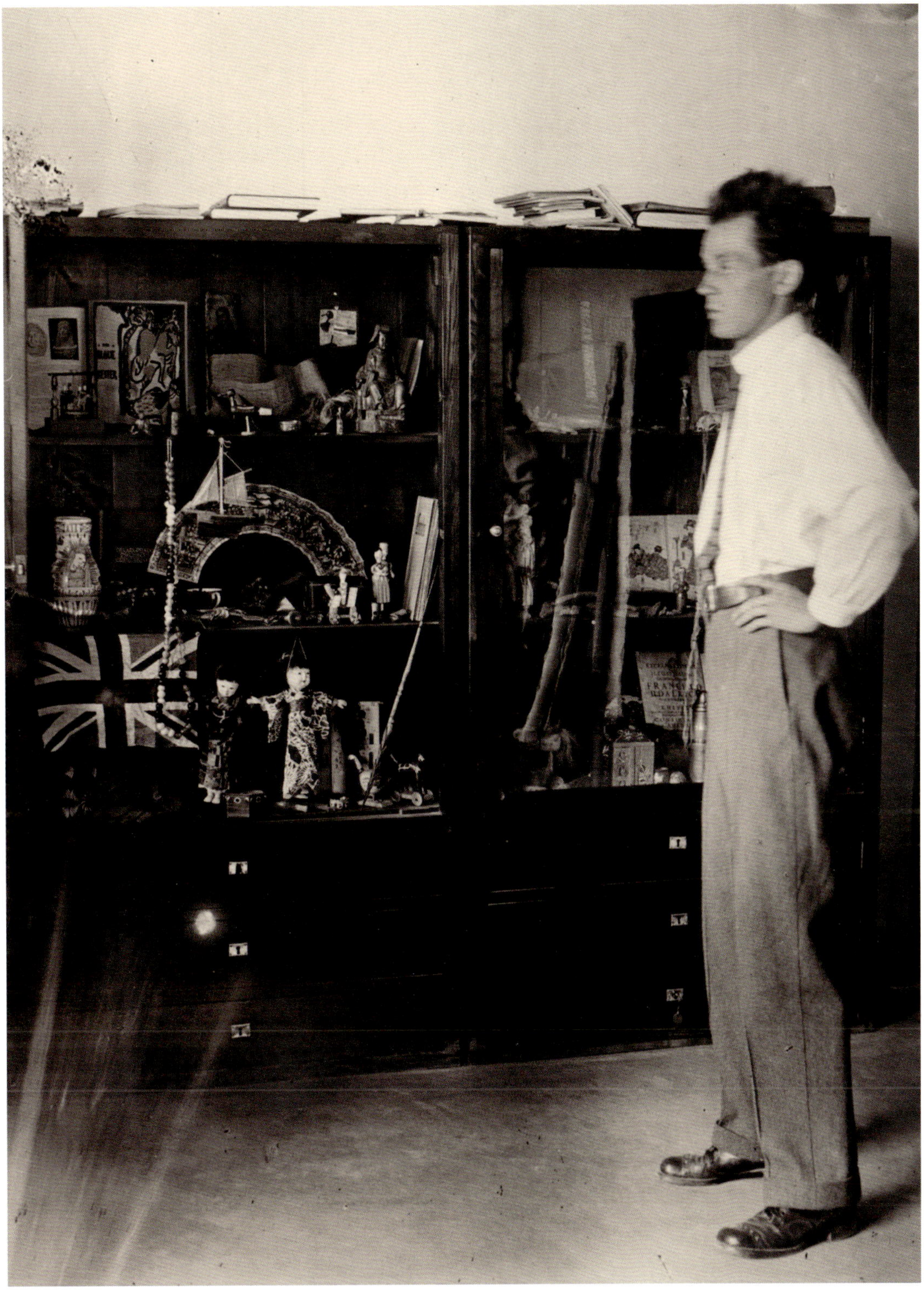

Egon Schiele with part of his collection, 1915,
photograph attributed to Johannes Fischer
Egon Schiele Archive, Albertina Museum, Vienna

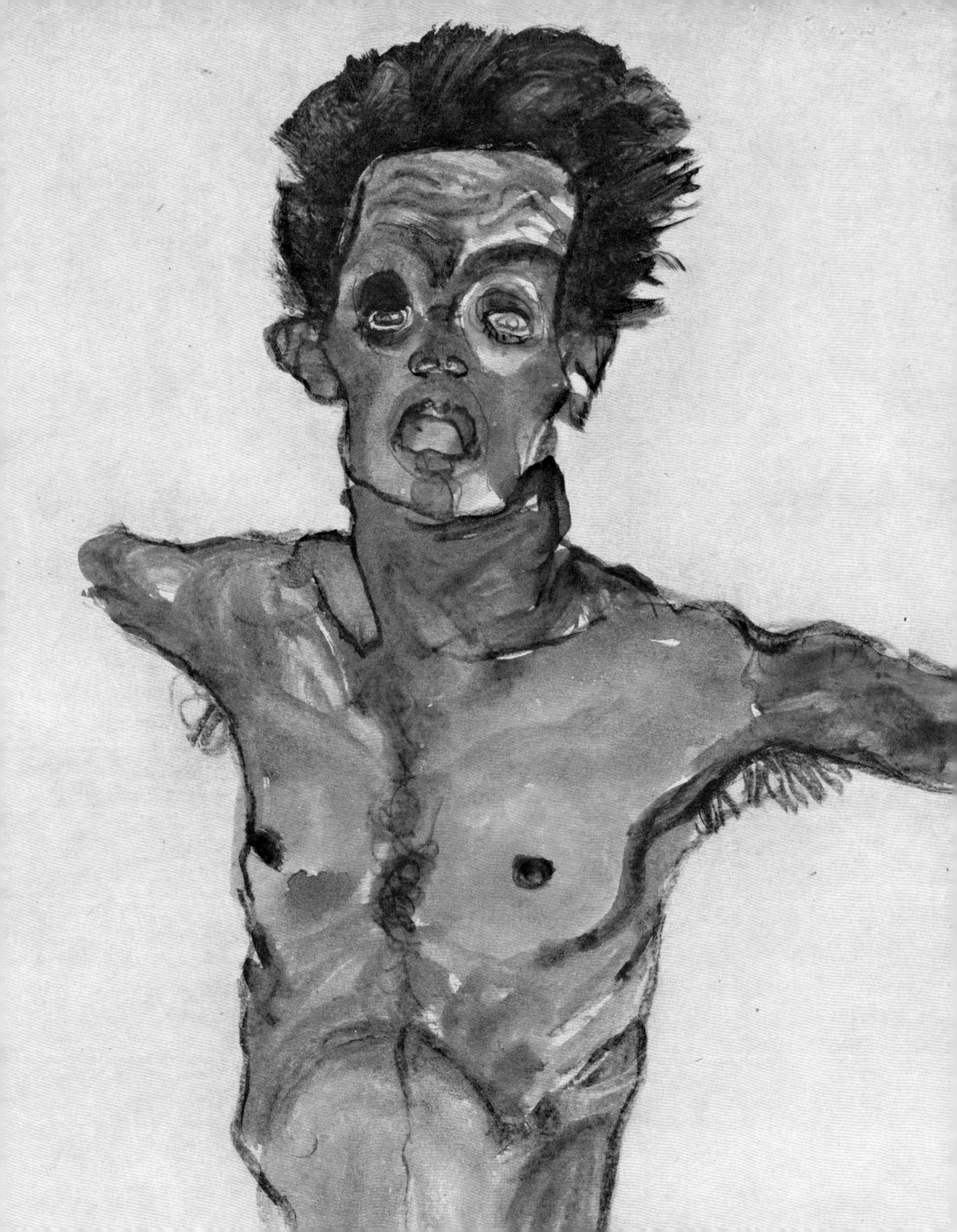

THE DEATH BENEATH THE SKIN

PETER VERGO

> Schiele has seen and painted the gem-cold eyes in human faces whose pallid sheen and sorrowful smiles resemble those of vampires starved of their grisly sustenance: faces that shimmer with the livid colours of putrefaction, and the death beneath the skin.
>
> **Arthur Roessler, review of Hagenbund exhibition, spring 1912[1]**

> The artist must be: the noblest of the noble, the most human and most responsive of beings. He must love death and love life.
>
> **Egon Schiele, 'Art and the New Artist', 1914[2]**

Visitors to the exhibition 'Egon Schiele: The Radical Nude' and readers of this catalogue may be surprised to discover that there is still no major work by Schiele in any British public collection. The general neglect that, until recently, has greeted him in this country contrasts starkly with the extent of his popularity elsewhere.[3] In most of Europe, the United States and Japan, his art has been widely collected, exhibited and written about. He has also been the object of a prolific myth-making industry that has resulted in sensationalised accounts of his life as well as novels and films.[4] For this, the artist himself must be held partly to blame. Anyone looking at the many artfully posed photographs of Schiele that have come down to us may well conclude that, whatever else was on his mind, this was someone unmistakably concerned with his own self-image, which he went to considerable lengths to propagate. In this, he was aided and abetted by several of his friends and contemporaries, including men of influence such as the critic and collector Arthur Roessler, whose portrait he painted in 1910 (fig. 2).[5] There is even a certain resemblance between the way Schiele depicts Roessler and the pose he himself adopts in one of those same photographs (fig. 1). Not only was the critic active in promoting Schiele during his lifetime; shortly after the artist's death in 1918 at the age of only 28, Roessler also published a memoir entitled 'Erinnerungen an Egon Schiele' (Recollections of Egon Schiele), in which many details were probably elaborated for the sake of a more vivid, at times even lurid story.[6] In addition, Schiele allegedly wrote a diary while awaiting trial in 1912 on the potentially serious charge of having had sex with a child, an accusation that was eventually dismissed.[7] This so-called 'Prison Diary', too, was posthumously published by Roessler, who is now thought to have written much of it himself, even if the text was perhaps partly based on what the artist said to him at the time.[8]

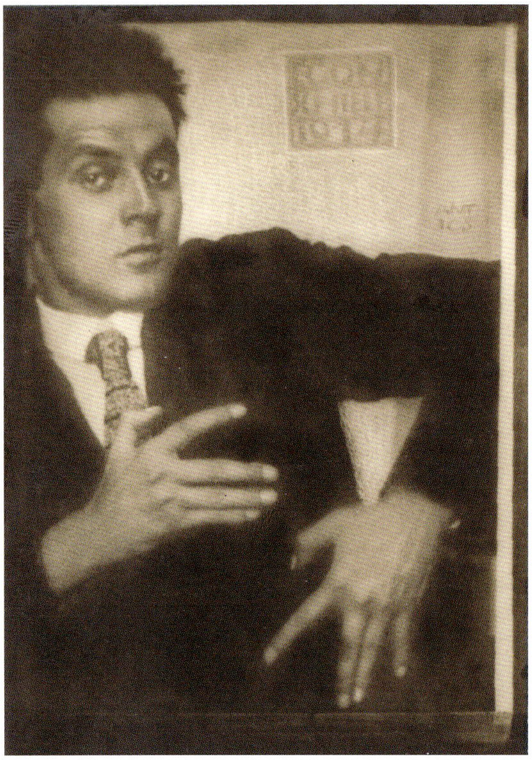

1
ANTON JOSEF TRČKA
Egon Schiele, 1914
Photograph
Egon Schiele Archive, Albertina
Museum, Vienna

VIENNA, CITY OF CLICHÉS

Since then, other writers have often been tempted to embroider stories about this celebrated *enfant terrible*, whose unconventional habits provided plenty of scope for creative fantasy. Added to which, the now vanished Habsburg Empire and its capital Vienna, where Schiele spent much of his life, when seen in retrospect have become more romantically alluring with each passing decade, and even some who could vividly remember the uncomfortable reality have assiduously perpetuated the consoling myth.[9] (Early twentieth-century Vienna, lest we forget, was a city where grinding poverty rubbed shoulders with ostentatious wealth, where a wartime Prime Minister could be murdered while lunching in a city centre restaurant and where, long before the horrors of Nazism were visited upon a hapless people, attacks on Jewish students attending lectures and classes at the university were commonplace.)[10] Stefan Zweig's *Die Welt von Gestern*, which paints a beguiling picture of ordered stability, and Arthur Schnitzler's *Jugend in Wien* are just two among many examples of this kind of myth making.[11] True, Zweig was well aware of the dark underworld of crime and prostitution that lay behind the "faultless, radiant façade" of the Austrian capital, which he describes together with social unrest and political tensions.[12] Schnitzler's account of his early years in Vienna also devotes a good deal of space to anti-Semitism and other forms of racial and political prejudice.[13] Yet one of his most sensitive commentators has remarked that even Schnitzler, a writer in many ways bound up with the distinctly dubious subterranean world that existed beneath that of pleasing but superficial appearances, subsequently became enmeshed in that same web of clichés that by now encompassed everything from the carefree charm of the Viennese waltz to the equally seductive melancholy of fin-de-siècle world-weariness.[14] More recent still is the acknowledgement that describing early twentieth-century Vienna in terms of these kinds of polar oppositions – dream and reality, appearance and substance, gaiety and despair – is itself yet another cliché.

In the essays and the catalogue entries that follow, I and my fellow contributors have tried to avoid regurgitating accepted 'truths' about a topic on which other writers have already expended an immense amount of literary and critical effort. In my case, I have endeavoured to view Schiele – himself just as much the object of mindless clichés as the city in which he lived – not through the rose-tinted spectacles of those still half in love with easeful myths regarding modern Viennese art and culture, nor from the more critical and analytical standpoint of those who favour a post-modernist account of art history.[15] Instead, I have to a large extent tried to see him through the eyes of his contemporaries – that is, through people who for the most part knew him well. Herein lies, of course, a danger already alluded to. Roessler

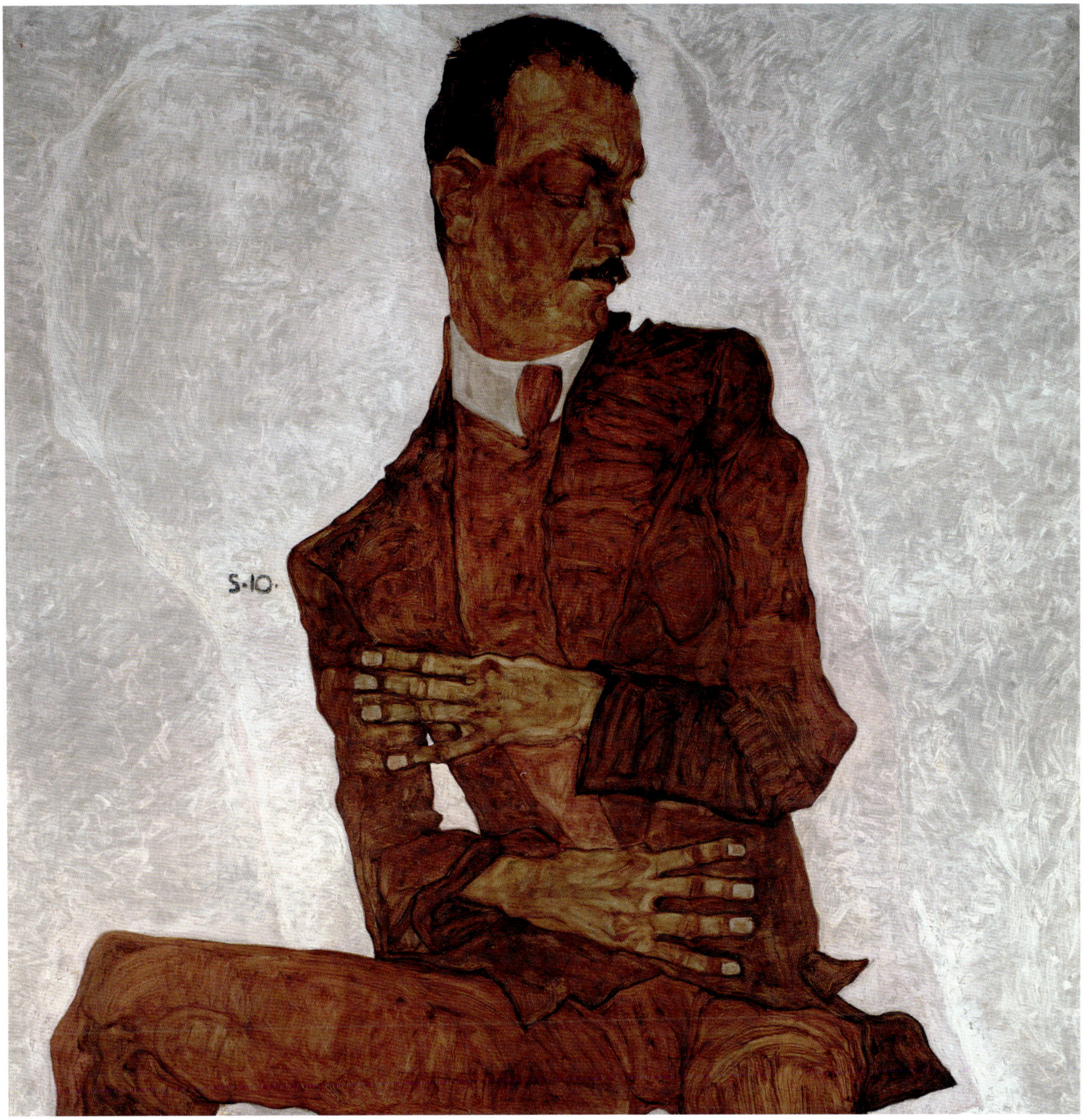

2
EGON SCHIELE
Arthur Roessler, 1910
Oil on canvas, 99.6 x 99.9 cm
Wien Museum, Vienna (Kallir P. 163)

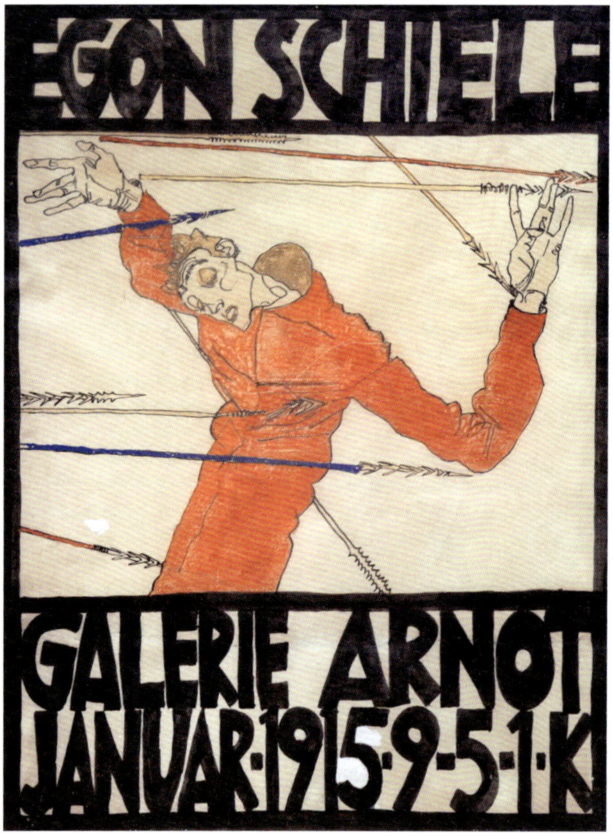

3
EGON SCHIELE
Poster design for his exhibition at the Galerie Arnot (*Self-Portrait as Saint Sebastian*), 1915
Wien Museum, Vienna

and others were undoubtedly complicit in fabricating an image of the artist-hero, misunderstood and persecuted for his art – an image given graphic form in the poster Schiele designed for his 1915 exhibition at Vienna's Galerie Arnot, which shows him in the guise of the early Christian martyr Saint Sebastian (fig. 3). Several of his self-portraits likewise imply an identification between his own image and that of Christ as the Man of Sorrows, a topos repeatedly invoked in some of the more recent literature on Schiele.[16] Only the very incautious would be willing to accept that such portrayals, like the words often put into the artist's mouth, should be taken at – in the most literal sense – 'face value'. At the same time, it must be acknowledged that Arthur Roessler, Heinrich and Otto Benesch and other friends and admirers of Schiele who wrote about his art were closer to his time than we are – closer, indeed, to the artist himself and thus more familiar with his way of thinking and expressing himself. Moreover, some of the best recent studies of Schiele have relied on a careful analysis of documents and other primary sources, which have shown that at least some of the stories told about him, although certainly embellished, were in essence true – that is, they can be proved to have a demonstrable basis in fact. Franz Wischin's close inspection of the evidence relating to Schiele's imprisonment in 1912 and subsequent trial is just one example of this kind of painstaking scholarship.[17]

As well as these kinds of material, we can turn to other, independent sources such as newspaper reviews in order to establish how the artist and, more important, his work were perceived and understood by his contemporaries. Of course, reviewers and critics are notoriously subjective and often have their own axes to grind. At least some of them were shocked by the subject-matter of Schiele's art – not only by overtly erotic (sometimes, in their terms, 'pornographic') depictions but also by what seemed to them an unhealthy obsession with topics such as mortality, sickness and death. Yet by no means all the critics who wrote about his art were hostile – another myth that has long since been laid to rest. By 1912, Schiele had already laid the foundations of an international reputation and had begun exhibiting abroad, for example at the Művészház (Artists' House) in Budapest and the epoch-making International Sonderbund exhibition in Cologne. By the time of his death in 1918, some reviewers at least were prepared to acknowledge him as the pre-eminent representative of modern Austrian painting. Writing about the 49th exhibition of the Vienna Secession, which included an important group of works by Schiele and for which he also provided the design for the poster, the unnamed critic of the *Wiener Abendpost* identified him as "following Klimt's death, the strongest and arguably the leading talent of the new tendency – or should one say tendencies, since there are now almost as many of these as there are individuals".[18]

DRAWING AS A WAY OF LIFE

While few would now question his outstanding abilities as a painter, another way of gaining a better understanding of Schiele is through a study of his numerous drawings in a variety of media – the focus of the present exhibition. His exceptional facility at drawing was evident at an early age. The apartment where he was born, the stationmaster's quarters overlooking the railway station at Tulln on the Danube, was soon filled with depictions of train tracks and locomotives he could see out of the window, delineated with extraordinary precision and an eye for minute detail. His speed of working was phenomenal. His father, station superintendent Adolf Schiele, who viewed the boy's precocious talent with some misgivings, was incensed to find that a bulky sketchbook he had given his son, which was meant to last him for several months, had been entirely filled up in only half a day. Other attempts to arrive at a compromise between schoolwork, which the young Schiele steadfastly neglected, and drawing, which became an obsession, proved equally unsuccessful.[19]

In later years, nearly everyone who visited the artist's studio remarked on his fluency as a draughtsman, his unerring confidence and his ability to execute a drawing in just a few rapid strokes. Accounts by Heinrich Benesch, one of his earliest patrons, and by Heinrich's son Otto, later director of Vienna's Albertina, both of whom posed for Schiele (see figs. 7 and 8), provide illuminating details of his working methods.[20] The elder Benesch was astounded to discover that Schiele habitually drew not only seated but also standing, with the drawing board resting on one knee, his left hand holding it in place while the drawing instrument (usually pencil, charcoal or black chalk), held in his unsupported right hand, would meet the paper almost vertically – "drawing from the shoulder, so to speak".[21] Corrections were virtually unknown. If , as happened very rarely, he made a mistake or was dissatisfied, he would throw the sheet of paper away. Or, as Otto Benesch observed, if the model shifted position during the course of a sitting, Schiele did not attempt to correct what he had already drawn but simply inscribed new lines and contours alongside the old ones.[22] However, only a small number of extant drawings betray alterations of this kind.[23]

Fluency and rapidity in drawing might well be thought desirable, indeed admirable qualities in a young art student. However, as Jane Kallir has pointed out, they did not endear Schiele to his teacher at Vienna's Academy of Fine Arts, the arch-conservative Christian Griepenkerl. Especially irritating was Schiele's habit of repeatedly missing classes and then turning up just before an assignment was due and dashing off a series of dazzling studies, to the despair of other students who had been working on the same exercise for hours.[24] On one occasion, he apparently produced entirely from memory a detailed and wholly accurate depiction of Vienna's Franz-Josephs-Bahnhof, a railway station he knew well, since it was from there that trains departed for Tulln.[25] Although the young Schiele was by all accounts shy and reticent, his very presence was considered disruptive. By the time he and some of his fellow students at the Academy declared their independence by exhibiting together as the Neukunstgruppe (New Art Group) at the end of 1909, the break with their teacher was complete.[26] Griepenkerl washed his hands of them; at the time of Schiele's departure from the Academy, he allegedly begged his former pupil: "For God's sake never tell anyone you studied with me!"[27]

Despite his obvious lack of affection for his teacher, Schiele did in fact owe a certain amount to Griepenkerl's classes. For one thing, his obsession with speed was almost certainly underlined by Gripenkerl's insistence on timed drawing exercises. His sister Gertrude, who often posed for him during the years around 1909–10, remembered his preoccupation with time and frequent recourse to a stop-watch.[28] For another,

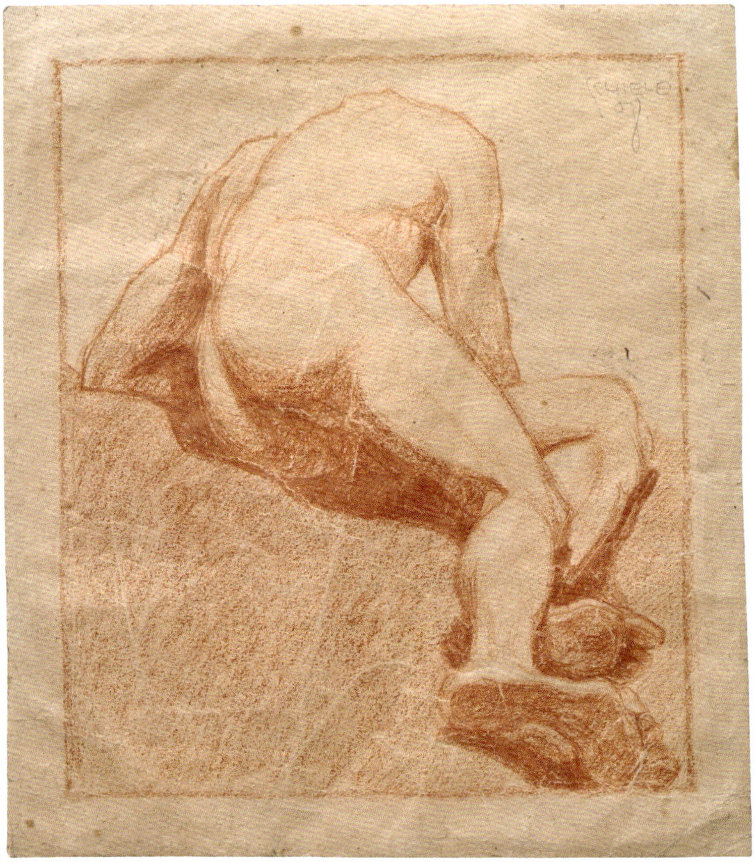

4
EGON SCHIELE
Male Nude (Study), 1908
Red chalk, 25 x 22.5 cm
Gradisch collection, Egon Schiele Museum, Tulln (Kallir D. 227)

the conventional academic routine of life drawing and copying from plaster casts is likely to have focused his attention on the subject he would treat more frequently than any other, the human body.

THE EXPRESSIVE NUDE

In his paintings and drawings, Schiele tackled just about every imaginable kind of subject-matter – landscapes and townscapes, interiors, still life and flowers, as well as a wide variety of depictions of the human figure including religious and allegorical subjects. But by far the greatest number of his drawings are devoted to the nude, not just studio models but pregnant women, mothers and babies, nude portraits and self-portraits, even dead bodies. One aim of our exhibition and its accompanying catalogue is to convey an impression of the extraordinary range and diversity of his works of this kind.

Some of Schiele's earliest nude studies demonstrate a high degree of technical competence but betray little by way of passion or real engagement with the subject (see fig. 4) – the result, almost certainly, of his disenchantment with his studies at the Vienna Academy. But from 1909 onwards, freed from any kind of academic strictures, he began to show an increasing, even obsessive interest in the expressive potential of the human figure. The nude models who posed in front of drawing classes at the Academy were often called upon to strike attitudes or mimic facial expressions traditionally associated with profound emotions like grief or anger. In this way, students were meant to acquire a vocabulary of visual forms that would serve the ends of narrative history painting, traditionally the most exalted genre to which a young artist could aspire.

However, Schiele's nude figure studies from 1910 onwards are quite alien to anything that can be understood solely in terms of the academic tradition. It has been suggested that, through his friendship with Max Oppenheimer, a painter better read and more intellectually inclined than Schiele, he may have been alerted to investigations conducted by psychologists Sigmund Freud and Josef Breuer which posited an association between convulsive gestures and psychological states.[29] The exaggerated poses and expressive hand gestures found in some of Schiele's self-portraits and in his portraits of other people – for example, the mime artist Erwin Osen (see cat. 13 and 14) – have been cited as evidence of his interest in such ideas. However, there is no proof that Schiele ever read any of Freud's scientific work or was even aware of it. Nor should we count on his having been an avid reader of Nietzsche, even though the climate of thought in Vienna at that time was pervaded by Nietzschean ideas, as Kathryn Simpson's essay in this catalogue on the 'Dionysian' artist ably demonstrates.[30] Gemma Blackshaw has suggested that Schiele's depictions of what she calls the 'body-in-pain' in his works of c. 1910–11 are more likely to have been influenced by images of patients in convulsive states or suffering from physical deformities reproduced in the illustrated journals of the Salpêtrière in Paris, well-known in Viennese medical circles.[31] If he did have access to this kind of material, it was probably through his friendship with the gynaecologist Dr. Erwin von Graff, who allowed the artist to draw and paint in the Frauenklinik (Women's Clinic) of Vienna University (see cat. 5 and 6).

Equally relevant and perhaps more reliable is the testimony provided by some of Schiele's contemporaries, who remembered how, as a young man, he was captivated by cabaret theatre and especially by dance.[32] Whereas traditional spoken theatre relies in the first instance on the power of words and only secondarily (albeit importantly) on gesture and movement, dance depends above all on bodily movements, although music, lighting, stage design and other constituent elements all contribute. During his first years in Vienna, nearly all the leading avant-garde dance practitioners visited the city, from Isadora Duncan via Loïe Fuller to Ruth St Denis. Schiele seems to have been especially taken with St Denis's performances, which he saw at the Ronacher variety theatre on Vienna's Seilerstätte. According to his biographer Fritz Karpfen, he contrived to meet the dancer, whose distinctive form of expressive movement particularly entranced him. In his illuminating article 'Attitudes and Gestures as Reflections of the Conception of Gender', Alexander Klee draws a parallel between Schiele's treatment of the human figure, especially the angular poses repeatedly captured in some of his nude studies, and the Viennese dramatist Hugo von Hofmannsthal's essay on pantomime.[33] Again, it is unlikely that Schiele read this essay, which did not appear until 1911 and then only in a German (rather than Viennese) periodical. However, Hofmannsthal had already pointed to the limitations of language in his earlier 'Letter from Lord Chandos', published in 1902. In either case, the similarities between the artist's and writer's conceptions of the expressive potential of both movement and dance are indeed striking. (From passing references to Nijinsky and – once again – Ruth St Denis in his essay on pantomime, it is obvious that the author also had dance clearly in mind.) Hofmannsthal writes about modern artists' compulsion to breathe new life into ancient forms and about the capacity of antique art

> to sum up a state of mind in a pose, in the rhythmic repetition of movements, thereby expressing our

relationship to the people around us in a form more concise, more pregnant with meaning than language is capable of doing, to bring to light something too grandiose, too universal, too immediate to be captured in words.[34]

During 1910, Schiele repeatedly depicted Osen's companion, the dancer Moa, whose slender outline and arresting features we can recognise from an old photograph showing the two of them apparently enacting a costumed play or pantomime (fig. 5). He also made a series of nude studies of Osen himself, usually striking a pose or gesturing. There are numerous affinities between these nude portraits and Schiele's depictions of his own body, among them the recurrence of the same expressive hand gestures, at times resembling an occult sign language whose meaning we can no longer decipher. But beyond these perhaps superficial similarities there exists a further resemblance between Schiele's depictions of Osen's body and his own, what one writer has called an "eerie, disquieting exaggeration" in the representation of the human form.[35] Equally disquieting is the realisation that, for Schiele, Osen's body appears to be an object of scarcely disguised erotic interest.

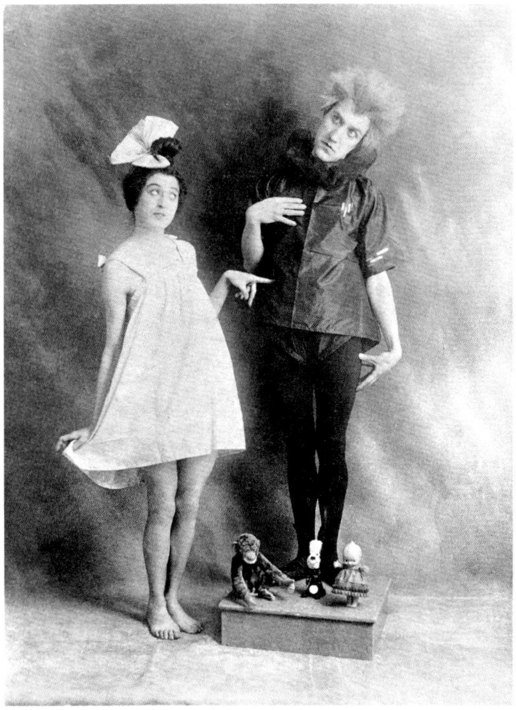

5
UNKNOWN PHOTOGRAPHER
Erwin Osen and the Dancer Moa,
c. 1910
Photograph
Egon Schiele Archive, Albertina
Museum, Vienna

THE RADICAL NUDE

In a penetrating study of Schiele's works on paper, gallerist and art historian Jane Kallir writes about the different, sometimes conflicting aspects of his self-portraits of the period during which he first attained artistic (if not emotional) maturity:

> In 1910, most of Schiele's feelings – sexual and otherwise – were focused on himself. The proliferation of self-portraits from this period can be likened to a kind of pictorial masturbation .... In addition to their ambiguous, abstracted sexuality, Schiele's 1910 self-portraits can also be shockingly ugly. At times, the artist resembles a corpse, with sunken eyes and a shrunken torso. Elsewhere, he grimaces ferociously or gesticulates wildly. And then again, he can be beautiful (as in reality he was and knew himself to be): preening, elegant and self-satisfied. Schiele was simultaneously probing his inner feelings and trying on a multitude of selves.[36]

This concise and evocative piece of writing summarises in one brief paragraph three defining characteristics of Schiele's self-portraiture that are essential to any understanding of his art. The first is its allusive or theatrical aspect – the artist's penchant for histrionics and role play, his tendency to adopt disguises or assume fictive identities. These included not only those of saint or martyr, as in the Saint Sebastian self-portrait mentioned earlier, but also of the adolescent tormented by erotic fantasies, the dandy or man about town and the artist sick unto death who sacrifices himself for his art.[37] For the painter to portray himself in various roles or guises was, of course, nothing new: artists have always taken an evident delight in depicting themselves and others in a variety of costumed parts as figures from drama or literature, ancient history or even the Bible.

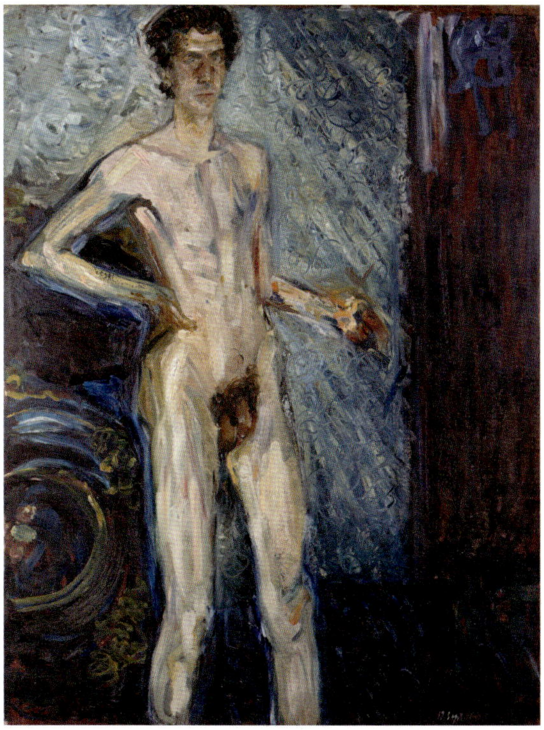

6
RICHARD GERSTL
Nude Self-Portrait with Palette, 1908
Oil on canvas, 140.5 x 119.5 cm
Leopold Museum – Privatstiftung, Vienna

More unusual in the history of art are nude portraits and self-portraits; among the latter, only the nearly contemporaneous *Nude Self-Portrait with Palette* by Austrian artist Richard Gerstl (fig. 6), a fellow student of Schiele's at the Vienna Academy, and (from several centuries earlier) Albrecht Dürer's nude portrait of himself spring readily to mind. Still more remarkable (and considerably more shocking) are Schiele's often gruesome depictions of his own flesh – the second aspect of his portraiture singled out by Kallir. Again and again, he paints limbs brutally truncated; in some cases, the entire torso appears to have been arbitrarily severed, with only the legs and abdomen remaining (see cat. 19). Far from being pink and healthy-looking, the flesh is mottled, with blues and purples predominating, like carcases seen hanging in a butcher's shop. Nor is it only his own body that he subjects to this kind of morbid, unsparing scrutiny. Confronted by his depictions of other people, some critics claimed to be horrified by what seemed to them his obsession with unhealthy subjects. Writing in Vienna's leading liberal newspaper, the *Neue Freie Presse*, about the spring 1912 exhibition of the Hagenbund, one reviewer alluded to Schiele's "sadistic-fantastic caricatures ... ghoulish lemurs with bloody spiders' fingers, deformed, half-decaying bodies, as if caught in a distorting mirror", at the same time acknowledging "these grotesque portrayals" as "the expression of a highly refined, playful virtuosity in drawing, a markedly individual feeling for colour".[38] But perhaps the most vivid evocation is to be found in Roessler's review of the same exhibition, where he wrote:

> For months he busied himself drawing and painting proletarian children. What fascinated him were the depredations wrought by the sordid sufferings to which these basically innocents were exposed. He marvelled at the curious changes in the skin, through whose flaccid vessels thin, watery blood and polluted juices trickle sluggishly; at the green eyes that avoided the light behind red-rimmed lids, the scrofulous finger joints and jaws, the slobbering mouths – and the souls that inhabit these ruined bodies.[39]

THE EROTIC NUDE

The third aspect of Schiele's depictions of the human figure highlighted by Kallir is possibly the most contentious – his preoccupation, bordering on obsession, with the topic of sexuality, both his own and other people's. Several of the artist's friends and champions were quick to defend him against any charge of pornography, an issue frequently raised in the Viennese press at that time.[40] Roessler dismissed as "beyond help" those people who could see "only obscenity" in the artist's depictions of nakedness. All Schiele wanted, according to Roessler, was to "achieve new conquests" for art.[41] The painter and writer Albert Paris von Gütersloh, in one of the first serious appreciations of his friend's work, wrote in similar vein, declaring that, even in the most shocking of Schiele's drawings

> the morbid, the vicious, the lewd aspect of a figure or line or gesture has, apart from its incidental meaning, a hidden meaning, like a cipher or shorthand character; in the artist's hurry to put it down on paper, it acquires an arbitrary significance and, when read together with other words, conveys a meaning that far surpasses anything one might suppose.[42]

In a sense they were right. Anyone who believes the principal aim of pornography is to arouse or titillate might argue that Schiele's nudes cannot be considered pornographic, because for many people there is little if anything titillating about them – "erotic representations without erotic content", in the words of one commentator.[43] The grimaces and convulsive gestures that characterise his depictions of himself masturbating, the diseased-looking flesh of children portrayed in deliberately provocative poses – all this seems to speak more volubly about the fear of sex rather than the joy of sex. Nevertheless, it can scarcely be denied that some of these poses are, indeed, provocative, while an exaggerated emphasis on erogenous zones such as nipples or pudenda, usually (though not invariably) achieved by the addition of a lurid red, characterises many of his drawings of children just as it does his studies of adult female models.

Several writers have maintained that Schiele, himself barely out of his teens and still preoccupied with his own sexuality, can scarcely be blamed for being equally fascinated by the sexuality of children, a topic that Freud had only recently explored in his *Three Essays on the Theory of Sexuality* of 1905. Thus (so the same argument goes) Schiele was merely reflecting the intellectual spirit of his times, or perhaps engaging through his art in a form of debate with his contemporaries – not only Freud but also writers such as Frank Wedekind – for whom the topic of adolescent sexuality was likewise a matter of absorbing interest. None of which quite succeeds in allaying our sense of unease when confronted not just by these explicit images but also by Roessler's remark about "proletarian children", quoted earlier.

Roessler was not alone in singling out this facet of Schiele's art. Other friends and acquaintances, too, commented in similar fashion. Anton Faistauer, likewise a founder-member of the Neukunstgruppe, described the Viennese suburbs with their "hunger, hatred and scowls", whose "tragic faces" stare disconcertingly at us from many of Schiele's early drawings.[44] Otto Benesch, too, alluded to the city's "proletarian district", by which he meant the urban periphery, whose "poverty" visibly characterised many of the young models who appear in those same drawings.[45] The truth of the matter was that down-and-out children, some of whom were almost certainly prostitutes, could easily be picked up off those grimy suburban streets and pacified with a few coins or perhaps just the promise of somewhere warm to stay. If, in reality, what that entailed was lolling around semi-naked while an artist drew and sketched, or even posing nude, it might still have seemed an acceptable bargain. What happened to them after that, no one seems to have cared very much – at least, not in Vienna.

DISASTER AT NEULENGBACH

However, in those days the morals of the big city and the *mores* of the Austrian countryside were very different. Even before what one might call the curious incident of the girl in the night-time, storm clouds had gathered on the horizon. In 1911, Schiele was forced to leave the Bohemian town of Krumau, his mother's birthplace, where he had intended spending the entire summer, because a local girl had been seen posing naked on the terrace of his rented garden cottage. His provocative behaviour had already alienated many of the townspeople; now, the scandal that ensued was enough to cause his landlord, one Max Tschunko, to demand his immediate eviction.[46]

Banished from the Garden of Eden, Schiele and his partner of those years, Wally Neuzil, again set up house together, this time on the edge of the small market town of Neulengbach, picturesquely situated amidst the Vienna Woods and less than an hour's train ride from the capital. But it soon proved to be a case of 'out of the frying pan and into the fire'. Many local residents belonged to the well-heeled bourgeoisie. Most of them probably kept quite a close eye on their children; certainly, they would not have countenanced their having anything to do with an outsider, worse still an artist, who, as soon became apparent, was openly co-habiting with his favourite female model. While you might have been able to persuade Viennese street urchins and 'proletarian' models to pose naked for you, it would have been sheer folly to attempt anything of the kind with children of the respectable inhabitants of Neulengbach. Nor is it likely that Schiele, still smarting from his experience in Krumau, ever seriously contemplated doing so – and especially not with a girl like Tatjana Georgette Anna von Mossig.

Tatjana was the teenage daughter of Theobald Ritter von Mossig, a retired officer in the merchant marine and former naval attaché.[47] The family rented an apartment in the country palace owned by the Princes Liechtenstein that occupies a dominant position immediately above the town. Whether Tatjana really turned up one night in the midst of a howling storm, telling Schiele and Wally that she had run away from home and insisting that they take her in, as Roessler claims in Schiele's 'Prison Diary', can no longer be verified. Benesch tells a different story, namely that the girl accosted Schiele and Wally on the platform of Neulengbach's railway station and demanded to be taken to Vienna to see her grandmother. What does appear certain is that Tatjana had indeed run away from home and that the local police, alerted by her father, had already instigated a 'missing persons' enquiry.

Thereafter, events took an ominous turn. Schiele was questioned on suspicion of child abduction, although it soon became obvious that there was no case to answer and the matter was dropped. He was, however, also suspected of sexual assault against a minor, so he was taken into custody and kept in the town gaol while investigations continued. Three weeks later, when tried at the district court in nearby St. Pölten, this charge, too, was dismissed for lack of evidence. However, the police who searched his studio had come upon a large cache of "indecent" drawings, which they confiscated. In Austria at that time, it was not an offence to be in possession of pornographic material; thus, a charge of making or keeping pornography did not arise. Unfortunately, Schiele appears to have allowed other local children to enter the house, thus giving them the opportunity of seeing one such drawing pinned up on the wall. This counted as an offence against public decency according to article 516 of the penal code, for which the artist was duly convicted and sentenced to 24 days' imprisonment. Because he had already spent 21 days in custody awaiting trial, the sentence was commuted to a further three days' detention. He was released on 7 May 1912.[48]

BEYOND SCANDAL

Schiele was evidently traumatised by his experience of prison. Just how anxious he was not to come into further conflict with the authorities may be judged from the fact that, after 1912,

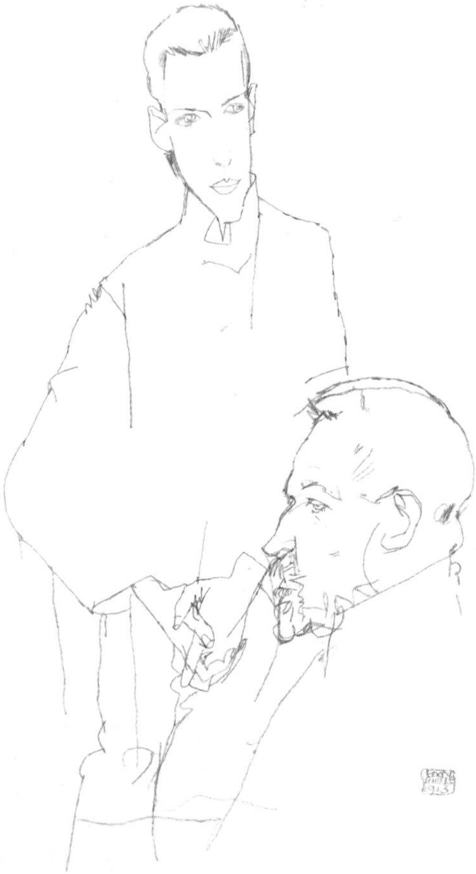

7
EGON SCHIELE
Heinrich and Otto Benesch, 1913
Pencil, 47 x 30.8 cm
Harvard University Art Museums,
Fogg Museum, Cambridge, Mass.
(Kallir D. 1403)

erotically charged depictions of children are almost entirely absent from his repertoire. He did not flinch from tackling what were, by the standards of his time, still taboo subjects such as female masturbation, nor does the wider topic of eroticism generally vanish from his art. But his manner of depicting erotic nudes now seems subtly different, closer to the contrived poses that characterised the nude photographs then widely (albeit surreptitiously) available, while lacking the sense of urgency that marked his earlier, often disturbing confrontations with the subject of child sexuality. This is not to suggest that he slavishly copied erotic photographs. On the contrary, he continued to draw and sketch mainly from life: indeed, both the elder and the younger Benesch insisted that Schiele invariably drew only in front of the model. However, from 1915 onwards his opportunities of doing so were more limited, for two reasons. In June of that year, having abandoned the faithful Wally in search of a more socially acceptable bride, he married Edith Harms, daughter of a railway employee, master locksmith Johann Harms.[49] Determined to keep a close eye on her potentially erring husband, Edith evidently put her foot down as regards the use of professional models, preferring if necessary to pose for him herself, although she appears to have been reluctant to adopt some more blatantly erotic poses, often hiding her face when these were demanded.

A more serious limitation on his artistic freedom was the fact that, within a few days of his wedding, Schiele was called up for military service. Unlike Oskar Kokoschka, who was seriously wounded on the Eastern front and who, as an official war artist, recorded incidents from the Italian campaign with shells bursting around him, Schiele spent the whole of the war in relative safely. Nevertheless, the tedious hours he spent on guard duty and the petty but time-consuming tasks he was given initially resulted in a dramatic decrease in his hitherto prolific output. Not until early 1917, with his transfer to the offices of the Imperial Military Supply Department, did he have the opportunity to draw and paint again more regularly, by which time both his style and his approach to the depicted subject had undergone a number of subtle but significant changes.

In his earlier drawings – for example, the small group of studies related to his magnificent 1913 double portrait of Heinrich and Otto Benesch (figs. 7 and 8) – outlines are often thin and precise. Here, line functions principally as contour; it is left to the viewer to imagine the plasticity and three-dimensionality of the two figures. Evidently, Schiele regarded highly finished drawings like these as independent works of art in their own right. They were also a useful source of income. Collectors like Benesch, whose financial resources were relatively modest, were more likely to acquire

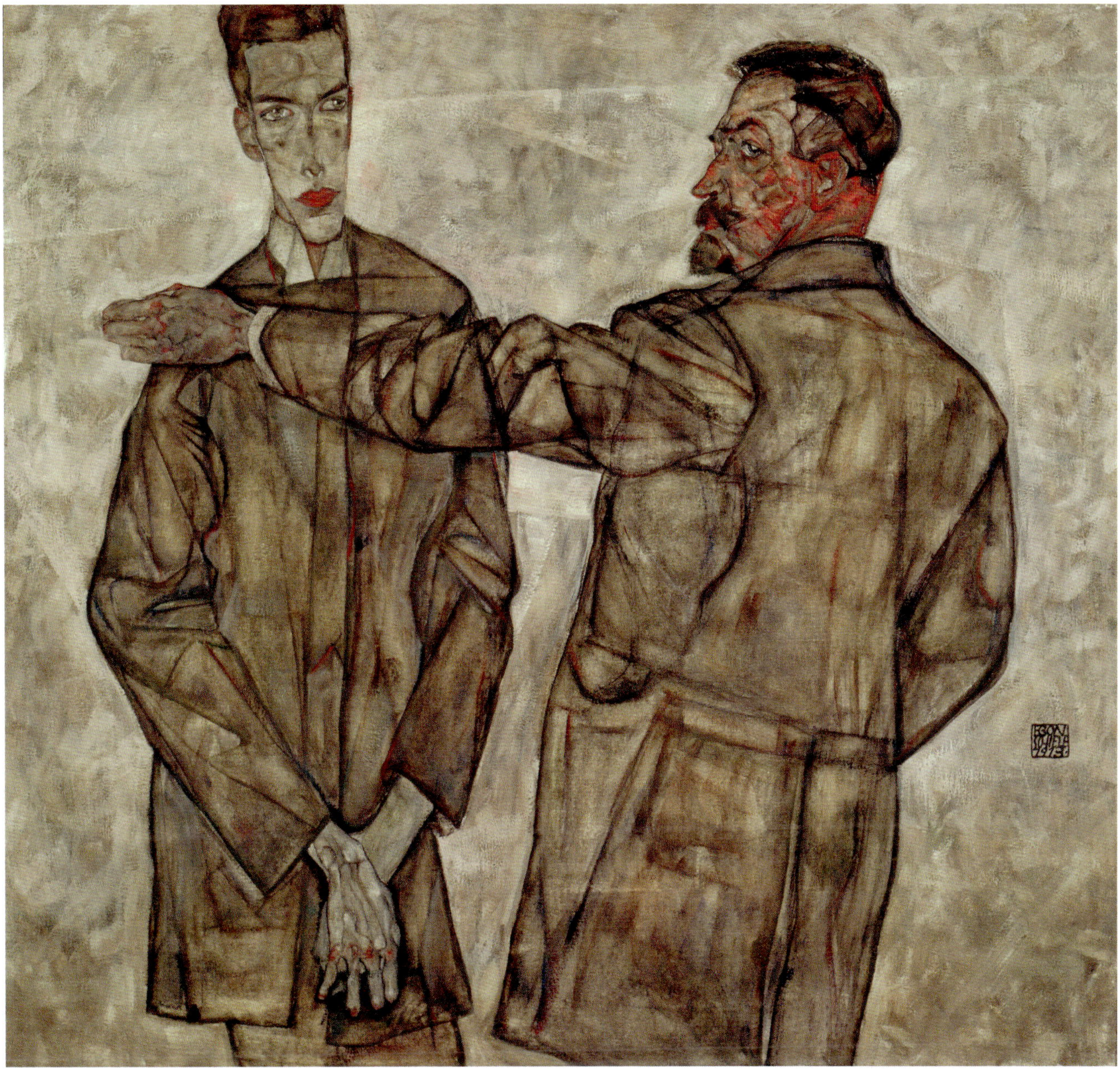

8
EGON SCHIELE
Heinrich and Otto Benesch, 1913
Oil on canvas, 121 x 131 cm
Lentos Museum, Linz
(Kallir. P. 250)

works on paper than major oils; indeed, he was unable to afford the finished portrait, which ended up in the collection of the wealthy industrialist Carl Reininghaus. Schiele also experimented briefly with drypoint, a print medium that he mastered with astonishing rapidity. Prints, too, were eminently saleable: moreover, since they were produced in multiple copies, they could be sold several times over. Nevertheless, having made six fine etchings during the early part of 1914, he then gave up. He seems to have resented how long it took him to create carefully worked prints of this kind, observing somewhat acidly that, in the time needed to etch one plate, he could create "fifty to sixty – no, even more, surely about one hundred drawings".[50]

In contrast to his earlier pencil studies, in later years Schiele often employed crayon or black chalk to create a softer, more palpable line, sometimes reinforcing it with further strokes in such a way as to suggest the solidity of forms. Several people who observed the artist at work also recalled that, when drawing from the model, he never used colour, which was added only later, if at all. However, during the last eighteen months of his life, with a few exceptions colour started to disappear altogether from his drawings. It has even been suggested that at least some watercolours and gouaches from 1918 are likely to have been products of 'posthumous colouring'. Their authenticity should therefore be viewed as to some extent problematic and the drawings themselves evaluated with caution.[51]

The motifs depicted in Schiele's last works on paper also pose something of a riddle. Female nudes and semi-nudes account for a noticeably large proportion of these, perhaps as much as two thirds of his total output. Many of them show women exposing themselves in what look like distinctly uncomfortable poses, seen from front or back, bending over or on their backs with legs splayed, sometimes masturbating. There are also studies of lesbian couples, some locked in a sexual embrace. Presumably Edith, who was pregnant by the spring of 1918, had now relaxed her ban on the use of studio models, leaving her husband free to draw pretty much what he liked. There was clearly a market for works of this kind: the artist was still in touch with some of his male buyers of pre-war years, to whom he had now added several new clients. Yet his attitude to the depicted subject appears far from straightforward. On the one hand, this seemingly endless succession of sexually explicit drawings might lead us to imagine Schiele creating them out of some kind of erotic frenzy. By now, he had evidently become a little bored with Edith and was perhaps seeking sexual gratification elsewhere, possibly with her sister Adele, with whom he had previously flirted. On the other hand, despite their explicit subject-matter, many of these images seem curiously detached, far removed from any real emotional involvement, closer to the more conventional erotica he had begun emulating as early as 1913.

Among his other drawings dating from the last year of his life, there exists a mere handful of landscapes and flower studies and a single drawing of Edith's dog Lord. Apart from these, the largest single category consists of studies for portraits, Edith's features and those of Schiele's mother Marie recognisable among them. After the resounding success of his participation in the Secession's 49th exhibition (Spring 1918), a growing number of paid portrait commissions meant that, for the first time in his life, he was comfortably off, able to afford the rent of a bigger studio and to purchase pictures by other artists. There was even a 'waiting list' of collectors anxious to buy his works.[52] This new-found affluence gives the lie to the fanciful tale, still widely believed, that when he died in October 1918 from influenza he was "poor as a beggar", misunderstood and scorned by his contemporaries.[53]

EPILOGUE

During the 1920s and 1930s, Schiele's reputation to some extent declined. In 1928 two exhibitions were held in Vienna to mark the tenth anniversary of his death; in 1930 there appeared the first oeuvre catalogue of his work by Jane Kallir's grandfather Otto Nirenstein, who later changed his name to Kallir. However, Schiele failed to achieve the same celebrity status that was accorded to Klimt. Somewhat surprisingly, in February 1943 Austria's Nazi rulers permitted a major Klimt retrospective in Vienna, thus missing by some six months the opportunity of marking the 80th anniversary of the painter's birth. By contrast, they explicitly prohibited the official public exhibition of any of Schiele's works, although it seems that the ban was not, in the end, strictly enforced.[54] Not until the 1950s did Schiele's star begin slowly to rise again, partly as a result of the activities of a small number of collectors and dealers. Prominent among the former was Austrian eye specialist Dr. Rudolf Leopold, whose passionate advocacy of Schiele helped lay the foundation of the artist's post-war reputation. His frequent purchases were also the starting point of what is now recognised as the most important single collection of Schiele's paintings, the Leopold Museum in Vienna, who are major lenders to the present exhibition.

A number of well-known Jewish dealers emigrated from Europe to the United States during the 1930s and 1940s, Nirenstein among them. Their unwavering promotion of modern German and Austrian painting helps partly to account for the now remarkable holdings of some of the major American museums which, during the post-war decades, seized the opportunity of buying important works by artists including both Schiele and Kokoschka.[55] Unfortunately, there was not really an equivalent phenomenon in Great Britain. As early as 1938, the New Burlington Galleries in London had shown one of the most significant counter-manifestations to the Nazis' public pillorying of 'degenerate' artists. Entitled 'Twentieth Century German Art', that exhibition showcased most of the leading Expressionists, including Max Beckmann, Wassily Kandinsky and Karl Schmidt-Rottluff. It also featured several important paintings by Kokoschka, among them his *Self-portrait as a Degenerate Artist*. There was, however, no mention of Schiele. After the war, and especially during the 1960s and 1970s, the major national collections in this country repeatedly missed or ignored the chance to acquire works not only by Schiele but also by important Expressionist artists such as Max Pechstein or Lyonel Feininger, despite the determined efforts of a handful of mostly London-based galleries and dealers, Marlborough and Fischer Fine Art prominent among them.[56] This studied neglect contrasts strikingly with the favour that modern French and British artists have usually found in the eyes of the British art establishment. It is our fervent hope that the present exhibition of Schiele's nudes will help to redress the balance while also underlining the crucial importance of this aspect of his art.

NOTES

All translations from German are my own unless noted otherwise.

1 In *Arbeiter-Zeitung*, 14 May 1912.

2 *Die Aktion. Wochenschrift für Politik, Literatur, Kunst*, IV. Jg., Nr. 20 (16 May 1914), col. 428.

3 According to Wolfgang Fischer, the Schiele exhibition at Marlborough Fine Art in London in 1964 was a "critical success but a commercial failure"; see 'Egon Schiele's Rise to Posthumous Fame', in Jane Kallir, *Egon Schiele. The Complete Works*, London (Thames & Hudson) 1998, p. 252. More recently, the exhibition organised by Bond Street dealer Richard Nagy in 2011, 'Egon Schiele. Women', attracted huge crowds of visitors; however, it is still the case that, until now, no major publicly funded institution in this country has taken up Schiele's cause.

4 Examples of fictionalised accounts of Schiele's life include Herbert Vesely's 1980 film *Exzess und Bestrafung* (*Excess and Punishment*, or *Excesses*) starring Mathieu Carrière and Jane Birkin, and Joanna Scott's *Arrogance: A Novel* (2004).

5 Kallir P. 163.

6 Arthur Roessler, 'Erinnerungen an Egon Schiele. Marginalien zur Geschichte des Menschentums eines Künstlers', first published in Fritz Karpfen (ed.), *Das Egon Schiele Buch*, Vienna (Verlag der Wiener Graphischen Werkstätte) 1921, pp. 29ff. In his important monograph on Schiele, collector Rudolf Leopold highlighted what he termed the "deplorable" aspect of Roessler's relationship with the artist, namely his habit of "free reporting" – that is, inventing or elaborating stories and incidents relating to Schiele: see Rudolf Leopold, *Egon Schiele. Paintings, Watercolours, Drawings*, London (Phaidon) 1973, p. 666.

7 See above p. 23.

8 Arthur Roessler, *Egon Schiele im Gefängnis: Aufzeichnungen und Zeichnungen*, Vienna (Carl Konegen) 1922. In an interview with Tobias Natter, Leopold roundly condemned this publication as an "outright forgery": see Tobias G. Natter and Ursula Storch (eds.), *Egon Schiele & Arthur Roessler. Der Künstler und sein Förderer: Kunst und Networking im frühen 20. Jahrhundert*, Vienna/Ostfildern-Ruit (Wien Museum/Hatje Cantz) 2004.

9 Over the past few decades, several volumes of memoirs by people who could recall or whose families experienced the stark realities of Vienna in the early twentieth century have served as a useful counterbalance to romanticised descriptions of the city and its changing fortunes. Especially noteworthy among them have been George Clare's *Last Waltz in Vienna* (1981) and, more recently, Edmund de Waal's *The Hare with Amber Eyes* (2010).

10 The Prime Minister in question was Karl Graf Stürgkh, assassinated in October 1916 by Friedrich Adler, son of Victor Adler, founder of Austria's Social Democratic Workers' Party. Being a politician with a taste for eating in public was then a perilous occupation, and not only in Austria. In Paris on the eve of the First World War, the Socialist leader Jean Jaurès was shot dead in the Café du Croissant while dining with a group of friends that included several Socialist Deputies.

11 Stefan Zweig, *Die Welt von Gestern*, Frankfurt (S. Fischer) 1970; Therese Nickl und Heinrich Schnitzler (eds.), *Arthur Schnitzler: Jugend in Wien, Eine Autobiographie*, Munich (dtv) 1971.

12 Zweig 1970, p. 70.

13 Nickl und Schnitzler 1971, esp. pp. 128, 137ff. Schnitzler's work appears to be largely unknown to English and American audiences, with the sole exception of his play *Reigen* (Round game), which was turned into the French-language film *La Ronde* by director Max Ophüls. Also Stanley Kubrick's *Eyes Wide Shut* was based on a novella by Schnitzler.

14 Friedrich Torberg, 'Nachwort', in Nickl and Schnitzler 1971, p. 196.

15 Jacques Le Rider stresses the similarities between many of the defining characteristics of Viennese modernism and certain 'central themes' addressed in more recent discussions of post-modernism: see 'Between Modernism and Post-Modernism: The Viennese Identity Crisis', in Edward Timms and Ritchie Robertson (eds.), *Vienna 1900 from Altenberg to Wittgenstein* (*Austrian Studies*, vol. 1), Edinburgh (Edinburgh U. P.) 1990, esp. pp. 3ff.

16 See, for example, Klaus Albrecht Schröder, *Egon Schiele: Eros and Passion*, Munich/New York (Prestel) 1995, pp. 53, 58ff.; compare also Gemma Blackshaw, 'Klimt, Schiele and Schönberg: Self Portraits', in *Facing the Modern: The Portrait in Vienna 1900*, London (National Gallery/Yale U. P.) 2013, p. 120.

17 Franz Wischin, *Egon Schiele, 'Ich Gefangener ...' Kunst oder Kinderpornographie: die Affäre von Neulengbach*, Vienna (Christian Brandstätter) 1998.

18 11 March 1918; the review is reprinted in Christian M. Nebehay, *Egon Schiele 1890–1918. Leben, Briefe, Gedichte*, Salzburg (Residenz Verlag) 1979, p. 457, doc. 1420.

19 For the anecdote about the early sketchbook see Alessandra Comini, *Egon Schiele's Portraits*, Berkeley (California U. P.) 1974, p. 10; for a detailed account of the artist's early life, based partly on recollections by his mother and sisters, see the recent catalogue edited by Christian Bauer, *Egon Schiele: Der Anfang/The Beginning*, Munich (Hirmer) 2013, esp. pp. 169ff.

20 Heinrich Benesch, *Mein Weg mit Egon Schiele*, New York (Verlag der Johannespresse) 1965; Eva Benesch (ed.), *Otto Benesch. Collected Writings*, vol. IV, London (Phaidon) 1973.

21 Benesch 1965, p. 26.

22 Otto Benesch, 'Egon Schiele', in Benesch 1973, pp. 185-86. Benesch's article was originally published in two parts in *Art International*, December 1958 and January 1959.

23 See, for example, the 1913 gouache *Female Nude with Yellow Cloth* (Kallir D. 1278) in the collection of the Leopold Museum, Vienna.

24 Jane Kallir, 'Early Works, 1906–1909', in *Egon Schiele: Self-Portraits and Portraits*, ed. Agnes Husslein-Arco and Jane Kallir, Munich/London/New York (Prestel) 2011, p. 63.

25 This story is based on a family memoir compiled by Schiele's nephew Anton Peschka Jr; see Kallir 1998, p. 44.

26 In addition to Schiele and Peschka, other founder members of the Neukunstgruppe included Anton Faistauer, Franz Wiegele, Albert Paris von Gütersloh and Hans Böhler: see Peter Vergo, *Art in Vienna 1898–1918: Klimt, Kokoschka, Schiele and their contemporaries*, London (Phaidon), 3rd rev. edn, 1993, p. 212.

27 According to Heinrich Benesch, who probably heard the story from Schiele himself: see Benesch 1965, p. 13.

28 Kallir 1998, p. 44.

29 Alexander Klee in Husslein-Arco and Kallir 2011, pp. 31ff., 40-41. Oppenheimer was personally acquainted with Freud, whose portrait he painted in 1909.

30 See above pp. 51-52.
31 Blackshaw, 'The Pathological Body: Modernist Strategising in Egon Schiele's Self-Portraiture', *Oxford Art Journal*, vol. 30 (2007), no. 3, pp. 377-401; see also Gemma Blackshaw and Leslie Topp, 'Scrutinised Bodies and Lunatic Utopias', in *Madness and Modernity. Mental Illness and the Visual Arts in Vienna 1900*, London (Lund Humphries) 2009, pp. 15-37. I am grateful to both Gemma Blackshaw and Kathryn Simpson for comments and suggestions they made in connection with the present essay.
32 The various influences discussed here were by no means incompatible, since some scholars have argued that the new language of the body articulated in illustrated medical journals also influenced Europe's cabaret theatre and dance; see for example Rae Beth Gordon, *Dances with Darwin, 1875–1910: Vernacular Modernity in France*, Farnham (Ashgate) 2009.
33 In Husslein-Arco and Kallir 2011, pp. 34-35.
34 Hugo von Hofmannsthal, 'Über die Pantomime', in *Reden und Aufsätze I, 1891–1913*, Frankfurt am Main (S. Fischer) 1979, p. 502. Hofmannsthal's article first appeared in *Süddeutsche Monatshefte*, IX. Jg., 1. Band (October 1911).
35 Patrick Werkner, 'The Child-Woman and Hysteria: Images of the Female Body in the Art of Schiele, in Viennese Modernism, and Today', in Patrick Werkner (ed.), *Egon Schiele: Art, Sexuality, and Viennese Modernism*, Palo Alto, CA (Society for the Promotion of Science and Scholarship) 1994, p. 59.
36 Jane Kallir, ed. Ivan Vartanian, *Egon Schiele, Drawings and Watercolours*, London (Thames & Hudson) 2003, p. 76.
37 Claude Cernuschi also comments on Schiele's inclination towards histrionics, comparing this with Kokoschka's adoption of assumed identities, for example as criminal or Christ; see his *Re/Casting Kokoschka: Ethics and Aesthetics, Epistemology and Politics in Fin-de-Siècle Vienna*, Madison, NJ (Fairleigh Dickinson U.P.)/London (Associated University Presses) 2002, p. 59.
38 'Feuilleton', *Neue Freie Presse*, 13 April 1912. For discussion of the widespread use of 'pathological' metaphors of this kind in contemporary reviews of Schiele's work see Blackshaw 2007, esp. pp. 400-01.
39 Nebehay 1979, p. 221, doc. 351.
40 And not only in relation to Schiele's art: Klimt, too, was accused of producing "painted pornography"; see Vergo 1993, p. 60.
41 'Egon Schiele', *Bildende Künstler* [Vienna], vol. I, no. 3 (March 1911), p. 118.
42 Paris von Gütersloh, *Egon Schiele: Versuch einer Vorrede*, Vienna (Verlag Brüder Rosenbaum) n.d. [1911], n. p. [p. 4].
43 Leopold 1973, p. 178.
44 Anton Faistauer, *Neue Malerei in Österreich*, Vienna (Amalthea Verlag) 1923, pp. 11ff.
45 Benesch, 'Egon Schiele', in Benesch 1973, pp. 182-83.
46 For an account of this incident, based on recollections by Tschunko's daughters, see Franz E. Wischin, *Die Stadt am blauen Fluß: Egon Schiele und Krumau*, Vienna (Wirtschaftstrend Zeitschriftenverlag) 1994, p. 48.
47 Wischin 1998, p. 33. Seemingly, when Schiele first encountered Tatjana she was not yet fourteen, then (as now) the age of consent in Austria.
48 I have mainly followed the account published in Wischin 1998; see esp. pp. 25ff. Much the same story is told at length in Kallir 1998, pp. 129ff., and, more briefly, in Kallir 2003, pp. 189ff.
49 See Nebehay 1979, p. 528. Schiele's friend and patron Heinrich Benesch, who rejoiced in the title of Chief Inspector, was also an employee of the Austrian State Railways, then regarded as a 'good' career. So were several members of the artist's own family, including his well-to-do uncle Leopold Czihaczek, who had initially helped to fund Schiele's studies.
50 Quoted from Kallir 1998, p. 646.
51 Kallir 1998, p. 602.
52 Kallir 2003, p. 441.
53 See, for example, the study by Karl Ruhrberg, who claimed that Schiele died "*bettelarm ... eine der größten Begabungen des Jahrhunderts, der an der Teilnahmslosigkeit der Zeitgenossen zugrunde ging*", in *Die Malerei unseres Jahrhunderts*, Düsseldorf/Vienna/New York 1987, p. 111, cited after Pia Müller-Tamm (ed.), *Egon Schiele: Inszenierung und Identität*, Cologne (DuMont) 1995, p. 7.
54 As documented in Leopold 1973, p. 674; for details of a Nazi-sponsored exhibition at Vienna's Albertina in February 1943 which included twelve drawings by Schiele see also Fischer, 'Egon Schiele's Rise to Posthumous Fame', in Kallir 1998, p. 249.
55 The useful check-list published in the Neue Galerie's catalogue of the Lauder and Sabarsky collections makes clear just how extensive were the acquisitions of works by Schiele made by a wide variety of American museums during the 1950s and 1960s: see 'Schiele in U. S. Public Collections', in Price 2005, pp. 453-71.
56 Fischer, 'Egon Schiele's Rise to Posthumous Fame', in Kallir 1998, esp. pp. 252ff.

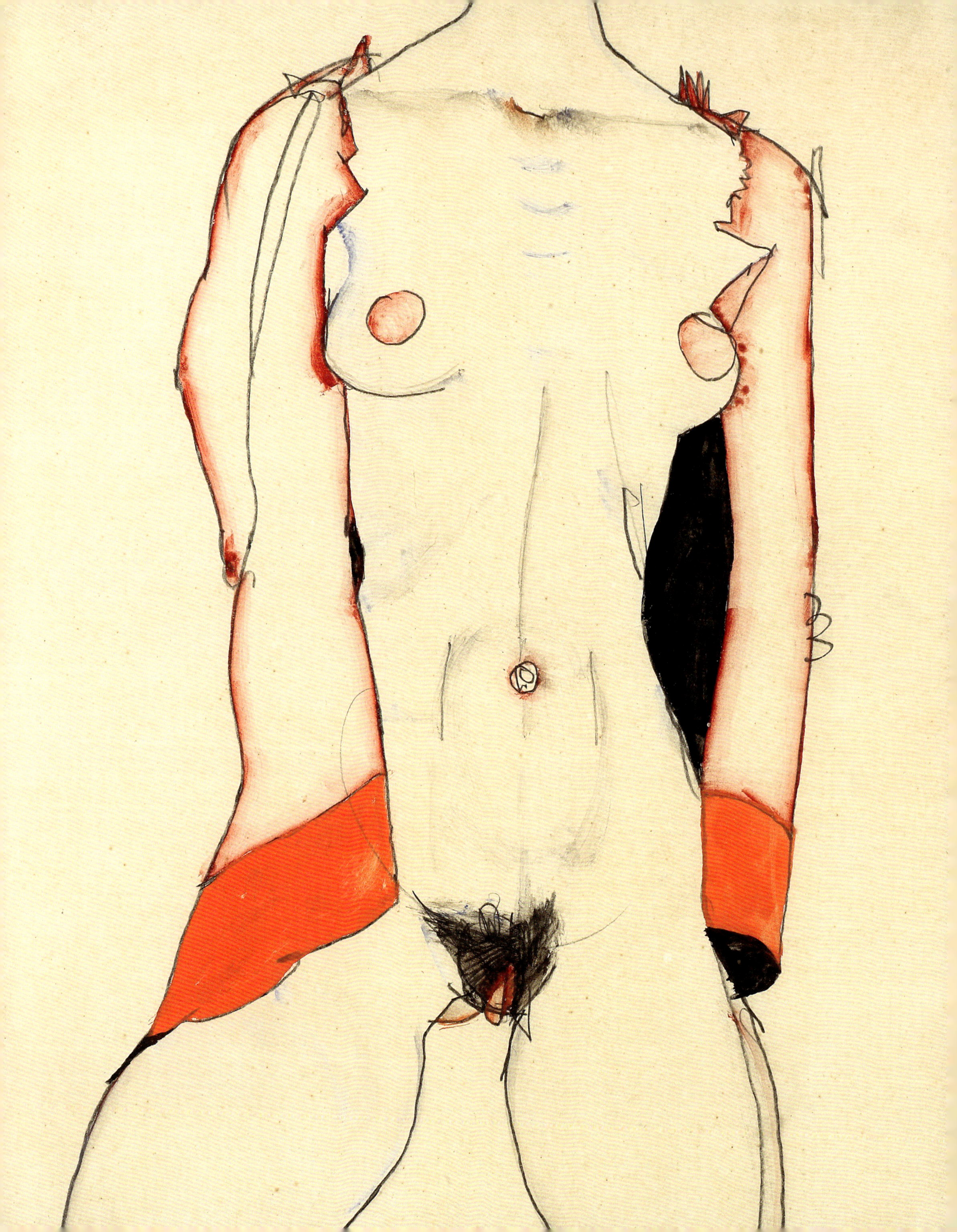

THE MODERNIST OFFENCE

SCHIELE AND THE NAKED FEMALE BODY

GEMMA BLACKSHAW

On 18 September 1923, the art dealer Karl Grünwald appeared before the Regional Court for Criminal Affairs on Hessgasse in Vienna's first district. He had been charged with the dissemination of obscene prints under paragraph 516 of the Strafgesetz, the penal code of Austria-Hungary of 1852, which stated:

> Whoever, by pictorial representations or immoral acts, grossly damages morality or public modesty by causing public outrage is guilty of misdemeanour and must be condemned to strict detention for a period of eight days to six months. If, however, such an infringement is committed by printed materials, that is an offence that must be punished by strict detention for a period of from six months to one year.[1]

The printed materials in question were colour lithographs after drawings of the naked female body by Egon Schiele, whom Grünwald had known personally and supported professionally from 1916 to 1918, during the last two years of the artist's life. They were not original prints: Schiele had not created the drawings for reproduction, or contributed to any part of the printmaking or printing processes.[2] Grünwald had purchased the facsimiles "cheaply" from an unidentified agent in January 1922, in the hope that he might use them in exchange for other works.[3] One year later, on a visit to Munich, he showed five examples to Hans Goltz, another art dealer based in the city with an intermittent history of representing Schiele. Goltz was not convinced by the demand for such work in Germany, so Grünwald put the prints in the post to be delivered to his home address in Vienna.[4] Before they could complete their return journey, however, they were seized by customs officials in Munich and identified as offensive pictures.

Following communication from Munich, the police in Vienna searched Grünwald's apartment. On finding a further 200 copies of the images, they confiscated them and arrested him. Grünwald pleaded not guilty to the charges, claiming that he had never intended to profit from the "questionable reproductions".[5] Showing, he argued, was different to selling and his prints had been kept under lock and key, revealed only to a select few identified by Grünwald as "art lovers".[6] They included the art historian Hans Tietze, who was at this time engaged in the reorganisation of Vienna's art museums, and another of his colleagues, an unidentified "gentleman from the Ministry of Education".[7] The president of the court argued: "If a businessman shows such pictures, he clearly wants to sell them".[8] Grünwald, however, maintained that he had purchased the copies "with a view to using them for purposes of exchange".[9] This was, in other words, a matter that only concerned those who were already invested in Schiele's work as "connoisseurs of art" and, as Goltz's response had shown, Grünwald's ambition to exchange the images for others had not, in this instance, been realised.[10]

Grünwald was acquitted by a majority of eight out of twelve jury votes. However, following an intervention from the state prosecutor, the president ordered the destruction of the 200 prints as "they offended public morality in the most extreme way".[11] Grünwald's lawyer appealed "for reasons of principle and the public interest, rather than solely in the interests of my client, for the pictures in question were of only insignificant value".[12] This was not, to the mind of the defence, about protecting Grünwald's assets. Rather, it was a matter of ensuring that the prints, as documents of art and of scholarship, could circulate with relative freedom in the public domain. The court records for the case are incomplete and journalists did not report on the result of the appeal.[13] Colour lithographs after such drawings by Schiele dating from this period do exist but they are scarce indeed, and this suggests that the president's ruling to destroy those seized from the apartment was upheld.

The case against Grünwald was covered extensively in the court report sections of the broadsheet press.[14] It provided the Viennese public with an opportunity to engage with the interlocking issues of art, morality and sexuality raised by Schiele's work and its circulation, and to identify their positions in broader debates on the modernist project as it was being historicised in the city by artists, their agents and apologists.[15] The trial lasted a single day, but it captured a decade-long reception of Schiele's drawings of the naked female body, a history that was troubled by questions, tensions and evasions. Were these works on paper art or pornography, and who was qualified to tell? Was this question a matter of attribution, of distinguishing the drawing, as the rare and expensive work of art, from its facsimile, its 'common', cheaper copy? What differentiated private from public dissemination and consumption, and how could these spheres be regulated and maintained as two 'discrete' entities? Such issues, which revolved around the problematics of the binary opposition – art/pornography, original/copy, private/public – were addressed in the courtroom on Hessgasse.

As interrogations, they were certainly not new. Schiele himself had appeared in court to answer comparable charges in what became known as the Neulengbach Affair of 1912, and from the very start of his short lived career, from one of his first group shows held in Prague in 1910, when police ordered the removal of fourteen of his drawings, authorities and 'art lovers' had battled over the status of his work.[16] The Grünwald case was, however, unusual in being a posthumous trial of the artist through his surviving dealer and of the artist's work through its reproduction. It was resolved through the declaration of difference – art from pornography, original from copy, private from public. What is fascinating is how this impulse towards distinction has become a defining feature of the discourse on Schiele's life, work and legacy, characterising the approaches of collectors and dealers, curators and scholars working in the latter half of the twentieth century and up to the present day. With this in mind, my aim here is to use the Grünwald trial as a window on to the artist's historiography: what was, and remains, at stake? As Abigail Soloman-Godeau has claimed in her exploration of photography and female subjectivity in the Second French Empire, "The barriers between what is deemed licit and illicit, acceptably seductive or wantonly salacious, aesthetic or prurient, are never solid because contingent, never steadfast because they traffic with each other – are indeed dependent upon each other".[17] How might such an engagement with difference, with the binary system, shift not only our understanding but also our appreciation of Schiele's representation of the naked female body, of what continues to be described and displayed as 'the nude'?[18]

ON TRIAL: GRÜNWALD, SCHIELE AND THE NAKED FEMALE BODY

Grünwald was tried five years after Schiele's death during the influenza epidemic of 1918. The two men had met during military service in the First World War; in 1916 Grünwald had arranged for Schiele's transfer to the Imperial and Royal Military Supply Service in Vienna, which allowed him to spend the remainder of the war re-engaging with his studio practice. Schiele drew Grünwald on nine occasions throughout 1917 (see, for example, fig. 9), in preparation for a large portrait on canvas. Delineating in the sparest of black crayon his elongated nose and high forehead, his arched eyebrow and pursed lip, Schiele created an image that recalled the distinctive representation of his own face; Grünwald's agitated fingers form a bridge over the artist's signature, encased within its own frame and placed centrally to the bottom edge of the sheet; portraiture and self-portraiture are in dialogue with one another here, and this was typical of Schiele's depictions of his male friends and patrons. After his death, Schiele remained an important artist for Grünwald, who consistently emphasised the closeness of their relationship; when he returned to business at the close of the war, he increased his own collection of paintings and drawings as well as purchasing and selling at least eleven of Schiele's major works on canvas.[19]

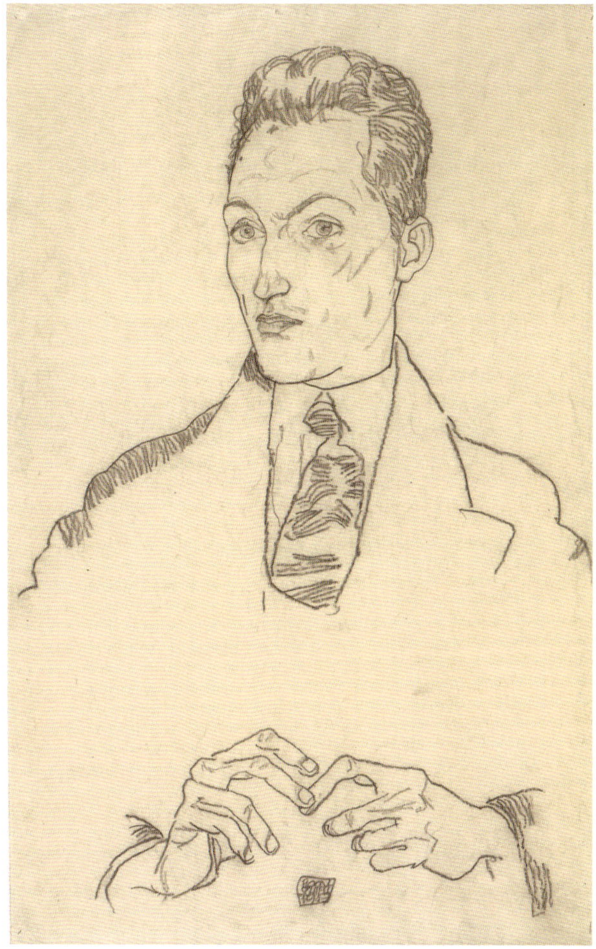

9
EGON SCHIELE
Karl Grünwald, 1917
Black crayon, 45.8 x 29.5 cm
Albertina Museum, Vienna
(Kallir D. 2074)

One of the paintings handled by Grünwald was Schiele's most provocative oil, *Reclining Woman* of 1917 (fig. 38, p. 145). He painted this major work, measuring 95.5 x 171 cm, in the same year as Grünwald's portrait, and it was exhibited at the Vienna Secession in 1918, in a group show organised by Schiele, who displayed his work prominently in the central room. The offer to curate that 49th exhibition of the Secession came as Schiele was working on this painting, and it is interesting to consider how the opportunity to display it publicly might have influenced his decision to 'cover' the vulva of the otherwise entirely naked woman's body. She lies on her back against a rumpled sheet; represented from a viewing position high above her, we are able to look down at her body, knees thrown apart to reveal conversely what has been so carefully concealed. The sheet – which has its own physicality, stretching and flexing across the canvas – is draped across her genitals; manipulated by Schiele into three narrow folds, the painterly pleats in this fabric evoke the form of the labia and clitoral hood. Placed centrally on the canvas, we can stare at this site unchallenged: though lying on her back, the woman's head is raised from the floor to look not at us, above her, but at someone else – the artist, we presume – who stands before her. With our presence unacknowledged, we can gaze as voyeurs at the sight of her sex, albeit one that has been fetishised in fabric.

Reclining Woman is in many ways unusual for being the most explicit of Schiele's works on canvas. However, as a 'major' painting as opposed to a 'minor' drawing, destined – initially, at least – for public display, it needed to function as a nude, and this meant having to suggest rather than represent the genitalia.[20] In his graphic work, however, Schiele could test such art historical categories by not only revealing the vulva but also exposing it as far as possible, depicting genitals that were shaved, or prepubescent, or parted with fingers. It was Schiele's drawings of the naked female body, and in particular such body parts, that so incited the authorities, and we see this with the response to his work on paper in Prague in 1910. Interestingly, the police suggested 'exhibiting' the offending 14 sheets removed from the gallery in a portfolio. The proposal, which was rejected, shows how the portfolio, the material object that could be opened but – more importantly – closed, was a means of mediation, of interceding in what could and could not be put on public display.[21] Such anxieties were heightened when it came to the reproduction of Schiele's work, to the facsimile copies of drawings that, by their very number, could not be contained within the walls of the gallery or concealed between the covers of the portfolio.

We do not know for certain what became of Grünwald's prints. The president's order to destroy the 200 copies found at the dealer's apartment was bound up in the legislation concerning public dissemination and it is possible that the original five sheets seized from the post office were returned to Grünwald on the condition that they remained for his private consumption. Alternatively, and I think more persuasively, they could have been retained by the authorities in Munich, as this was typical of German police action against the pornography industry.[22] We also do not know how many of the prints had been produced in the first place, and whether Grünwald had been able to exchange them for other images, as he had planned, in the twelve months between his purchase and his visit to Goltz's gallery. It seems likely that there were more than those implicated in the trial, or that some sheets evaded destruction, as there are at least two portfolios containing five colour lithographs after drawings by Schiele that were printed around 1920 that have survived (figs. 11–15). One is to be found in a private collection in Munich, and the other, reproduced here, is held at the Galerie St. Etienne in New York; the portfolio covers for each are slightly different but

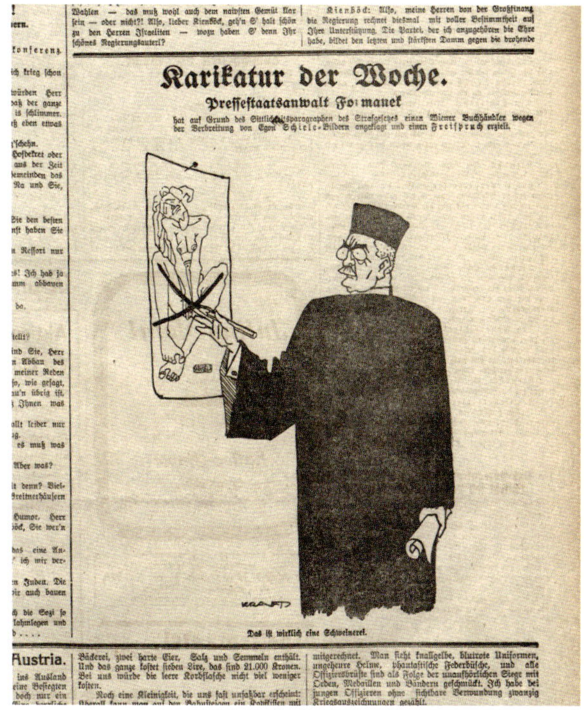

Karikatur der Woche.

Pressestaatsanwalt Fo: manek

hat auf Grund des Sittlichkeitsparagraphen des Strafgesetzes einen Wiener Buchhändler wegen der Verbreitung von Egon Schiele-Bildern angeklagt und einen Freispruch erzielt.

Das ist wirklich eine Schweinerei.

10
Caricature published in
Der Morgen, 24 September 1923
Austrian National Library, Vienna

the contents are the same. In her catalogue raisonné of 1998, Jane Kallir states that these were possibly Grünwald's prints and that the portfolio covers (rather interestingly) were probably added later.[23] In the catalogue accompanying the exhibition *The Naked Truth: Klimt, Schiele and Other Scandals* of 2005, the Munich portfolio's cover and contents are reproduced, with the prints identified definitively as those from the Grünwald trial. The authors suggest further that the initials 'AK' that appear on both sets of the actual sheets refer to the Photochemigraphische Kunst-Anstalt, A. Krampolek, a specialist printing firm based in Vienna.[24] But another compelling argument for these being Grünwald's prints is to be found in their contents. Paragraph 516 of the Austro-Hungarian legal code was concerned with those pictorial representations that "grossly damage morality or public modesty". The disparate images of girls and young women in varying states of undress across initialled pages measuring 50 x 32.5 cm in both landscape and portrait orientation have just one feature in common: they all depict the genitals exposed and in this they all conform to the description provided by the Munich police of offensive pictures.

The facsimiles were produced by a specialist firm from works in pencil, black crayon, watercolour and gouache created by Schiele across a considerable period of time, from 1910 to 1916. Of the five original drawings, only two are now traceable. The first, *Die Traum-Beschaute* (*Girl Seen in a Dream*) of 1911, now held by the Metropolitan Museum of Art, New York, is the only one from the group with a title written on the sheet and it is also the most explicit. Anatomical precision, so characteristic of Schiele's practice, is sacrificed here to the view of the vulva, opened out by the woman's jewelled fingers – glittering rings that rarely feature in Schiele's figure or portrait studies. The genitals are similarly exposed in the second traceable drawing, *Reclining Semi-Nude with Legs Spread* of 1916 (cat. 34), reproduced as the lithograph fig. 14. This drawing relates directly to the painting *Reclining Woman* (fig. 38), although the model used for the study was Schiele's wife Edith, and the perspective of the drawing is different to that of the painting. In his drawing practice, Schiele often used his signature to alter the position of the sheet, changing in the process the viewer's relationship and response to the body represented. In this case, the portrait format presents the vulva in an even more spectacular display for the viewer's consumption. Turned vertically, the drawing offers the genitals in place of the face and this is emphasised by the fact that, no matter what the sheet's orientation, Edith's chin remains tucked into her neck, face obscured, hidden from the viewer, who can thus look on unhindered.

The significance of this site of the genitals to Grünwald's trial can be seen in the image published as 'Caricature of the Week' in the Viennese newspaper *Der Morgen* (fig. 10). We see the state prosecutor Dr Formanek, who was well known in Vienna for his pursuit of pornography traders in the book and picture businesses, standing in his black robes and hat next to a sheet by Schiele. Tacked up on a wall with a single pin

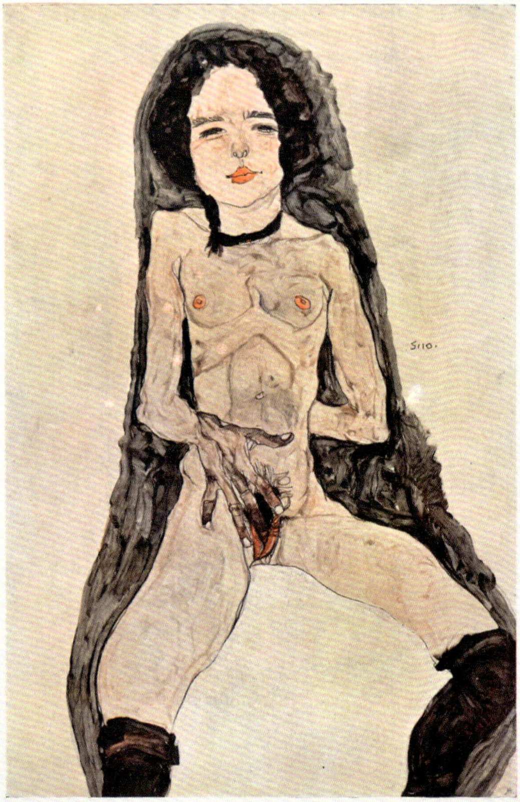

11

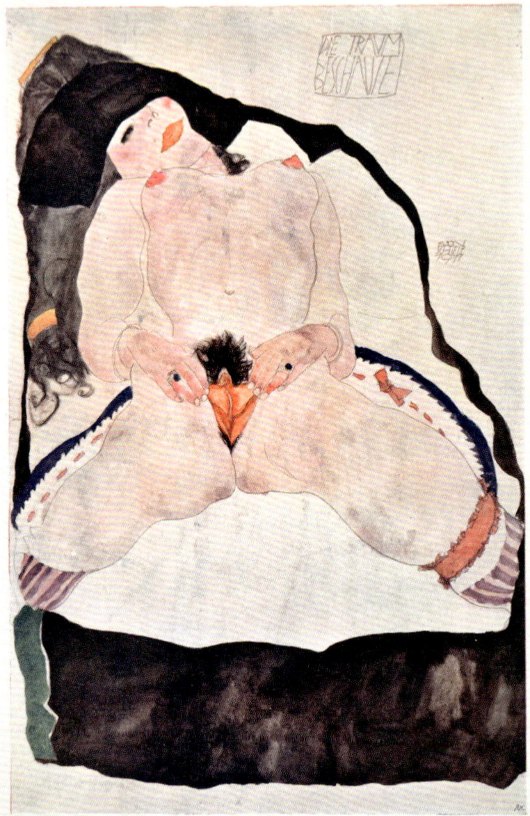

12

11–15

'Five Drawings', Portfolio of lithographs after drawings by Egon Schiele, Vienna, c. 1920
Galerie St. Etienne, New York

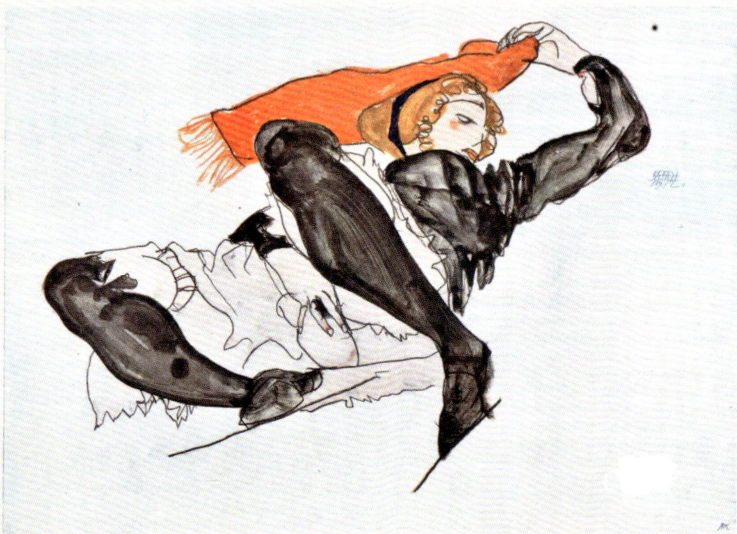

13

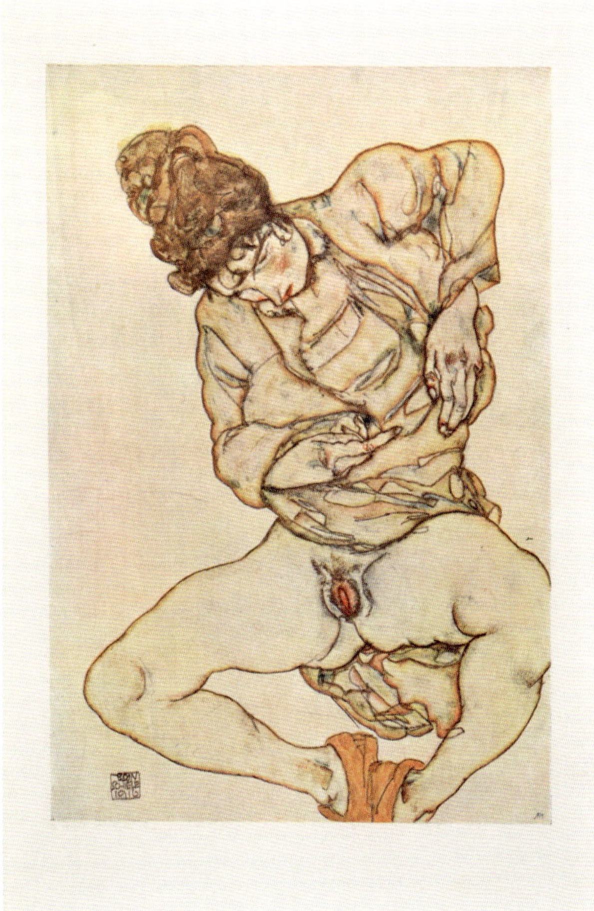

14

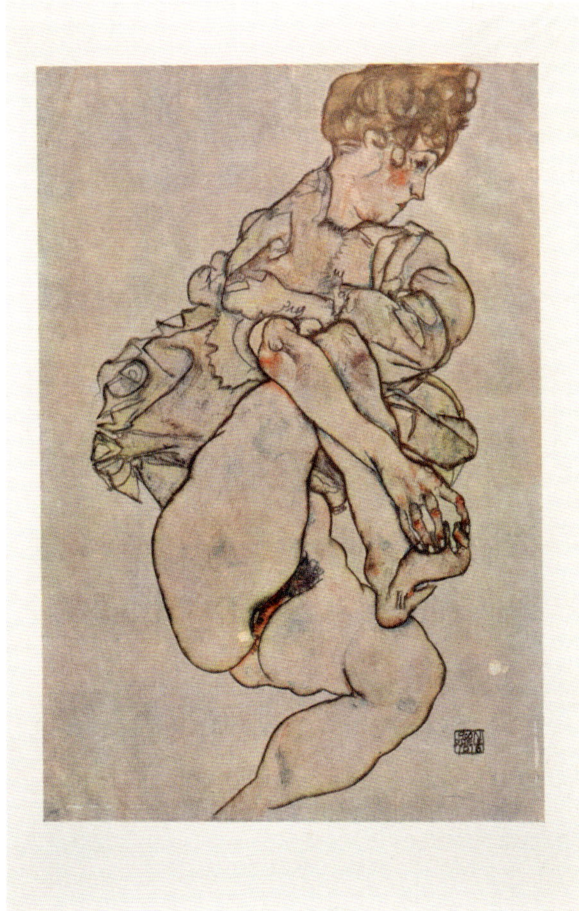

15

to emphasise not only its low value but also its portability, its potential for dissemination, the sheet shows the naked, seated body of a woman with legs splayed. Her hands are brought down to her genitals to open her sex further for the viewer, but there is nothing to see as this site has been covered by the centre of a black cross painted by Formanek with a large brush because, as the caption underneath the image states, "That is absolute filth." The caricature pokes fun at the frowning Formanek as it is introduced with his failure to have Grünwald convicted: "State Prosecutor Formanek has, on the basis of the paragraph concerning morality in the legal code, accused a Viennese book-dealer of disseminating pictures by Egon Schiele and has achieved an acquittal." But the words uttered by 'Formanek' – *that* (the image of the vulva and hence, I would surmise, the vulva itself) is absolute filth – gives the prosecutor, the censor, his voice nevertheless. This was not, however, Formanek's statement; it does not appear in any of the reports of the trial in the press. Rather, the words were put into his mouth by the humorist for *Der Morgen* and this shows that, even in caricature, a domain of visual culture that destabilised authority, the representation of the female genitalia was an opportunity to exercise power, to express disgust.

In keeping with court regulations, members of the public would not have seen the prints; they were viewed only by court officials and members of the jury, and this makes the representation of the incriminating picture by Schiele in the caricature all the more interesting. It relates rather loosely to two of the five lithographs included in the portfolio (figs. 11

and 12), but it is very much of the caricaturist's own invention, a representation of what would be recognised by readers of *Der Morgen* as a typical 'Schiele' drawing. And in this, in its legibility, it shows how effectively the female body with exposed genitals signified Schiele's work on paper. As his rival Oskar Kokoschka commented, "Pornography always flourished in Vienna – you know, in the Schiele style. The more pornographic, the easier it was to sell."[25]

DRAWING TO DEMAND: THE 'SCHIELE STYLE'

It scarcely needs to be said that Schiele was a prodigious and provocative draughtsman with a confidence in his materials that was unrivalled in early twentieth-century Vienna, even by his mentor Gustav Klimt. Schiele's drawings of the body unclothed or in a state of undress have become the signifiers not only of his life and work (a conflation that typifies modernism) but also of the conflicts between the social and the sexual, the conservative and the liberal that we identify as characterising 'Vienna 1900'. A precocious student, Schiele entered the city's Academy of Fine Arts in 1906 at the age of sixteen. Life drawing was central to his training, though from the early works that have survived it would seem that he did not encounter female life models until he turned eighteen. On leaving the Academy in 1909 – a move that enraged his uncle, guardian and benefactor Leopold Czihaczek – his drawing practice shifted fundamentally. By 1910, working from his own studio with models of his choosing, and financially cut off from his family, Schiele had radicalised his tuition to produce explicit images of the female body that quickly found their market.[26]

In the drawings dating from this time onwards, Schiele adopted unusual viewing positions to emphasise his spatial association and sexual connection with the model as the object of his gaze. He rarely included himself in these images, but asserted his physical presence nevertheless by cropping the female body. Cut off at the knee, the neck, the waist, the thigh, such depictions as *Standing Nude in Red Jacket* of 1913 (cat. 24), with their dramatic, foreshortened distortions, established the close proximity of artist to model. Frequently, positions were taken up to facilitate Schiele's focus on the genitalia: single hairs were picked out in sharp pencil, swollen lips were highlighted in crimson gouache. These intimate, spectacularising details, which we see in such works as *Woman with Black Stockings* of 1913 (cat. 23), were described by Heinrich Benesch, one of Schiele's early patrons, as being added after the event of the life drawing, "from memory and without reference to the model".[27]

Schiele's repeated return to the image suggests not only a re-experiencing of the encounter between the desiring subject and his object but also an intensifying of their original exchange: through the re-touching of the drawing, the all-seeing artist can look ever closer in improbable, incredible detail at a site he might have been shown fleetingly, or reluctantly, if indeed at all. Schiele's omnipresence was founded further on the dynamism of the models' poses – their arched backs and spread legs, their opened chests and flung-back heads – which extended the artist's role to directing as well as looking, touching as well as drawing. As Klaus Albrecht Schröder has argued, Schiele's practice was not, then, that of the voyeur, peeking through the curtain at the woman unawares; rather, the female body was represented as continually reacting to that of the artist-spectator.[28]

Schiele captured this responsive aspect of his image-making in a somewhat uncharacteristic work from 1910 (fig. 16). The model stands before a mirror with her back to him, looking at her own pose and pout; he sits close behind

16
EGON SCHIELE
Self-Portrait drawing a Nude Model before a Mirror, 1910
Pencil, 55.2 x 35.3 cm
Albertina Museum, Vienna
(Kallir D. 737)

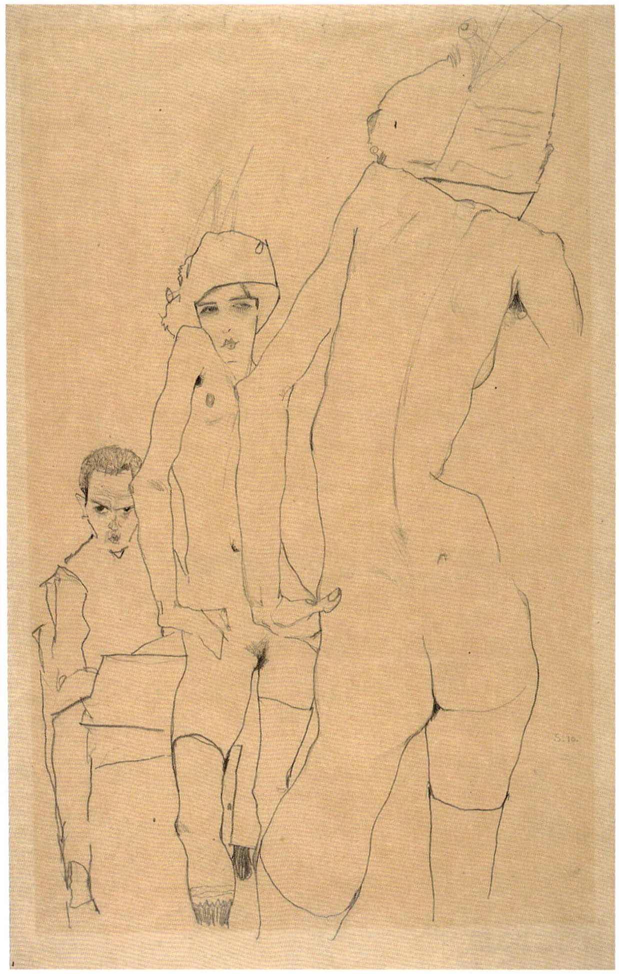

her with a board on his knees, drawing her back view, the reflection of her front view and, beyond that, his own reflected image. The studio environment is both nowhere and everywhere: there is no mirror, no furniture beyond a cursory line describing the arm of a chair, no heap of clothes or pile of materials, and yet all this is conjured nevertheless by the positions these two figures take up in relation to each other, and by the model's state of undress – naked except for her stockings and boots. The image is intriguingly atypical: ordinarily, Schiele worked to suppress all traces of the mechanisms that drove the production of his drawings – the boards and ladders, the brushes and pencils. As we see in *Squatting Girl* of 1917 (cat. 35) and *Female Nude, Back View*, also of 1917 (cat. 36), his models stand, sit and stretch in voids. They recline on absent beds, bend over missing chairs. Framed not only by the limits of the paper but also by their clothing – the garter fastened above the knee, the petticoat pulled up to the waist – their bodies are viewed in ways that draw the formal and the sexual together. Partially exposed to heighten their nakedness, the contrasts between the models' white skin and black stockings, their full skirts and narrow hips, serve both to abstract the body and focus the gaze on what *can* be seen, on what *has* been revealed. There is no narrative beyond this undressing, the strip tease for the artist who almost always remains 'off-paper', and the projected fantasy of the sexual encounter that, we imagine, will soon follow.

This focus on the model's body to the exclusion of everything incidental around her was the 'Schiele style', and it accounts for the seemingly eternal appeal of his images, a timelessness his contemporaries were keen to emphasise. As Schiele's friend and fellow painter Albert Paris von Gütersloh so vividly described, the models would respond to the artist's soft call to 'stop':

17
UNKNOWN PHOTOGRAPHER
Pornographic photograph, c. 1900
Formerly Uwe Scheid Collection, Munich

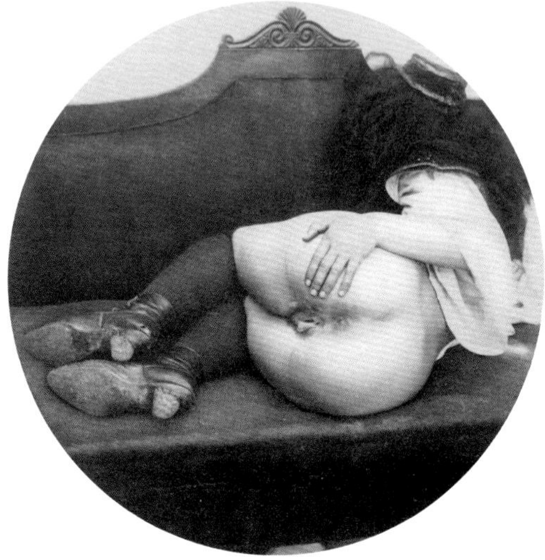

> And now, as if under the spell of his magic, they froze as they were – lying, standing, kneeling, relaxing, tying or untying, pulling down or up, combing themselves or scratching themselves – as though they had been banished to timelessness or covered with lava, and then, in a twinkling, brought back to life. That is the immortal moment in which the transitory is transformed into the eternity of art.[29]

This language, with its emphases on immortality and universality, on transformation and contemplation, is typical of that used to describe the high art category of the nude. The female body represented by Schiele was far from idealised – Gütersloh also commented on the models' dirty skin and tangled hair – but it was elevated to the realm of perfection nevertheless, and this meant having to divest it of its sexuality.[30] In the process, Gütersloh polarised art and pornography, disassociating Schiele's 'nudes' from the arousing, seemingly accessible female bodies they referred to. The power of this emphatically modernist discourse goes a long way towards explaining why the precedents for Schiele's drawings of the female body in pornographic photography have been largely suppressed in the scholarship.[31]

PORNOGRAPHY, PHOTOGRAPHY AND THE 'SCHIELE STYLE'

From the first daguerreotypes of the 1840s to the cheaper and more widely disseminated albumen prints of the late nineteenth century, pornographic imagery was very much a part of modern photographic production. But as Solomon-Godeau has pointed out in her work on the nineteenth-century French context, pornographic photography is "empirically elusive": it is seldom discussed in histories of the medium, despite the contribution it made to the driving of technical innovation. Private holdings and public collections of pornographic photographs from this period are rarely made accessible to scholars or to wider audiences through the exhibition or book.[32] The archive's resistance to research on pornographic photography is down in part to the fact that the creation and circulation of these pictures was illegal. In response to the rapid proliferation of the industry across Europe, legislation such as Paragraph 516 of the Austro-Hungarian penal code criminalised the production and public dissemination of pornographic images; the Grünwald case is one of many examples of the prosecutions that took place in Vienna alone.[33] As Gary D. Stark has revealed in his research on pornography in Imperial Germany, photographic studios and publishing houses operated on a Europe-wide basis: material was produced in Vienna or Budapest (identified as "the largest producers of pornography in Europe, perhaps in the world"), but subsequently sold in Munich or Berlin in an attempt to outwit the authorities.[34] The expansion of this 'under the counter' industry across national borders ensured that pornographic images resisted being traced to named photographers, studios, cities or even countries; this, then, was a wholly ubiquitous yet largely anonymous body of work that was central to modern European visual culture. Unauthored, undated and unregulated, pornographic photography could be placed by authorities and 'art lovers' in

18
UNKNOWN PHOTOGRAPHER
Pornographic photograph, c. 1900
Formerly Uwe Scheid Collection, Munich

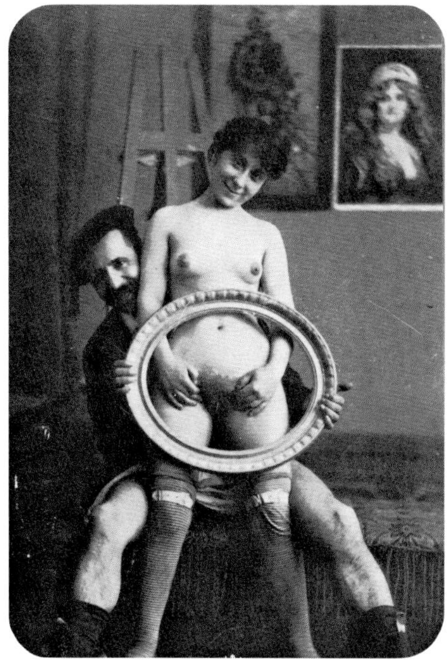

opposition to the high art culture described by Gütersloh in his celebration of Schiele's "eternal" nudes. Such a distinction between high and low, the masterly and the mass-produced, the timeless and the timebound was, however, replete with tension, and we appreciate this all the more when we consider the traffic across the lines that demarcated drawing from photography.

In a photograph formerly in the collection of Uwe Scheid that is tentatively dated at around 1900 (fig. 17), a woman lies on a polished wooden bench with her back to the viewer. She has removed her skirts, but not her stockings, boots, blouse, shawl or hat. The clothing has a number of functions: it frames her exposed bottom, anus and genitals, abstracting the body and focusing the spectator's gaze; it emphasises the nakedness of this part of her body, uncovered, pale and dimpled; it conceals her head and face, eliminating the potentially disruptive signifiers of her subjectivity; and it locates her as a woman of a particular social class, wearing everyday boots with heels worn from walking, a woman you might meet on the street. The image's pornographic content lies not only in its fixation on her sites of penetration but also in these faint traces of her contemporaneity. Unlike erotic, legally sanctioned photographs of the period, for which women posed as Venus, for example, artfully concealing their sex with a scallop shell, pornographic photographs exposed the genitals in ways that emphasised the entirely unremarkable reality of the body and the encounter, closing the gap between the real and the imagined.[35] The viewing subject is invited in to such images, towards the object of representation, as opposed to being kept at a respectable arm's length. In the case of this photograph, we see such a beckoning through the inclusion of the woman's hand, pulling her cheeks apart, and in the round, lens-like structure of the image itself, which draws the spectator's eye ever closer.

Scholars have convincingly demonstrated how such a focus on the single, framed body part was photography's invention, with poses developed for the practical and technical specificity of the camera expanding modes of representation in fine art practice.[36] Photography, then, played the leading role in culturally establishing what constituted the pornographic image, but photographers often made references to the painter's studio in their construction of these images. Sexual relations between artists and models were an established trope of pornographic imagery and literature, and photography referred to this through the staging of sexual encounters in studio spaces, amongst paintings and easels. In a second image from Scheid's archive (fig. 18), set in what looks suspiciously like a fabricated atelier, a model parts her labia for the spectator; her hands and genitals are encircled by an empty, oval picture frame held up by the artist she is poised to have intercourse with; doubly-framed, her sex is twice reinforced as the subject of the image.

Such material was very much in focus when Schiele embarked on his exploration of life drawing in 1910. In the same year, Austria-Hungary signed an international treaty with fourteen other countries, including Germany, to cooperate in the pursuit and prosecution of traders in pornography; the communication between the authorities in Munich and Vienna that resulted in the arrest of Grünwald thirteen years later was facilitated by this agreement.[37] I would argue even further that the distinctive formalism of Schiele's drawings – the framing of penetrable body parts, the positioning of hands in relation to genitals, the juxtaposing of fabric and flesh – evolved out of the pornographic photographs that so pervaded the city's visual culture, despite the watchful eye of the authorities. As a journalist for the *Arbeiter Zeitung* commented in relation to the trial of the Viennese businessman Carl W. Stern for the dissemination of pornographic pictures and texts in 1912 (the year of Schiele's arrest in Neulengbach): "Pornographic literature appears here on a weekly basis and remains, essentially, unchallenged. So many of our Viennese satirical magazines are in the habit of consciously and consistently publishing pure filth .... These are available in every coffee-house and enjoy a very considerable circulation." The article was entitled 'Eroticism and Pornography' and it considered the challenges in policing the distinction between the two; the journalist argued that "nobody can dispute the fact that there is a state of crisis with regard to pornographic portrayal".[38]

This "state of crisis" defined the cultural and commercial context in which Schiele was struggling to establish himself as an artist – a struggle that resulted in his attracting the attention of a substantial group of collectors and dealers.[39] The appeal of Schiele's work to his patrons, I suggest, lay in its traversing of the borders between not only the drawing and the photograph but also, and in relation to this, between art and pornography; this was the source of its frisson, and its fundamental collectability.[40] But with the city's public attacks on the progressive visual arts in mind, these borders, on being crossed, had to be reinstated by the modernists who trafficked across them in the first place; art had to remain Art. We see this process of recuperation at work in the tortuous defence of Schiele's practice by Hermann Bahr, the writer and critic who so fervently supported Klimt:

> The many, far too many sheets of this kind that Schiele drew under the pressure of his never-ending problems of feeding himself and for the sake of a particular circle of customers, both harmed him and was of value to him; harmed him, because this eroticism, which had to draw its justification from inner experience, had to be reduced to common fluency by the way it was turned out as if by some artisanal process; was of value, because it was precisely this dissipation of his fire that allowed the artist to gain distance from his work and thus make possible the formal development of his art.[41]

Erotic, critical and formal, Schiele's drawings of the female body were elevated to a higher art-form and thus recovered for the modernist offensive. Bahr's argument was somewhat harder to make when it came to Grünwald's prints, the offensive pictures described by the prosecutor, Formanek, as "cheap", "insignificant" and "obscene" – but only if the distinctions between the artist and the dealer, the original and the copy were maintained, and on this point Formanek faltered.

"EROTIC IS FAR FROM BEING IMMORAL": THE MODERNIST DEFENCE

Grünwald's lawyer, Dr. Schäfer, took up this quintessentially modernist defence of Schiele's practice when he intervened in the cross-examination of his client in the courtroom on Hessgasse on 18 September 1923.[42] Formanek had asked the accused why he had purchased the prints in the first place, "if you did not wish to sell them and if the material gives you no pleasure?"[43] Insinuating that Grünwald's pleasure in looking was a matter of sexual as opposed to aesthetic gratification – which was not technically an offence – Formanek connected the dealer's desire to the market, to the issue of dissemination and ultimately to the charge of damaging public morality. To emphasise the condemnable and expendable nature of the prints, he followed his question up with the statement: "In my opinion these are reproductions of the worst quality, mass-produced items". Grünwald countered: "They are lithographs, but of good quality".[44] After a lengthy discussion concerning the value of the prints – a debate in which Grünwald, as an art dealer, must have had the upper hand – Formanek changed his line of questioning, shifting the focus from the copies of Schiele's drawings to the original work, and from the dealer to the recently deceased artist. Blurring the investigation, he reminded the courtroom of Schiele's own brush with the authorities in the Neulengbach Affair of 1912 for what he described as the artist's "extreme erotic ..."[45] and at this point Schäfer, seizing the opportunity provided by Formanek's conflation of the drawing and its reproduction, and the artist and his agent, interrupted him with the rebuttal, "Erotic is far from being immoral".[46] The coverage of the case in the press varied from paper to paper, but, irrespective of the length of each article, this exchange was repeated, word for word; it was the hinge of the trial.

Schäfer's response had the weight of Vienna's 'art lovers' – apologists like Bahr, who championed the creative, moral and sexual freedom of the artist – behind it. His legal defence was an echo of an earlier, albeit recent defence of Schiele's work from the city's modernist community that arose out of his arrest in Neulengbach for the abduction and sexual abuse of a minor (charges that were dropped) and the display of obscene drawings to further children (for which he was imprisoned for twenty-four days). In 1922, just one year before Grünwald's trial, Arthur Roessler published *Egon Schiele in Prison*, a diary of dubious authorship that covered the artist's period of confinement. It included 'Schiele's' account of his practice: "I do not deny it: I have made drawings and watercolours that are erotic. But they are still always works of art – that I can attest, and people who understand something of this will gladly affirm it."[47] 'Schiele's' call to "people who understand" was significant, and in his foreword to the book Roessler responded, declaring the artist's arrest and imprisonment "the ill-intended blunder of overly enthusiastic moral busybodies and the pitiful martyrdom of an artist who was misunderstood in his lifetime". Forced to "tread paths completely overgrown with the weeds of prejudice" through his affront to moral and sexual proprieties, Schiele was a genius martyred for his art, a Christ-like figure who needed the protection of his fellow modernists.[48]

Roessler had already gathered this support in his publication *In Memoriam Egon Schiele* of 1921, an edited collection of appraisals of Schiele's work that included a contribution by the art historian Hans Tietze, who had seen the incriminating prints at Grünwald's invitation. Collectively, the authors all presented Schiele as an artist driven by anxieties that were as spiritual as they were sexual. For Roessler, "His religiosity, turned inward so as to become mystical, drove Schiele towards eroticism, an eroticism that ranged from the sentimental all the way to the perverse, and that made him an abomination for all narrow-minded moral hypocrites".[49] And for Kurt Rathe, Schiele's eroticism was "absolved by showing figures that are bloodthirstily ascetic, figures who reveal the torments of their souls no less passionately than the nudes reveal their nakedness".[50] In the same year as *In Memoriam*, Roessler published a collection of letters and poems by Schiele, and one year later, in 1922, his *Recollections of Egon Schiele* appeared, accompanying the publication of the Prison Diary; deluxe editions were produced as collectors' items for all publications except the Diary.[51] This construction of Schiele's life, work and legacy ran in parallel with a series of exhibitions in Vienna, including a major retrospective selected to inaugurate Otto Nirenstein's (later Kallir) Neue Galerie, which opened just two months after Grünwald's trial in the winter of 1923.[52]

This was the backdrop against which the drama of the Grünwald trial was staged, and these were the actors, men invested in Schiele's work as collectors and critics, as connoisseurs. Their professional status, their ability not only to discern high from low quality work but also to uphold this distinction through the mythology of genius, was all brought to bear on the case against Grünwald. As he declared, his prints – his colour lithographs of "good quality" – had been shown to a select few, including representatives of the Ministries of Art and Education, with the knowledge and authority to recognise and maintain the difference between art and pornography. Disinterested and, we might say, disembodied – able to respond to the work in ways that were not entangled with the world of sex – these men did not desire; they were not susceptible. The modernists' use of the word 'erotic' was significant here as it established a safe distance between image and viewer, working to suppress their corporeality; this was about sight as opposed to touch, a way of looking at the naked female body that emphasised the spectators' critical detachment, their moral faculties, their non-arousal.[53] At his trial, Grünwald called the ministers who had seen the prints "art lovers", but this was about the love of Art – not what was often described as "the art of the brothel"[54] – and to emphasise this point he told the court "they were certainly not considering a purchase".[55] This position provided Grünwald with his response to the charge of obscenity. Fixated on the work of art as it referred to itself and its creator – the work of art that was erotic and, if not moral, certainly not *im*moral – the modernist defence marshalled for the Grünwald trial also gave the art establishment its conventions for the discussion and display of Schiele's work throughout the twentieth century and up to the present day.

SAFEGUARDING SCHIELE

Grünwald was tried at a time when Schiele's supporters were working intensively to establish his posthumous reputation in the German-speaking world. In his overview of the twentieth-century reception of the artist's work, Wolfgang G. Fischer considers the challenges such individuals faced in maintaining this reputation through the First World War but also, and far more significantly, the Second.[56] It was not until the last half of the twentieth century that Schiele's somewhat neglected position in the history of modern Austrian art started to shift, and this was primarily through the work of dealers and collectors.

Such efforts were not confined to Austria, but were also achieved to a great extent in the English-speaking world: Kallir, for example, who, like Grünwald, had emigrated to the United States after the *Anschluss*, mounted a series of retrospectives at the Galerie St. Etienne in New York in the 1940s through to the 1960s, raising Schiele's profile in America. This process was not, however, without its controversies and we see this in a remark of Kokoschka's, relayed by Fischer, who had organised the first exhibition devoted to Schiele's work in London at Marlborough Fine Art in 1964: "he put me on the spot: 'So you've been having a show of that little crook, that pornographer!'"[57] The denigration of Schiele's work as pornography typified many of the critical responses to this mid-twentieth-century resurgence of interest in the artist. As Keith Roberts wrote in his review of Schiele's work at the

Marlborough exhibition for *The Burlington Magazine*: "His most typical works are the sketches and watercolours of girls, lolling about in various states of calculated undress ... these are more like inspired *graffiti* from some public lavatory frequented by old men".[58]

This disdain accounts in part for the recuperation of Schiele's drawings as 'erotic' works of art in more recent years, particularly by those who played important roles in bringing the artist to international attention in the post-war period.[59] In the last decades of the twentieth century, when Schiele's images of the naked female body have appeared in the public domain, many writers have reactivated the modernist defence of his work, with its emphases on the artist-martyr and the sacred-sexual.[60] The 'erotic' has continued to operate powerfully in this context as what Lynda Nead has identified as a middle term that mediates between art, on the one hand, and pornography, on the other. She writes: "Since pornography may be defined as any representation that achieves a certain degree of sexual explicitness, art has to be protected from being engulfed by pornography in order to maintain its position as the opposition to pornography".[61] The category of the 'erotic' provides a middle ground which separates these two forms of cultural production whilst also allowing them to mingle with one another, and this permissive policing has been crucial for the appreciation of an artist like Schiele. Ultimately, the safeguarding of his work as 'erotic' and through this, as art as opposed to pornography – depends upon the disavowal of the interested and embodied subject. This goes some way towards explaining why the late twentieth-century reception of his drawings has been so very preoccupied with questions of form, style and aesthetic significance.

An interesting exception to this discourse of the disinterested, disembodied subject is a review of an important exhibition of Schiele's work at the Museum of Modern Art, New York, held in 1997, by the writer John Updike.[62] In his article entitled 'Can Genitals Be Beautiful?', Updike also addressed the question as to whether Schiele's work was art or pornography. He concluded – somewhat problematically – that Schiele's nudes were too gaunt to excite the male viewer sexually, and hence could not be considered pornographic; genitals could be beautiful, or rather, they could be displayed on the walls of the Modern. Unusually, Updike did not justify this through evasive descriptions of line, colour and contour. By contrast, having safeguarded Schiele's work as non-arousing, as art as opposed to pornography, he then proceeded to write in vivid detail about the artist's depictions of the female sex, the "secret cave", the "densely curly pudenda", the "genitals – lit as if by a fire within", and the labia, indistinguishable from "the fingers and the folds of her red slip".[63] Such "peeps", as he described them, were the source of the exhibition's "electricity" because, as he noted rather wistfully: "Women in the age of voluminous long skirts and petticoats, we are more than once reminded, did not wear underpants, and a casual flash was more possible then than in our age of short skirts revealing only the impregnable crotch of pantyhose".[64]

Updike's piece shows that ultimately the distinction between art and pornography is a capricious one in that it continually resists our attempts to define and secure it. His writing – his aroused response to visual material that was not, apparently, arousing – also prompts us to question the dispassionate detachment of the viewer from the image that modernism insisted it could achieve. The case against Schiele, through his surviving dealer, and against his drawings, through their reproduction, was so fraught because it raised the very question of desire and susceptibility that his supporters worked so assiduously to suppress. Schiele's work was about the world of sex and, as Updike's lament about the age of the impregnable crotch of pantyhose reveals, it remains about the world of sex.

REPRESSIVE MODERNISM

The power and authority of modernism originates in its ability to offend, to transgress. Schiele's status as the *enfant terrible* of early twentieth-century Viennese art was achieved through his challenge to the 'repressive' moral and sexual *mores* of his time. The impact of his drawings of the female sex – works that were removed from exhibitions and destroyed in courtrooms – lay in their violation of the boundaries between art and pornography, between what was and was not 'acceptable', and this affront provided Schiele with his identity as an avant-gardist. The case against Grünwald and his offensive pictures, along with such events as Schiele's own arrest in the Neulengbach Affair, seems to confirm the force of the artist's attack on society, and this is how it is represented in much of the scholarship.[65] But was the atmosphere of 'Vienna 1900' as reactionary as the reception of Schiele's work suggests? As Michel Foucault considered in his *History of Sexuality*:

> If sex is repressed, that is, condemned to prohibition, nonexistence, and silence, then the mere fact that one is speaking about it has the appearance of a deliberate transgression. A person who holds forth in such language places himself outside the reach of power; he upsets established law; he somehow anticipates the coming freedom.[66]

Foucault was critical of what he termed the 'repressive hypothesis', the assumption that the modern period was one of censorship and of silence as far as matters relating to the body and to sex were concerned; new legislation – such as the international anti-pornography agreement of 1910 that, we should remember, coincided with Schiele's first explicit drawings – did not mean that sexuality was repressed; rather, as Foucault writes, it was almost the opposite case. He argues that, in fact, there was a remarkable proliferation of discourses on sex at this time, a "discursive ferment" that had been gathering in momentum as far back as the eighteenth century.[67] This makes the "if" at the start of Foucault's proposal above so crucial, as it suggests that Schiele's work was not as offensive as we might like to think. However, the securing of his position in the narrative of an embattled Viennese modernism meant that it needed to be proclaimed as such. Schiele had to appear to "upset established law" and, in terms of the historiography, this is what made the legal actions against him and his agents so very useful.

In an essay published in the collection *Rethinking Vienna 1900* of 2001, Robert Jensen reflected on the market-led generation of Schiele's drawings of the female body, their circulation amongst his clients, and their modes of delivery around the city. Schiele's lover Wally Neuzil, whom he considered too lower-class to marry, was reputedly asked to hand over in person the explicit drawings he produced of her to his patrons. According to Alessandra Comini, she was occasionally subjected to "lewd interrogation by some of the more curious customers", encounters that made her cry.[68] Jensen does not pursue the sexualised transactions at work in this "new traffic in pictures" but, in a reading that is also indebted to Foucault, he proposes that Schiele's "sexual truth-telling" did not signify a revolt against society; rather, it was "precisely oriented toward meeting a societal demand": "His work sustained rather than fundamentally criticised the social order".[69] Jensen's reading is an important corrective that encourages us to interrogate how Schiele's drawings did not just point to unequal sexual relations between men and women in early twentieth-century Vienna but also perpetuated them.

How, then, might we start to engage with Schiele's work differently, outside the modernist discourse that circumvents the social and sexual politics that informed the production and dissemination of his drawings? The trial of Grünwald is such an interesting case because it shows how the opposition between art and pornography mapped on to other, equally value-laden binaries – between the original and the copy, the private and the public, the legal and the illegal. Schiele's work was so problematic (and hence remains so interesting) because it continually called these distinctions into question, highlighting their instability and contingency. In his practice, Schiele collapsed the binary system, trafficking back and forth between the high and the low, the licit and the illicit; this is what I find so very compelling about his work. In the modernist defence of the artist by the critics who established his reputation, and those who have maintained it since, these borders between art and pornography and their associated domains, are, however, reinstated to protect an 'offensive' position that, I would argue, we no longer need. What lies behind this continued urge to categorise and contain Schiele's work? And how might we develop alternative approaches that engage rigorously with not only its content and context but also its consumption? Schiele's drawings of the naked female body invite us to be radical in our revisions.

NOTES

1 Strafgesetz 1852 (Österreich); retrieved 14 April 2014 from http://de.wikisource.org/wiki/Strafgesetz_1852_(Österreich).
2 Schiele produced just seventeen prints during his career. For more information on his work as a graphic artist see Jane Kallir, *Egon Schiele: The Complete Works*, London (Thames & Hudson), 1998, pp. 646-50. In 1917 he published a portfolio of copies of twelve drawings through the Viennese book dealer Richard Lanyi's publishing house. It was not what was termed an 'erotic' portfolio; it included self-portraits, family portraits and images of children as well as single- and double-figure studies. It was produced as an edition of 400 copies, numbered and signed by Schiele, and is the only portfolio attributed to the artist.
3 *Wiener Allgemeine Zeitung*, 19 September 1923.
4 *Neue Freie Presse*, 19 September 1923; *Wiener Allgemeine Zeitung*, 19 September 1923.
5 *Neue Freie Presse*, 21 September 1923.
6 *Neue Freie Presse*, 19 September 1923; *Wiener Allgemeine Zeitung*, 19 September 1923.
7 *Neue Freie Presse*, 19 September 1923.
8 *Neue Freie Presse*, 19 September 1923.
9 *Neue Freie Presse*, 19 September 1923.
10 *Neue Freie Presse*, 19 September 1923.
11 *Neue Freie Presse*, 19 September 1923. The president of the court was Hofrat Dr Barasch. Utilising Paragraph 42 of the new Press Law, the state prosecutor petitioned the president to consult with the jury on the fate of the reproductions. Their discussion was the first of its kind to happen under this legislation, and as it had to take place in private, away from the journalists gathered in the court, there is no record of the debate that ensued beyond the president's subsequent decision to declare the prints forfeit. This was reported in *Arbeiter Zeitung*, 19 September 1923.
12 *Neue Freie Presse*, 21 September 1923.
13 The case is indexed in the Register of the Regional Court for Criminal Cases WStLA Landesgericht für Strafsachen B14 2346/1923. No further paperwork has survived.
14 The material presented here has been gathered from the following newspaper sources: *Arbeiter Zeitung*, 19 September 1923; *Neue Freie Presse*, 19 and 21 September 1923; *Neues Wiener Journal*, 19 September 1923; *Neues Wiener Tagblatt*, 19 September 1923; *Die Neue Zeitung*, 19 September 1923; *Wiener Allgemeine Zeitung*, 18 September 1923.
15 As Frederic Schwartz has argued in his reconstruction of two early twentieth-century trials involving the doctor Theodor Beer, Professor of Medicine at the University of Medicine, and the architect Adolf Loos, who both stood to answer charges of child pornography and molestation: "A close look at scandals and court proceedings can reveal how practices of the case cut through a variety of different media, how forms of knowledge intersected, how matters of public concern at a specific moment of modernity were negotiated": Schwartz, 'Architecture and Crime: Adolf Loos and the Culture of the "Case"', *Art Bulletin*, vol. 94, no. 3 (September 2012), pp. 437-57, at p. 437.
16 Schiele exhibited with the Neukunstgruppe

(New Art Group), a collective of sixteen artists formed in 1909; Schiele was president of the group. For more information on the scandal of the exhibition see Irmgard Hütter, 'Gütersloh: Die ersten zwanzig Jahre (1899–1918)', in Heribert Hutter (ed), *A.P. Gütersloh: Zum 100 Geburtstag*, Vienna (Österreichischer Kunst und Kulturverlag) 1987, p. 42.

17 Abigail Soloman-Godeau, 'The Legs of the Countess', *October*, vol. 39 (Winter 1986), pp. 65-108, at p.104.

18 The nude as an art historical category that stands apart from the 'base' matter of sexuality was encapsulated by Kenneth Clark in *The Nude* (Harmondsworth: Penguin, 1976) and problematised by John Berger in *Ways of Seeing* (London: BBC and Penguin, 1972). Feminist art historians have since probed their formulations and developed new ways of thinking about the relationship between sex and spectatorship. See, for example, Anthea Callen, *The Spectacular Body: Science, Method, and Meaning in the Work of Degas* (New Haven, London: Yale University Press, 1995); Tamar Garb, 'The Forbidden Gaze: Women Artists and the Male Nude in Late Nineteenth-Century France' in Nicholas Mirzoeff (ed.), *The Visual Culture Reader* (London: Routledge, 1998), pp. 415-22; Lynda Nead, *The Female Nude: Art, Obscenity and Sexuality* (London: Routledge, 1992).

19 This is based upon a discussion of the fate of Grünwald's art collection, which was broken apart in World War Two, in Melissa Müller and Monika Tatzkow (eds.), *Lost Lives, Lost Art: Jewish Collectors, Nazi Art Theft and the Quest for Justice*, London (Frontline Books) 2010, pp. 172-85.

20 It is interesting to note that, following the Secession exhibition, this painting has an uninterrupted history of private male possession, from Grünwald, its first owner, to the present day The owners of the painting are as follows: Karl Grünwald; Richard Lanyi; Otto Kranz; Friedrich Wolff (Frederic Knize); Fritz Kamm; and finally, Rudolf Leopold. See Kallir 1998, p. 336.

21 Tobias G. Natter reflects on such issues in 'On the Limits of the Exhibitable: The Naked Body and Public Space in Viennese Art around 1900', in Max Hollein and Natter (eds.), *The Naked Truth: Klimt, Schiele and Other Scandals*, exh. cat., Schirn Kunsthalle, Frankfurt, and Leopold Museum, Vienna, 2005, pp. 17-42. We cannot identify the drawings by Schiele that were implicated in the Prague exhibition scandal.

22 For a discussion of these actions which included raids on bookshops and postal embargoes, see Gary D. Stark, 'Pornography, Society and the Law in Imperial Germany', *Peer Reviewed Articles*, Paper 12, 1981, pp. 200-29, at pp. 218-19; retrieved 2 January 2014 from http://scholarworks.gvsu.edu/hst_articles/12.

23 Kallir 1998, p. 697.

24 Hollein and Natter 2005, pp. 240-41. Andreas Krampolek established his printing practice in 1905, opening a further branch in Stuttgart in 1914. He also worked for the Board of Trade for Lower Austria and in 1923, the year of the trial, he became a member of the Viennese Society of Fine Arts; he therefore had the credentials to be associated with this network of artists and dealers that stretched across Austria and Germany.

25 Oskar Kokoschka, 'Drei Fabriken fälschen meine Bilder: Ein interview mit dem Spiegel', *Der Spiegel*, xx/44 (24 October 1966), p. 172.

26 As Robert Jensen has argued, "What is most striking about Schiele's career is that by the age of 20, he had already discovered many of most important and influential patrons": Jensen, 'A Matter of Professionalism: Marketing Identity in Fin-de-Siècle Vienna' in Steven Beller (ed.), *Rethinking Vienna 1900*, New York/Oxford (Berghahn Books) 2001, pp. 195-219, at p. 207.

27 Heinrich Benesch, *Mein Weg mit Egon Schiele*, New York (Verlag der Johannespresse) 1965, p. 26.

28 Klaus Albrecht Schröder, *Egon Schiele: Eros and Passion*, Munich/New York: Prestel, 1995), p. 112.

29 *Gustav Klimt – Egon Schiele: Zum Gedächtnis ihres Todes vor 50 Jahren*, Albertina, Vienna, 1968, p. 74, quoted in Kallir 1998, p. 75.

30 As Lynda Nead has argued in her analysis of twentieth-century debates on art and pornography: "Emphasis was placed on the nude as an ideal form that embodies perfection, universality, and unity. These conventions were in opposition to the codes and functions of pornography – fragmentation, particularity, titillation. Above all else, paintings of the female nude had to be closed off from any associations with commercialism or sexual arousal. Refusing the connotation of commodity, the discourse of high art retreated into a vocabulary of contemplation and aesthetic response": Nead, 'The Female Nude: Pornography, Art and Sexuality', *Signs*, vol. 15, no. 2 (Winter 1990), pp. 323-35, at p. 329. Schiele's drawings, as works on paper as opposed to canvas, were especially difficult to 'close off' from the visual culture of pornography.

31 One exception is Schröder, who mentions the influence of what he identifies as "left-hand pictures" (which he cites as a specifically English term) on Schiele's drawings. However, no visual examples are provided or discussed and ultimately this maintains the distinction between art and pornography: Schröder 1995, p. 112.

32 Soloman-Godeau 1986, pp. 94-104.

33 Another example is the 1912 trial of the book dealer Carl W. Stern for the dissemination of pornographic literature and illustrations that reputedly spread the fame of the Austrian publishing house as far as Australia. Stern was acquitted on the basis that he had submitted the material to the Ministry of the Interior, as was required by law, ahead of printing. In a leading article for the *Arbeiter Zeitung* which was entitled 'Morality', the case was considered as an exposé of the hypocritical Austrian legal system: *Arbeiter-Zeitung*, 1 June 1912.

34 Stark 1981, p. 207. Stark identifies the largest firms as Gustav Grimm and Sachs & Pollack in Budapest, and C.W. Stern and the Wiener Verlag, under the ownership of Fritz Freund, in Vienna.

35 Vienna's erotic photography industry was dominated by the studio of Otto Schmidt. For more information on Otto Schmidt see Michael Ponstingl, '"Die grosse Abwechslung der gebotenen Stellungen und Modelle ... wird jeden Künstler befriedigen" [The great variety of poses and models ... will satisfy any artist]: Die Geschäfte des Wiener Berufsfotografen Otto Schmidt mit dem Nackten', in *Die nackte Wahrheit und anderes: Aktfotografie um 1900*, exh. cat., Museum für Fotografie, Berlin, 2013, pp. 43-51.

36 Soloman-Godeau 1986, p. 97. See also Kelly Dennis, 'Seeing and Touching: Photography and the Birth of the Modern', in Dennis, *Art/Porn: A History of Seeing and Touching*, Oxford/New York (Berg) 2009, pp. 57-123.

37 Stark 1981, p. 218.
38 *Arbeiter-Zeitung*, 11 June 1912.
39 For a list of the collectors and dealers who knew the artist see Kallir 1998, pp. 684-86.
40 Schiele knew this through the example of Klimt, whose "obscene" drawings were criticised in the press on their display at the Galerie Miethke in 1910. As Hugo Ganz commented, "Nudity, with or without details, is artistically quite unobjectionable. But the exposure, the shameless presentation of the genitals is the art of the brothel and for it to be exhibited is a gross violation of one's feelings of shame and we cannot reject it too vigorously .... The directors of this exhibition should exercise some censure unless they want to awaken the suspicion that they have some dealings in pornography": Ganz, 'Erotik und Obszönität: zur neuen Klimt-Ausstellung', *Frankfurter Zeitung und Handelsblatt*, 3 December 1910, third morning edition. The exhibition was a commercial success: Klimt sold eleven drawings: see Tobias G. Natter, *Die Galerie Miethke: Eine Kunsthandlung im Zentrum der Moderne*, exh. cat., Jüdisches Museum der Stadt Wien, Vienna, 2003, p. 216.
41 Hermann Bahr, *Die bildenden Künste: 1910-34*, Vienna (Akademie der bildenden Künste) 2007, p. 61.
42 Dr. Hans Arthur Schäfer was assisted by Dr. Fritz Wagschal: *Die Neue Zeitung*, 19 September 1923.
43 *Neue Freie Presse*, 19 September 1923.
44 *Neue Freie Presse*, 19 September 1923
45 *Neue Freie Presse*, 19 September 1923
46 *Neue Freie Presse*, 19 September 1923. Journalists did not report on the debate about quality between Grünwald and Formanek beyond its being "lengthy".
47 Alessandra Comini, *Schiele in Prison*, New York (New York Graphic Society) 1973, p. 58. This is a translation of the original text of Arthur Roessler (ed.), *Egon Schiele im Gefängnis: Aufzeichnungen und Zeichnungen*, Vienna/Leipzig (Verlag Carl Konegen) 1922.
48 Comini 1973, p. 40.
49 Arthur Roessler, *In Memoriam Egon Schiele*, Vienna (Richard Lanyi) 1921, p. 22.
50 Roessler 1921, p. 45.
51 Roessler was not the only agent involved in this consolidation of Schiele's reputation: in 1921, Fritz Karpfen published 1000 copies of *Das Egon Schiele Buch* through the printing arm of the Vienna Workshops.
52 The exhibition at the Neue Galerie included a number of drawings. It was preceded by Gustav Nebehay's display of 162 works on paper in 'Die Zeichnung: Egon Schiele' in the spring of 1919, and was followed by a further one-man show at the Kunsthandlung Würtle in the winter of 1925, which included 109 drawings.
53 Such a distinction between the erotic and the pornographic, and between sight and touch, has been convincingly dismantled by Dennis, who argues: "In contemporary mainstream debate, to defend erotica as 'leaving room for the imagination' and to condemn pornography as being 'too close' is actually to replay an ages-old antithesis between sight and touch – an antithesis regulated in centuries past not by the media and the courts but by the reception and criticism of historical works of art": Dennis 2009, p. 3.
54 Ganz, 'Erotik und Obszönität', as note 40.
55 *Neue Freie Presse*, 19 September 1923.
56 Wolfgang G. Fischer, 'Egon Schiele's Rise to Posthumous Fame', in Kallir 1998, pp. 247-55. See also Sophie Lillie, 'A Legacy Forlorn: The Fate of Egon Schiele's Early Collectors', in Renée Price (ed.), *Egon Schiele: The Ronald S. Lauder and Serge Sabarsky Collections*, exh. cat., Neue Galerie, Museum for German and Austrian Art, New York (Prestel) 2005, pp. 111-39.
57 Kallir 1998, p. 253.
58 Keith Roberts, *The Burlington Magazine*, vol. 106, no. 741 (December 1964), p. 584.
59 See for example Serge Sabarsky, 'Egon Schiele at Face Value', in Price 2005,, pp. 43-45.
60 This is just beginning to change. We see this in the work of Tobias Natter, and also in Jane Kallir's latest publication, *Egon Schiele's Women*, Munich/London/New York (Prestel), 2012.
61 Nead 1990, p. 324.
62 The work was compiled from the Leopold Collection, the world's largest inventory of Schiele's paintings and drawings amassed by the collector Rudolf Leopold from the 1950s onwards, which was due to be displayed in its own dedicated space, the Leopold Museum in Vienna, which opened in 2001; John Updike, 'Can Genitals Be Beautiful?', *New York Review of Books*, vol. 44, no. 19 (1997), pp. 10-12.
63 Updike 1997, p. 12.
64 Updike 1997, p. 12.
65 See, for example, Franz Wischin, *'Ich Gefangener, schuldlos gestraft, gereinigt!': Kunst oder Kinderpornographie: Die Affäre von Neulengbach 1912*, Vienna (Christian Brandstätter) 1998. Tobias Natter, however, counters this in his recent essay 'Egon Schiele and the Neulengbach Affair' in Price 2005, pp. 140-57.
66 Michel Foucault, *The Will to Knowledge. The History of Sexuality: Volume One*, London (Penguin) 1990, p. 6 (first published in 1976).
67 Foucault 1990, p. 18.
68 Alessandra Comini, *Egon Schiele's Portraits*, Berkeley (University of California Press) 1974, p. 99. This is not supported with documentary evidence, though it is likely to have emerged in the interviews Comini conducted with Schiele's family and friends in the 1960s. For an overview of these fascinating experiences see Comini, 'Pilgrimage to Schiele's Past: Forgotten Sites, Still-Living Sitters and Early Collectors', in Price 2005, pp. 72-101.
69 Jensen 2001, p. 214.

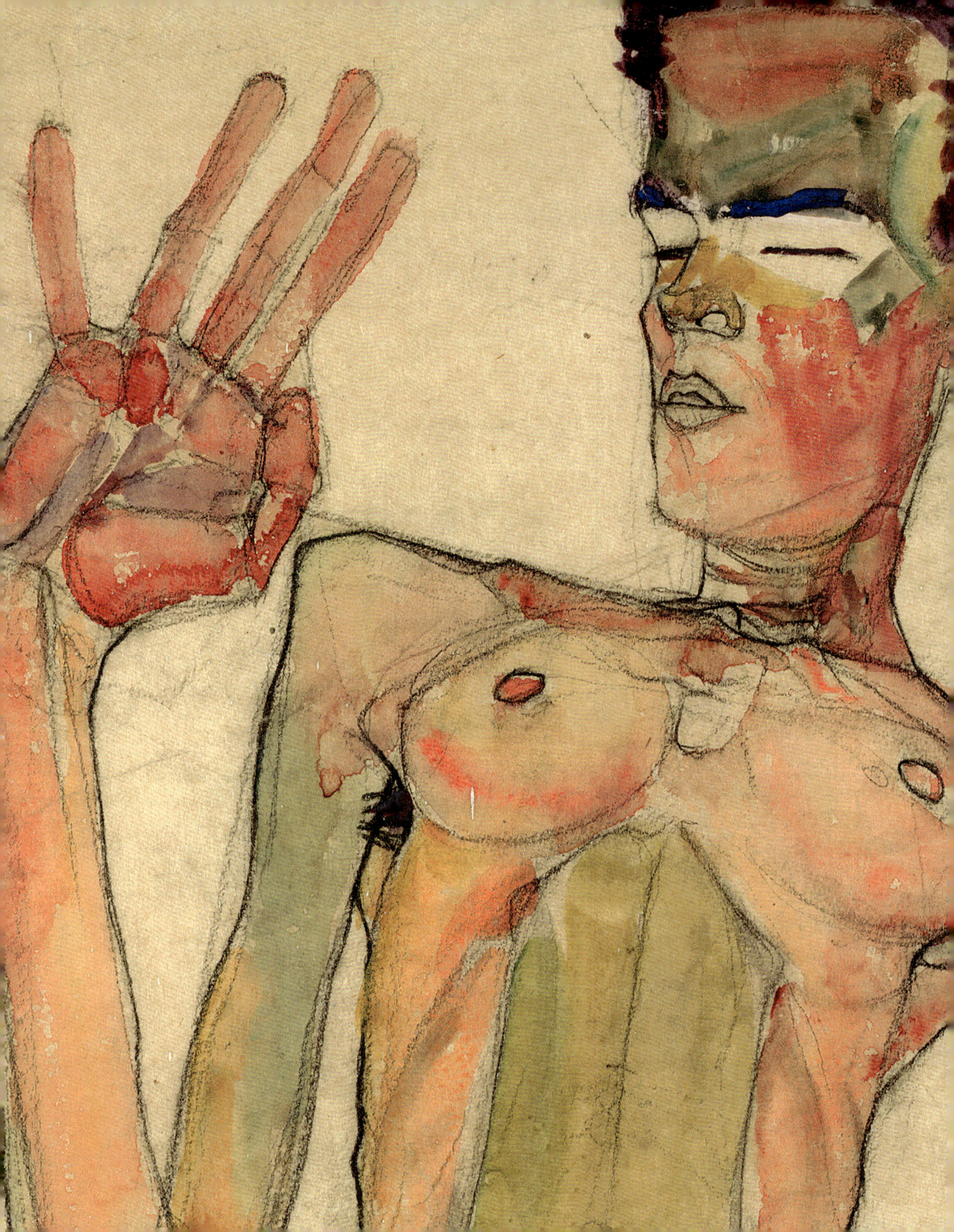

DIONYSIAN UGLINESS AND RADICAL BEAUTY IN EGON SCHIELE'S OEUVRE

KATHRYN SIMPSON

Like other precocious artists, philosophers and prolific self-portraitists, Egon Schiele favoured the metaphor of 'giving birth to oneself'. His true origins were almost as striking: Schiele's mother Marie met her future husband when she was a mere twelve-year-old, convent-educated little girl. Adolf Schiele was twenty-three and apparently vowed on the spot to make this child his wife. Five years later, in 1879, Marie married Adolf – only to be infected by the deadly syphilis her husband carried silently within him.

Less than three years after Adolf and Marie were married, the German philosopher Friedrich Nietzsche penned these words in the aphorism 'On female chastity':

> There is something quite amazing and monstrous about the education of upper-class women. What could be more paradoxical? All the world is agreed that they are to be brought up as ignorant as possible of erotic matters, and that one has to imbue their souls with a profound sense of shame in such matters ... they are supposed to remain ignorant even in their hearts; they are supposed to have neither eyes nor ears ... for this – their 'evil'; and mere knowledge is considered evil. And then to be hurled, as by a gruesome lightning bolt, into reality and knowledge, by marriage .... In sum, one cannot be too kind about women.[1]

The reality of the Schiele wedding night – gruesome or otherwise – may never be known; but Egon's brother-in-law later claimed that the adolescent Marie ran away from Adolf in terror.[2] Her retrospective diary entry,[3] however, reads like the polite reminiscence of a proper young lady. After the wedding began a series of pregnancies and miscarriages that, while common enough at the time, could nevertheless have been very traumatic – Marie's body was dedicated to a dance of death masquerading as the cycle of life. By the time she bore Egon Marie had already given birth to no fewer than four babies, only one of whom would survive beyond childhood. Egon, the male heir, was brought into a world in which sexuality, disease and death were not only inextricably intertwined but also oppressively omnipresent, and his art evinces this fearsome reality most memorably in his brutal treatment of the naked body.

Initially allied with Gustav Klimt and the Vienna Secessionists, by 1910 Schiele was creating original works that focused on themes of sexuality and death, ugliness, masking, sickness and transformation. These themes share a kinship with Nietzsche's philosophy, particularly his later concept of the Dionysian. While we have no reason to imagine Schiele as a reader of Nietzsche, Vienna was saturated both with Nietzsche's actual writings and with multiple and various Nietzscheanisms. Already by 1876, at a time when Nietzsche had few readers in Germany, university students in Vienna had formed a Nietzsche society known as the Pernerstorfer circle and written to the philosopher to express their admiration for his work.[4] Viennese composer Gustav Mahler originally intended to name his Third Symphony (completed in 1896) 'Meine fröhliche Wissenschaft' in homage to Nietzsche's book *Die fröhliche Wissenschaft* (*The Gay Science* [1882/87]) and incorporated Nietzsche's 'Night Song' from *Thus Spoke Zarathustra* (1883–85) into the fourth movement of that symphony.[5] Max Burckhard, who directed the Burgtheater, the national imperial theatre in Vienna , from 1890 to 1898, apparently worshipped Nietzsche.[6] The Vienna Psychoanalytic Society discussed the philosopher frequently.[7] Irascible Viennese architect and art critic Adolf Loos named *Trotzdem* (1931), a collection of his writings from 1900 to 1930, after Nietzsche; in Nietzsche's autobiography *Ecce Homo* (completed 1888) he used the term '*trotzdem*' in a claim that can be translated as "everything decisive comes into being 'nevertheless' [*trotzdem*]".[8] Loos paraphrased this passage as the epigraph for his *Trotzdem*. Klimt's Secession-era work, for example his Beethoven frieze for the Vienna Secession's Beethoven exhibition of 1902, shows the influence of a contemporaneously popular, romantic synthesis of the ideas of German polymath Johann Wolfgang von Goethe, composer and theorist Richard Wagner, philosopher Arthur Schopenhauer and Nietzsche.[9]

Thus there were certainly myriad different manifestations of the Viennese Nietzsche cult. Nevertheless Nietzsche's first book, *The Birth of Tragedy out of the Spirit of Music* (1872/86), was particularly influential in artistic and literary circles, and his iconoclastic ideas regarding classical culture, the Dionysian, music, poetry, the visual arts, the higher man, embodiment and the unconscious were widely discussed. In an oft-quoted passage from *Gustav Klimt, The Beethoven Frieze* (1980) author Marian Bisanz-Prakken states succinctly: "every educated person was familiar with Nietzsche's philosophy".[10] Indeed, the ubiquity of Nietzschean influences in Schiele's Vienna can barely be overstated.

In such a cultural context it is not surprising that Schiele developed a visual vocabulary well suited to Nietzschean interpretation. Nietzsche's philosophical and psychological themes are admittedly prolific and protean: those most fruitful when put into dialogue with Schiele's oeuvre include his notions of embodiment and his Dionysian perspectives on beauty and ugliness, transformation and masking, health and sickness (including his 'great health', which incorporates sickness) and self-creation. Schiele's art highlights the emergence, from pathology and paroxysm, of a philosophy of embodiment as the source of a Dionysian power, and his profoundly anti-classical presentation of the body, especially the naked body, continues to have radical implications for our understanding of aesthetics and existence today.[11]

In *The Birth of Genius* (*Dead Mother II*) (fig. 19), which Schiele painted at the age of twenty-one, we are confronted with an emphatic declaration of self-creation. He pictures a living baby, an expression of shock consuming his round face, who struggles against his containment within his dead mother's torso. The dead mother's head slants horizontally in one direction at the top of the image while her long, bony fingers splay outward, in the opposite direction, at the bottom – this visually frames the baby, who pushes against his enclosure with eerily adult hands. One digit extends beyond the border. This image of a baby struggling for life, trapped within the womb of a dead mother, is in keeping with Egon's frequent complaints about Marie's cold, unloving nature – her deadness, essentially – and his descriptions of himself as an autogenetic genius. However, one can plainly

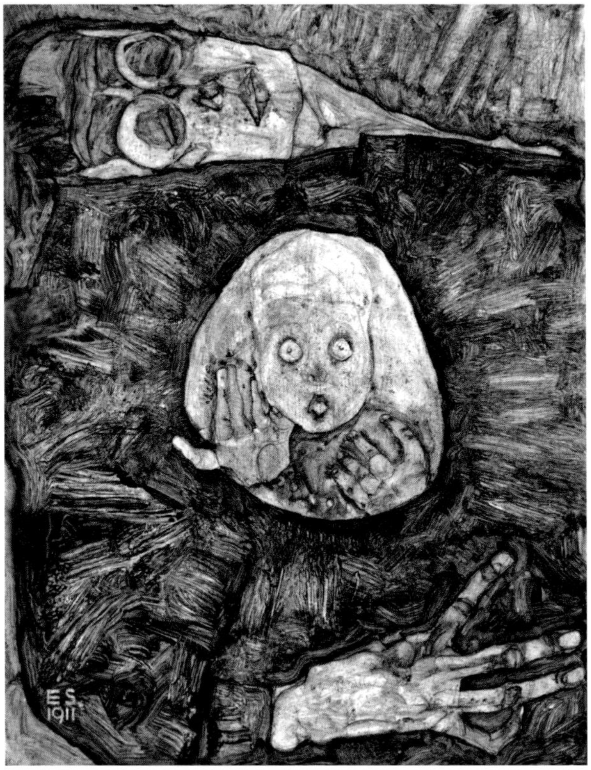

19
EGON SCHIELE
The Birth of Genius
(*Dead Mother II*), 1911
Presumed destroyed (Kallir P. 195)
Photograph Galerie St. Etienne,
New York

see that, regardless of what Egon's conscious intentions were, the artist has given the dead mother the features he normally gives himself – his own face and hands as pictured in many contemporaneous self-portraits. This, arguably, bespeaks apprehension about the Schiele family stain and the terrifying possibility that he himself might also be a 'dead mother'. Paralysed into deadly inertia by congenital sickness, then resentment, a 'dead-mother Schiele' might never be able to breathe life into the potential creations gestating within.[12] Artistic anxieties regarding fecundity are common: Cecile Nebel asserts that "self-doubt, a sense of impotence, anguish, inadequacy, uncertainty have more often than not accompanied artistic creativity".[13] The ambivalent treatment of sexuality, creation and death in *The Birth of Genius* exemplifies not only Schiele's own idiosyncratic turmoil but also his ability to refract the larger dramas of human existence through extreme representations of the human body.

As Sigmund Freud examined his own psyche during self-analysis, so Schiele looked at his own body as an object of and tool for experimentation. Nietzsche did both; he referred to the history of philosophy as that of a grand misunderstanding of the body, and philosophers as thwarted men who mistook their symptom for a system. Nietzsche's radical originality – his self-designations included philologist, philosopher, psychologist and anti-Christ – was due in no small part to the way in which he turned this misunderstanding of the body on its head by striving to articulate and legitimate precisely a philosophy of the body. In *The Gay Science*, a book written after convalescence from a lengthy and harrowing illness, Nietzsche declares his aim explicitly: "To what extent can truth endure incorporation? That is the question; that is the experiment."[14] This evokes both gleaning the truths of the flesh and making truth something lived corporeally – truth is now of, and in, the body. In *Thus Spoke Zarathustra*, conceived while Nietzsche was writing *The Gay Science*, he discusses the embodied self, which controls the ego self, as the 'it' – the same 'das Es', in German, that later, English readers would encounter in Freud's work as 'the Id'. That this 'it' rules over our egos and minds should in fact inspire joy, because the body is the source of the soul and of our most valuable forms of knowing:

> 'I,' you say, and are proud of the word. But greater is that in which you do not have faith – your body and its great reason: that which does not say 'I,' but does 'I' .... Behind your thoughts and feelings, my brother, there stands a mighty ruler, an unknown sage – whose name is self. In your body he dwells; he is your body. There is more reason in your body than in your best wisdom .... I want to speak to the despisers of the body. It is their respect that begets their contempt. What is it that created respect and contempt and worth and will? The creative self created respect and contempt; it created pleasure and pain. The creative body created the spirit as a hand for its will.[15]

20
EGON SCHIELE
Female Nude, 1910
Gouache, watercolour and black crayon with white heightening, 44.3 x 30.6 cm
Albertina Museum, Vienna
(Kallir D. 555)

Unsympathetic critics have lambasted Schiele for his adolescent portrayals of the self controlled and tortured by the pains and pleasures of the flesh; from a Nietzschean perspective, however, Schiele shows great wisdom. He, too, experimented to see how he could represent the experiences and knowledges of the body – truth incorporated, pain and pleasure, indivisible, creative and willed to power.

In Schiele's works around 1910–11, especially, the creative and destructive forces of this corporeal self – the 'it' – are pictured provocatively in various stages of sexuality, sickness and death. Schiele objectified and amputated sexualised bodies, both as life-giving vessels and as corpses, in *Nude Pregnant Woman Reclining* (cat. 5), *Female Nude* (fig. 20) and *Male Lower Torso* (cat. 19). In *Nude Pregnant Woman Reclining* we already see him ruminating visually on the same thematic question that still clearly occupied him a year later in *The Birth of Genius* (*Dead Mother II*): what are the relations between sexuality, reproduction and death, between creation and destruction? But *Nude Pregnant Woman Reclining* is less allegorical, more gynaecological. On 18 May 1910, the gynaecologist Dr. Erwin von Graff wrote to the artist regarding a woman who Schiele had apparently impregnated and subsequently deserted, leaving her with the doctor.[16] The doctor allowed Schiele to paint a portrait of him and granted the artist access to pregnant patients and babies for the same creative purpose. Even within an artistic corpus known for its tendency towards the macabre, the portraits Schiele created in this context are notably morbid. Schiele insisted that "everything is living dead",[17] and almost none of his other works capture this philosophy as vividly and aggressively as his pictures of rigid, discoloured babies and limp, forlorn pregnant women – who look more like cattle doomed for slaughter than powerful, creative vessels.

Unlike some of the other pregnant women Schiele portrayed, whose very misery denotes them as alive, the subject in *Nude Pregnant Woman Reclining* could easily be a corpse. The work is unfinished, and Schiele has chosen to represent the pregnant woman's body with a dark rusty red resembling dried blood. Her face is like a smooth clay mask – a mask of death– with holes for eyes and a mouth and no nose. Arms and legs are spread akimbo, arms amputated at the wrist and legs at the knee. We see engorged nipples like ripe plums, a hugely swollen belly on a body that, otherwise, is typically Schielian in its emaciation, thick pubic hair and the tops of dark knee stockings, which remind us of the subject's origins in the profane real world.

Schiele's striking *Female Nude* (fig. 20) embodies the sinister complicity between sex and death. This nude, unlike the pregnant one, seems individual, animated, even alluring: her eyes almost sizzle, her body seems to undulate toward us and her hair – a rose, blue and mauve nimbus – is like a seductive halo. At first glance she looks like someone we might want to touch; at second glance we notice that she may in fact be a corpse, that asymmetrical eyelids hang loosely over empty eyes, that she is missing her arms and legs. The hand that seemed a moment ago to be caressing her torso suggestively now looks rigid and claw-like from rigor mortis. Thus whereas in *Nude Pregnant Woman Reclining* Schiele pictures the sexual, pregnant woman as dead, in *Female Nude* he represents a dead woman as desirable. In Schiele's visions we see that death may be not only the result but even the object of the sexual drive.

Schiele shows dangerous sexuality in *Male Lower Torso* as well. Discolouring naked flesh, which we see only from the waist down, with a wounded palette of indigo, violet and magenta, Schiele paints legs splayed exaggeratedly outward, which emphasises the subject's thinness and creates a large

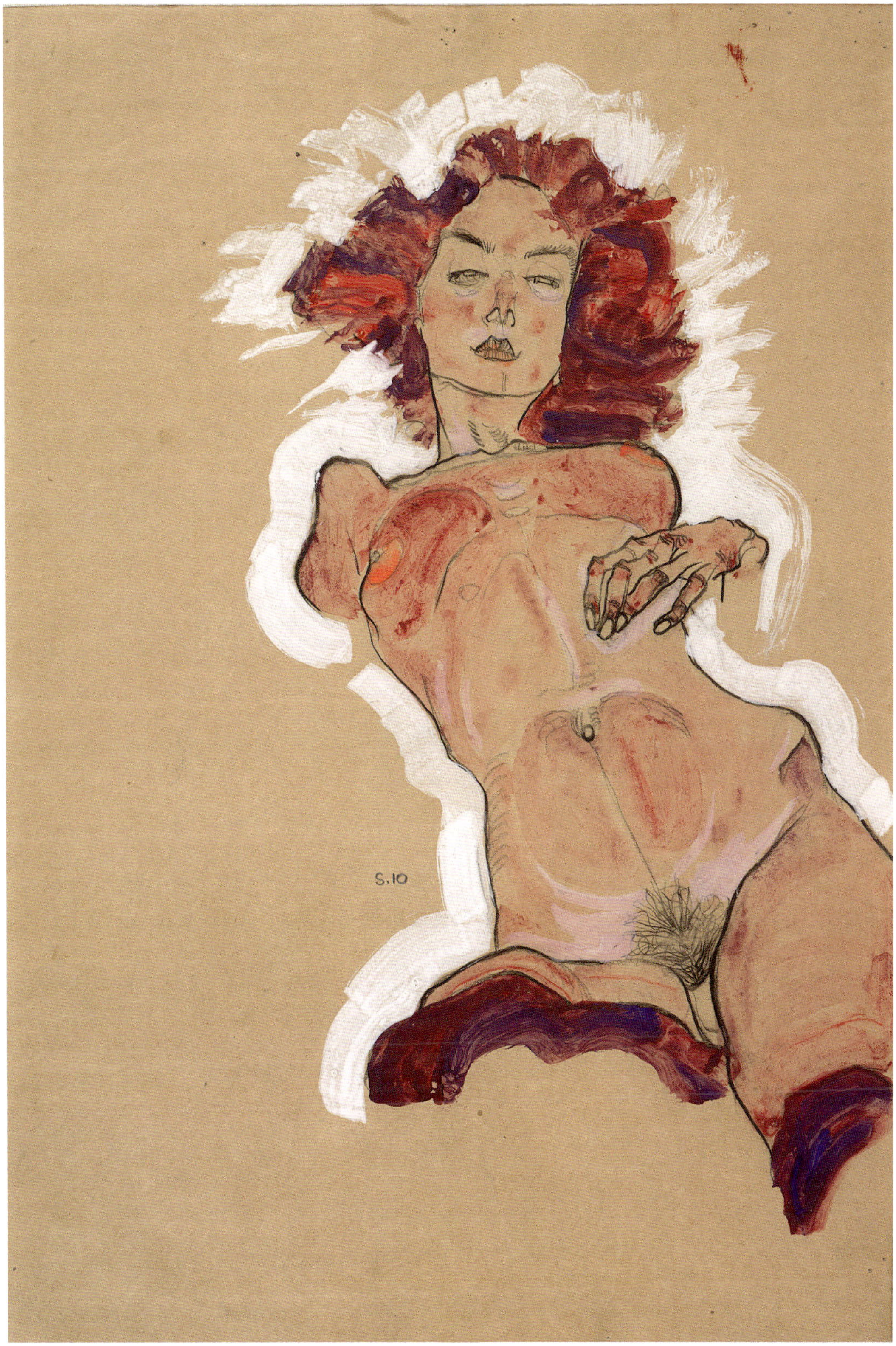
S.10

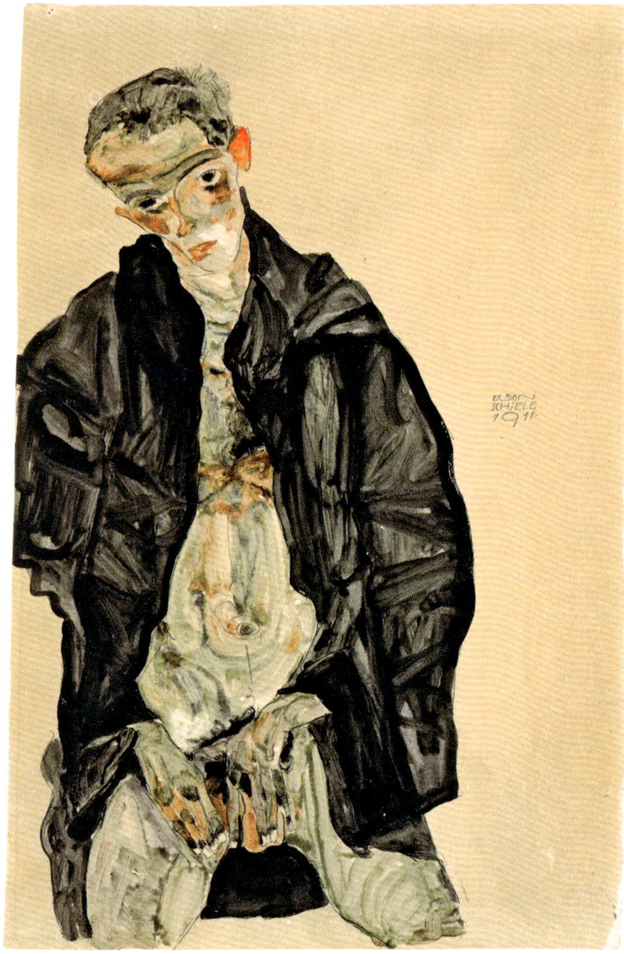

21
EGON SCHIELE
Self-Portrait in Black Cloak, Masturbating, 1911
Gouache, watercolour and pencil, 48 x 32.1 cm
Albertina Museum, Vienna
(Kallir D. 947)

'V' shape. The focus on the male lower torso could have been meant to represent the full force of male sexuality, but instead Schiele's battered and emaciated flesh looks juvenile and flaccid. A profusion of long abdominal hair dwarfs a genital area that is small, limp and ill-defined – like empty little flesh bags. Thus the sexual body is here threatened with pain and castration. While Schiele virtually collapses the genital organs in on themselves he by contrast takes care to represent the fibula, or calf bone, which he paints with a lighter rose wash that darkens into fuchsia and magenta at the base. This representational strategy makes the bone look like it is resting in a pool of blood. In an image that, compositionally, foregrounds the sexual organs Schiele shifts focus to the skeleton, which threatens to burst through translucent flesh across which bruises bloom like dark flowers.

Schiele pictures himself doomed by Eros and Thanatos together, coiled tightly like a snake about to execute a lethal strike in *Self-Portrait*, 1911,[18] where he appears as a kind of neutered vampire; and in *Self-Portrait in Black Cloak, Masturbating* (fig. 21), he likewise looks unsexed and inhuman. In this image of onanism Schiele's hand completely covers his penis and with the position of his fingers makes the scrotal sack into a kind of labial fold. The paint application itself is streaky and scatological, and Schiele shows himself with an ominous blankness of mien.

One way of understanding Schiele's tendencies toward inconsistent application of paint, aggressively anti-classical cropping and composition, the representation of pervasive skin diseases, misshapen or missing genitalia and amputated limbs is as a strategic use of visual ugliness. Schielian ugliness can be better understood alongside Nietzschean thought, especially Nietzsche's redemptive philosophy of Dionysian ugliness. In his late notebooks Nietzsche opined that the "nihilist's eye idealises in the direction of ugliness"[19] – but what does this mean? For Nietzsche there are two different types of nihilism, which in turn dictate two types of ugliness. He says: "Nihilism. It is *ambiguous*. A. Nihilism as a sign of increased power of the spirit: as *active* nihilism. B. Nihilism as decline and recession of the power of the spirit: as *passive* nihilism."[20] Each form of nihilism has a corresponding kind of ugliness based on either a lack or a surplus of power; whereas passive nihilism is decadent pessimism, and pessimistic ugliness signals a hatred of life itself, for Nietzsche active nihilism is Dionysian affirmation – and Dionysian ugliness is part of the highest affirmation of life and its powers.

In *Twilight of the Idols* (1889) Nietzsche noted that "the tragic artist is *not* a pessimist: it is precisely he who *affirms* all that is questionable and terrible in existence, he

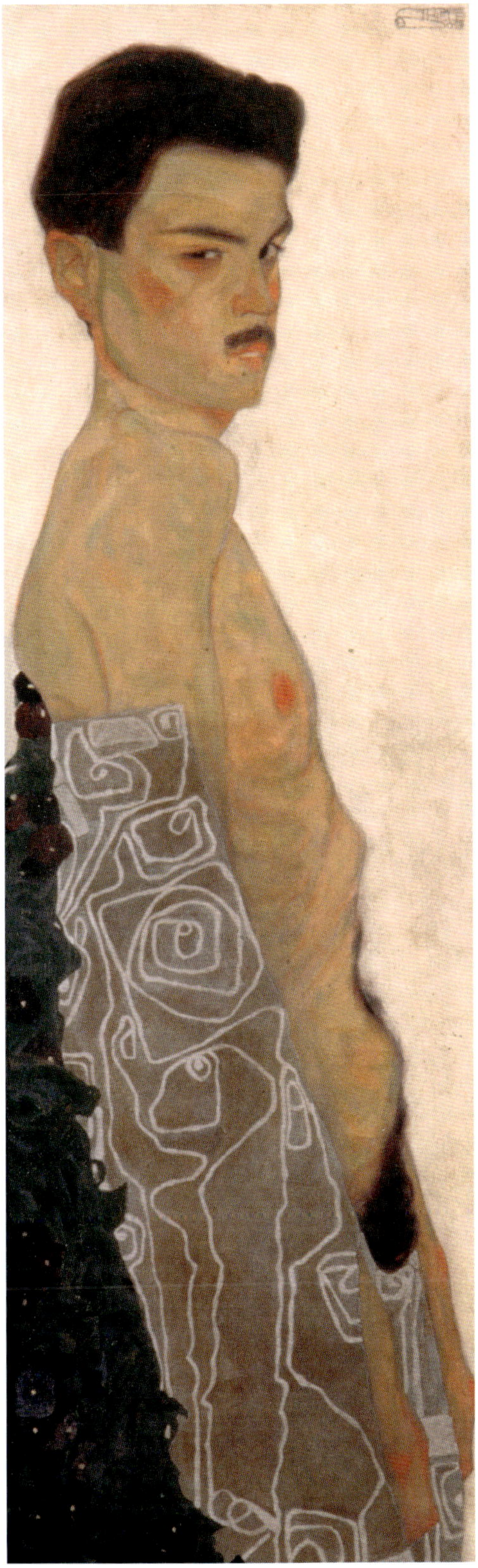

22
EGON SCHIELE
Nude Self-Portrait with Ornamental Drapery, 1909
Oil and metallic paint,
110 x 35.5 cm
Private collection (Kallir P. 154)

is *Dionysian*".[21] Whereas Nietzsche has great contempt for those who would make of existence something small and ugly, the Dionysian person, and particularly the artist, overcomes the preoccupation with superficial beauty to pay homage instead to something more profound than pretty: the creative will itself. In this view ugliness, sickness, disaster and decay are all simply transitory phases of the total, timeless, protean power that is life itself. Nietzsche saw that the art of becoming often requires us to embrace ugliness, pain and destruction on the path to richer existence and greater truth. He declared both that truth was ugly and that art saves us from perishing of the ugly truth. Schiele shows us his ugly truths, but with artful style.

In the 1909 *Nude Self-Portrait with Ornamental Drapery* (fig. 22) Schiele had subtly evinced a turn from conventional beauty toward the possibility of Dionysian ugliness. Using an attenuated vertical composition, metallic paint and a sultry gaze out at the viewer, Schiele seems to have constructed a typically pleasing image. He shrugs his shoulder out of the ornamental drapery, which shrouds his genitals. His thin moustache and eyebrows are precisely groomed. But ugliness is creeping in here – in the strange way Schiele purses his mouth, in the use of agitated, curved lines, in the dark plants encroaching upon the image from the frame.

In his *Seated Nude (Self-Portrait)* (fig. 23) of the following year Schiele alights on the combination of Dionysian ugliness and radical beauty that characterises his most impressive work. In this large, oil-on-canvas self-portrait Schiele's whole body, which is painted in greenish-yellow hues, seems as though it is being blown up and backward. He leans to one side; his raised arms cover his mouth and frame his face; his hair streams out behind him. But Schiele's eyes, which glow vivid red like his nipples, are wide open: he stares down this unseen force with a power of his own.

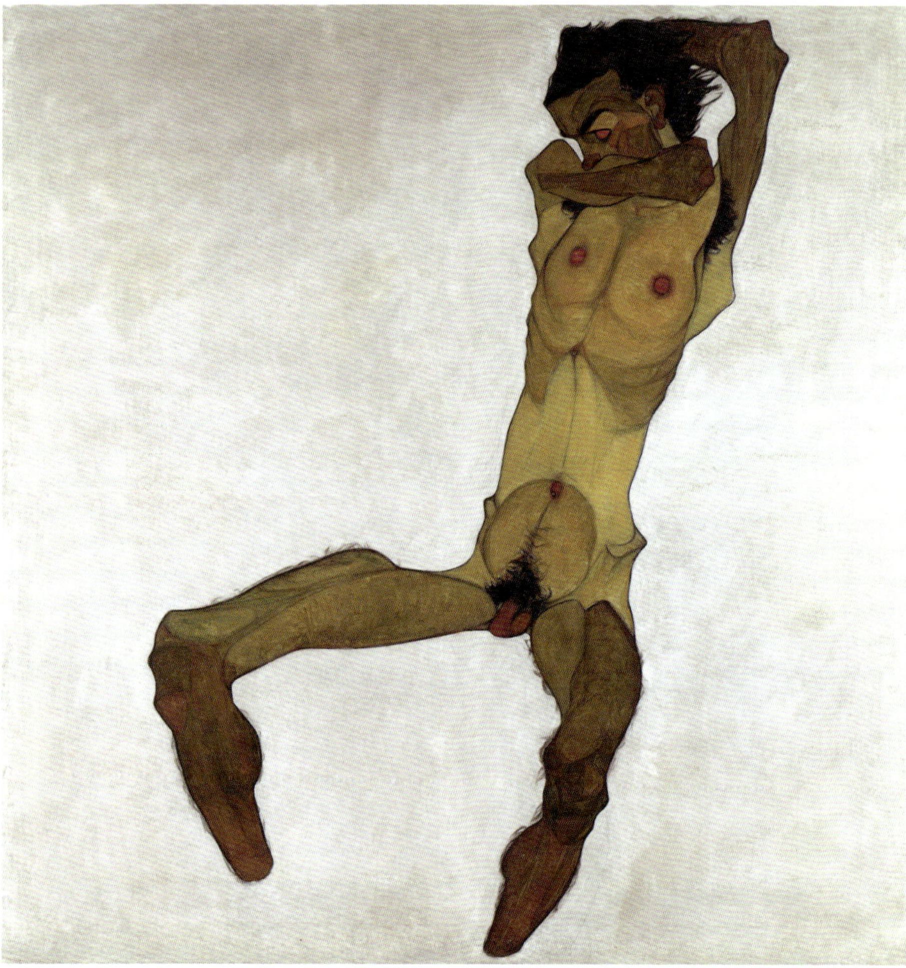

23
EGON SCHIELE
Seated Nude (Self-Portrait), 1910
Oil and gouache on canvas,
152.5 x 150 cm
Leopold Museum – Privatstiftung,
Vienna (Kallir P. 172)

There is a marvellously precise linearity to this and much of Schiele's other work, but what those deft lines are used to represent is often rather horrible. The artist's raised left arm in this painting, for example, shows extremely distorted edges and warps that in real life would signal a serious sickness. But Schiele's disturbed and disturbing imagery takes on a different cast – albeit perhaps a no less threatening one – if we consider it alongside Nietzsche's notion that the artist's practice is an embodied Dionysianism. Selfhood involves constant becoming and periodic sickness; practising selfhood in art involves moments of monstrousness. Indeed Nietzsche suggests that it is "exceptional states that condition the artist – all of them profoundly related to and interlaced with morbid phenomena – so it seems impossible to be an artist and not to be sick".[22] Schiele's black chalk and gouache paint *Nude Self-Portrait in Grey with Open Mouth* (cat. 16) shows the artist himself as the morbid phenomenon: his mouth slack and open, his limbs and penis amputated, with proliferating hair, jutting cheek and hip bones and blank eyes, Schiele's self-image here is dreadful and deathly. This is a cruel and ugly self-portrait of the artist as a dirty corpse.

Schiele's *Self-Portrait, Nude* (1910; cat. 17) is similarly cadaverous and frightful. His flesh, rendered loosely in shades of brown, orange and red, appears to be decomposing, his arms are amputated and he is exceptionally skeletal, a mere sliver of a being. Paint drips from eyes of different colour and size and the nose is flat and unmodelled, halfway between a nose and an alarmingly empty pit. Thin and brittle bones jut out painfully. The neck is very unsightly: it is excessively long, has lumps near the base and shows exposed sinews and folds of flesh that furthermore suggest organic decay. But perhaps the most striking element of Schiele's self-presentation is the castration; he not only amputates his image right at the genitals, but also scoops out the entire pelvic area, revealing only a shadowed hollow and some spidery lines in a shaft-like area beneath his hips. While it would perhaps be understandable to regard such relentlessly grisly imagery as an indication of Schiele's hateful nihilism, Nietzsche's portrait of the Dionysian being suggests we interpret otherwise. He insists:

> He that is richest in the fullness of life, the Dionysian god and man, cannot only afford the sight of the terrible and questionable but even the terrible deed and any luxury of destruction, decomposition, and negation. In his case, what is evil, absurd, and ugly seems, as it were, permissible, owing to an excess of procreating, fertilizing energies that can still turn any desert into a lush farmland .... The desire for *destruction*, change and becoming can be an overflowing energy that is pregnant with future.[23]

Schiele's early nudes indubitably make deliberate use of visual strategies of ugliness; nevertheless both the cause and effect of such ugliness may look less unattractive if we frame our looking with radical, Nietzschean ideas about beauty and Dionysian ugliness.

Regarding the tragic Dionysian artist's embrace of precisely those aspects of life that offend weary nihilists, who hate existence itself, Nietzsche suggests:

> It is a question of *strength* (of an individual or of a people), *whether* and *where* the judgment 'beautiful' is applied. The feeling of plenitude, of *damned-up strength* ... applies the judgment 'beautiful' even to things and conditions that the instinct of impotence could only find *hateful* and 'ugly' .... It is a sign of one's *feeling of power and well-being* how far one can acknowledge the terrifying and questionable character of things .... 'Love of beauty' can therefore be something other than the *ability* to *see* the beautiful, *create* the beautiful; it can be an expression of the very *inability* to do so.[24]

As a symptom of strength, love and life, Dionysian ugliness can therefore be considered a form of radical beauty, originary and potent. Art, likewise, is "an excess and overflow of blooming physicality into the world of images and desires";[25] it represents our animality, and excites those impulses.

This understanding of the impulse towards and function of art actually sees pleasure in the ugly insofar as it "still communicates something of the artist's victorious energy which has become master of this ugliness". For Nietzsche such mastery can include "even a desire to harm *ourselves*, self-violation – and thus the feeling of power over ourselves".[26] Moreover the transformation toward animality and artistic self-mastery is individual, and beauty looks different to everyone because everyone experiences it differently. Nietzsche concludes: "*The* beautiful exists just as little as does *the* good, or *the* true. In every case it is a question of the conditions of preservation of a certain type of man: thus the *herd man* will experience the value feeling of the beautiful in the presence of different things than will the *exceptional* or over man."[27] The exceptional person pushes past conventional understandings to perceive ugliness and beauty in their own exceptional way.

Could Schiele's art, which actually aims at ugliness, also save us from its threatening grasp? Yes, in a manner of speaking, because it is only by accepting the negativity of our ugly selves that we can hope to transform into creatures of radical beauty. And as readers of Nietzsche or viewers of

Schiele we are invited to do just this kind of self-overcoming. In *The Gay Science*, in the aphorism 'In favour of criticism', Nietzsche tries to convince us of the value of negation, or criticism. He explains:

> When we criticise something, this is no arbitrary and impersonal event; it is, at least very often, evidence of vital energies in us that are growing and shedding a skin. We negate and must negate because something in us wants to live and affirm – something that we perhaps do not know or see as yet. This is said in favour of criticism.[28]

Not only does Schiele picture precisely this kind of skin shedding in his art, he also articulated himself in poems and letters using similar imagery. Indeed Schiele could have been responding to Nietzsche rather than his patron Dr. Oskar Reichel when he wrote:

> I bring forth out of myself always more, always something further, an endlessly brighter shining, as far as love, which is everything, enriches me .... I want to tear into myself so that I may create again a new thing which I, in spite of myself, have perceived. My existence, my decay, transposed to enduring values, must sooner or later bring my strength to other strongly or more strongly developed beings .... I am so rich that I must give myself away.[29]

By exposing – spotlighting – the ugliness, sickness and negativity he saw both within himself and in those around him, Schiele was in fact practising an art of revelation, catharsis and overcoming that is likewise central to Nietzsche's philosophy.

According to Nietzsche, the power of these transforming and transformative relationships between the forces of destruction and creation, ugliness and beauty, negation and affirmation, the death of an old self and the birth of a new one, compels artists to mask themselves and their creative concepts. He explains that "every profound spirit needs a mask; more, around every profound spirit a mask is continually growing, thanks to the constantly false, namely *shallow*, interpretation of every word, every step, every sign of life that he gives".[30] Thus for the sake of self-protection the tragic Dionysian artist "finds all forms of disguise necessary".[31]

Schiele's *Sneering Woman* (cat. 15) masks herself, perhaps, as armament and protection in a gambit to wage war; as Nietzsche notes, free spirits are warriors.[32] Importantly, while the woman's breasts are exposed above her crossed and folded arms, they are not arranged 'on display', nor does she look vulnerable. This sneering young woman seems almost to have torn off her shirt in a moment of mischievous antagonism; she gives the definite impression of belonging to a social class of proper ladies (indeed the subject is Schiele's younger sister Gerti) and of rejecting this legacy unashamed. The overriding sense of hostility is pictured most clearly in her facial expression: her scornful mask of disgust is simultaneously a frown, a sneer and an open-mouthed, tongue-lolling and abject objection to the world outside the frame.

This mask, then, both signifies her own criticism and protects her from others' as she transforms herself into something greater than negation. In this respect she is an embodiment of Nietzsche's "imperious and domineering" free spirit who, with a "not altogether innocent readiness ... to deceive ... and to dissemble ... enjoys the cunning and multiplicity of its masks ... for it is precisely through its protean arts that it is best concealed and protected!"[33] Further forms of masking and transformation include the uneven washes of white paint applied to the surface of Gerti's skin, which give her a sickly appearance, the giant orange protuberance above her head, which distorts hair and hat, and the haunting hint of a shin bone Schiele leaves unpainted – another of his myriad

24
EGON SCHIELE
Self-Portrait, Grimacing, 1910
Gouache and black chalk,
45.3 x 30.7 cm
Leopold Museum – Privatstiftung,
Vienna (Kallir D. 705)

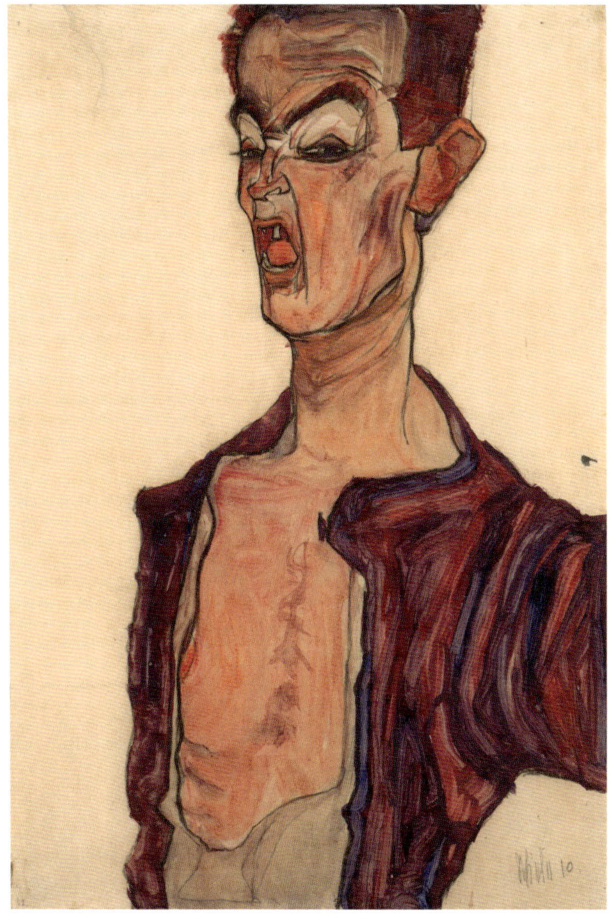

reminders that life itself is merely a mask for death. With these tokens Schiele's sneering woman also opposes the misogyny of her culture, which tells her that her fundamental impulse is toward self-adornment, for, although she masks herself, she does not thereby seek the "appearance and beauty" to which Nietzsche, too, in his less Dionysian moments, reduces women.[34]

In *Self-Portrait, Grimacing* (fig. 24) the paint itself, viscous and erratically applied, becomes a kind of disguise, as does the use of distorted and often unappealing details such as purple ribs and mismatched eyes and teeth. Schiele presents an unforgettable grimace, an alarmingly hideous mask of rejection that functions both as an attack against a society that viewed this art and artist as ugly and sick, and as an attack against himself insofar as he exaggerates just those qualities decried by the conservative viewer. The artist described his frustration with the moral majority in Nietzschean terms: "The 'many' are those who are dependent upon each other – the people. The 'few' are the direct leaders of the world because they introduce only that which is new and are therefore repugnant ... it is tactless to hold accountable a person with a free soul and to level 'moral' charges against him ... whatever desires to hinder ... development is possessed by evil intentions ...."[35] At times Schiele felt constrained by such evil, as in 1910 when he wrote to his friend and future brother-in-law Anton Peschka: "I wish to leave Vienna, very soon. How ugly it is here. Everybody is envious ... and deceitful ... there is only shadow .... I have to see new things and learn about them .... [I] want to see light, the sun ...."[36] *Self-Portrait with Hand to Cheek*, 1910,[37] which could almost form a diptych of dissatisfaction with *Self-Portrait, Grimacing*, also captures this tension impressively. Schiele tugs at his face with palpable weariness and dismay; he looks infinitely disappointed but still takes care to offer the viewer interesting and attractive visual elements – like the spiky pink, purple and blue hair, or the flaming lines on ears, eyes and finger. Schiele was, as he himself reiterated frequently, able to "see beauty in everything in the world";[38] paradoxically, the ugliness he saw and reflected in his art was part of this fundamental beauty.

Nietzsche observed that, for the "eternal child", even "the most solemn concepts which have occasioned the most strife and suffering" become material for play and experimentation. Remarkably, in his own writings Schiele likewise referred to himself as an "eternal child".[39] What mattered for both was not the fact of suffering but how it could be transformed; moreover both Nietzsche and Schiele approached this question with a stance of childlike experimentation and a focus on the body. Nietzsche explains that "every art, every philosophy may be viewed as a remedy and an aid in the service of growing and struggling life; they always presuppose

25
EGON SCHIELE
For Art and for My Loved Ones I will gladly endure to the End!, 1912
Watercolour and pencil,
48.2 x 31.8 cm
Albertina Museum, Vienna
(Kallir D. 1189)

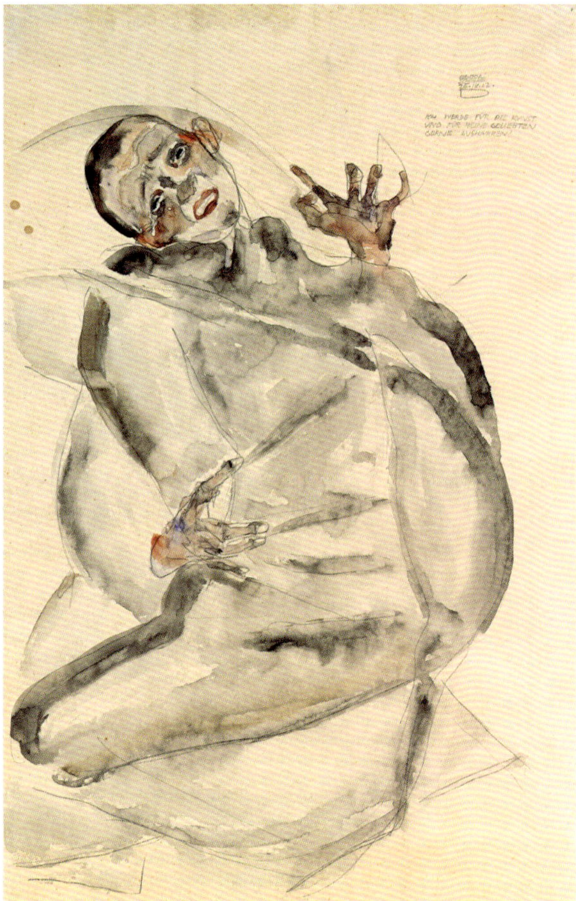

suffering and sufferers".[40] Thus for the Dionysian artist suffering, sickness, ugliness and death can all be transformed into art, and thereby redeemed – as a revelation of life itself. It is this embrace of the art of becoming, this eternal affirmation of eternal transformation, that produces what Nietzsche refers to as 'the great health'.

Nietzsche describes those who suffer from this "more audacious" kind of health as "premature births of an as yet unproven future". In "a world so overrich in what is beautiful, strange, questionable, terrible and divine", such new beings can become "dangerously healthy, ever again healthy". This is "the *great health* – that one does not merely have but also acquires continually, and must acquire because one gives it up again and again, and must give it up".[41] Nietzsche likens himself and other such premature births to Dionysus, as "Dionysus cut to pieces is a *promise* of life: it will be eternally reborn and return again from destruction".[42] The vision of well-being that Schiele offers ultimately resembles Nietzsche's great health: his oeuvre enacts a process of becoming, often destructive, that concretises the sacred in the representation of the profane.

Seen from this perspective, the stark image of a twisted body in one male nude (cat. 11), the spastic contortions in the prison self-portrait *For Art and My Loved Ones I will gladly endure to the End* (fig. 25) and the frenzied Dionysian dance of *Nude Self-Portrait, Grimacing* (fig. 26) all document stages in the eternal cycles of great health. Along the way every tragedy may become joyous, every ugliness beautiful. For both Nietzsche and Schiele the "deification of the body" leads to a state in which "the most sensual functions are finally transfigured by a symbol-intoxication of the highest spirituality"; indeed, the "highest and most illustrious human joys" are those in which "existence celebrates its own transfiguration".[43] The creation of a corporeal art is therefore a form of reverence toward the inherent divinity of the body. Through repeated acts of such reverence Schiele, the Dionysian artist, becomes himself: he becomes himself by creating himself anew, again and again.

Schiele's self-portrait *Kneeling Male Nude with Raised Hand* (cat. 10) is an eloquent testament to such deification of the body, symbol-intoxication and continual self-creation. In an unusual frontal pose that is half defensive, half open, Schiele

26
EGON SCHIELE
Nude Self-Portrait, Grimacing, 1910
Gouache, watercolour and white heightening, 55.8 x 36.9 cm
Albertina Museum, Vienna
(Kallir D. 720)

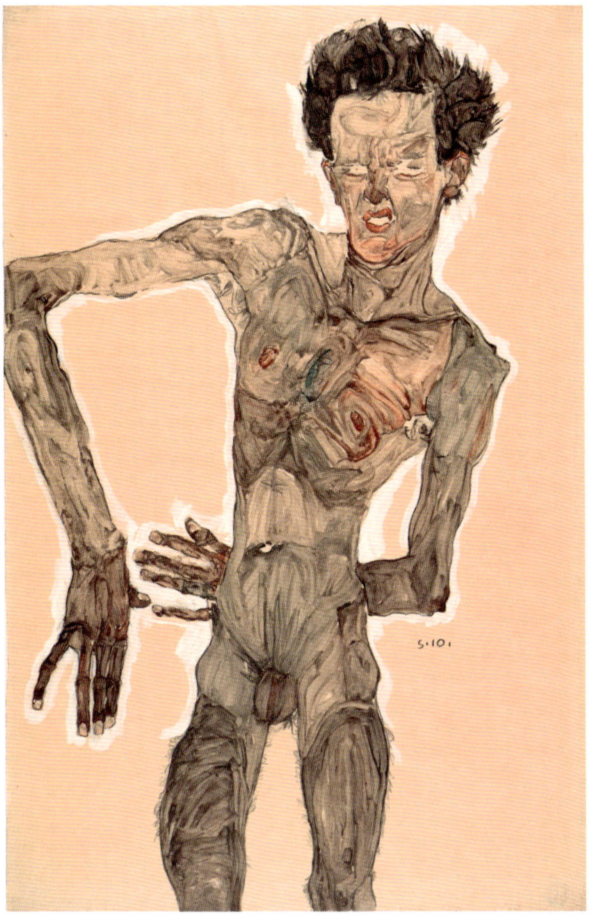

paints himself with a palette that, although characteristically anti-naturalistic, is more rainbow- than wound-toned. His face, raised leg and hands are a feverish red, his torso is a gangrenous yellow, pubic hair a rich, deep blue, and his face has green and blue accents that appear as an enigmatic eye-mask around closed eyes.

Schiele's fears of death, sexuality and disease, his ambivalence about beauty and ugliness, both his own and that of the world he was part of – all of these conflicts play out across the surface of the skin and are transformed in Schiele's radical nudes. Reinhard Steiner proposed that the nude self-portrait was, for Schiele, "the most radical form of self-expression not because the body is exposed but because the self is grasped entire".[44] I would suggest that what we see in Schiele's naked self-portraits is the self not grasped but rather *created* – and through the body. Being is not penetrated; becoming is embraced, in the form of a Dionysian dance of joyful nihilism and self-creation.

Such embodied Dionysianism is the basis for the great health that results when we "*become those we are* – human beings who are new, unique, incomparable, who give themselves laws, who create themselves".[45] Such health is often misidentified, according to Nietzsche, "because we ourselves keep growing, keep changing, we shed our old bark, we shed our skins every spring, we keep becoming younger, fuller of future, taller, stronger, we push our roots ever more powerfully into the depths – into evil – while at the same time we embrace the heavens ever more lovingly, more broadly, imbibing their light ever more thirstily".[46] Schiele uses this same metaphor of thirst in his poem 'A Self-Portrait', in which he declares: "I am for me and those to whom the thirsty drunkenness for freedom presents everything with me, and for everyone as well, because everyone I love as well .... I am among the most noble .... I am human, I love death and love life ...."[47]

In *Self-Portrait with Splayed Fingers* (fig. 27) we glimpse the promise of health and beauty contained in these acts of becoming and self-creation. The work shows Schiele looking back over his left shoulder, his right arm raised with his hand in a characteristically ambiguous and stylised gesture. Complex shades of forest green, rust, purplish-brown, indigo and light yellow are scattered so gently over the body that

27
EGON SCHIELE
Self-Portrait with Splayed Fingers, 1911
Pencil and gouache, heightened with white, 53 x 29.1 cm
Leopold Museum – Privatstiftung, Vienna (Kallir D. 952)

the figure itself appears almost gossamer. Schiele's look contains both haughtiness and vulnerability, and the white outlining he used so frequently appears here more than ever as a halo. The Dionysian god and man tears into himself so that he can recreate himself, eternally. Schiele here shows us one moment, in the blink of an eye, of his becoming: he looks back briefly at what has been destroyed in creation, before continuing his demiurgic odyssey.

For Nietzsche, writing was a way to metabolise the circumstances of his life; through writing he could plumb his own depths and transform sickness into health, doubt into faith. Writing allowed him to move from the passive nihilism he abhorred to the active nihilism of the Dionysian artist. Schiele offers us similar experiments with his art and so, too, are their Dionysian visions related. By moving past his own most superficial beauty and past the clever aesthetic formulas around him into vital, transformative zones of powerful, pulsating and chaotic ugliness Schiele created himself continually in the image of a far more radical beauty. By 1914 Schiele finally smiles at his reflection (photograph reproduced page 6). Even before that, though, during the years of great ugliness, what he was really sketching out was love – for himself, for the world, for life itself. Schiele created his ugly art out of his love for life and its beauty. And in so doing he also created himself, as the Dionysian artist whose affirmative gaze sees the power and possibility of life in death, health in sickness and beauty in ugliness.

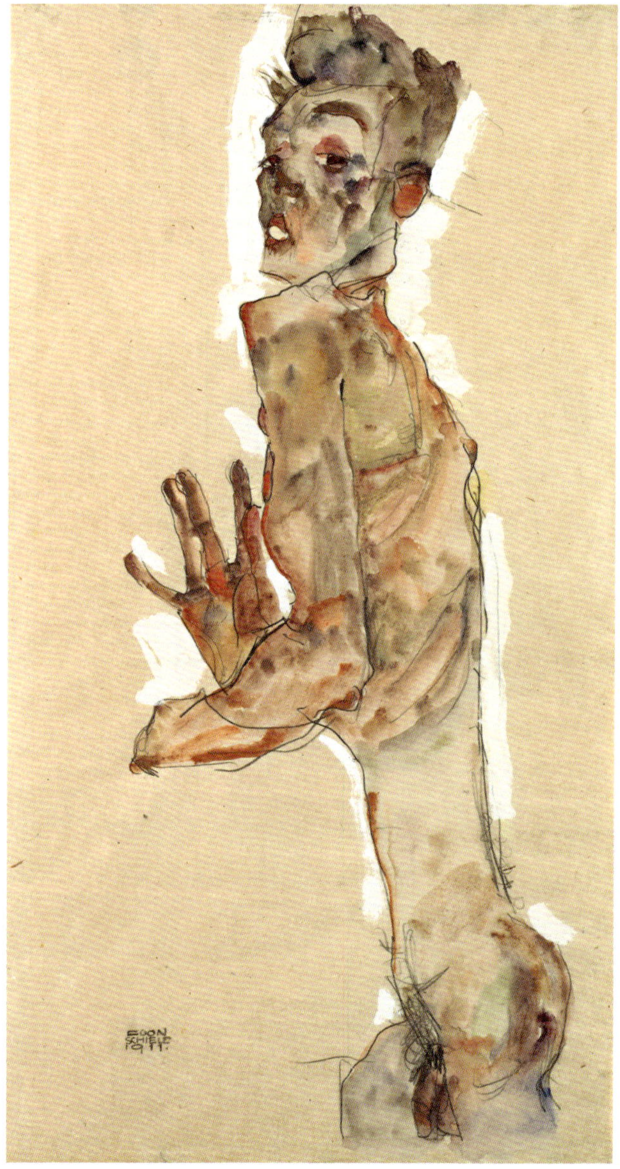

NOTES

1 *The Gay Science*, §71 (Friedrich Nietzsche, *The Gay Science*, translated by Walter Kaufmann, New York [Vintage Books] 1974).

2 Anton Peschka, Jr., *Die Wahrheit über Egon Schiele* (unpublished manuscript), p. 15, cited in Jane Kallir, *Egon Schiele. The Complete Works*, London (Thames & Hudson) 1998 (first published 1990), p. 27; Lewis Crofts's novel *The Pornographer of Vienna* (2007) also begins with a lurid fictionalisation of this purported event.

3 Christian M. Nebehay (ed.), *Egon Schiele: 1890–1918: Leben, Briefe, Gedichte*, Salzburg (Residenz Verlag) 1979, p. 12; cited and translated in Kallir 1998, p. 38, n. 7.

4 William J. McGrath, *Dionysian Art and Populist Politics in Austria*, New Haven and London (Yale University Press) 1974, p. 218.

5 McGrath 1974, pp. 226-27.

6 Clare A.P. Willsdon, 'Klimt's Beethoven Frieze: Goethe, *Tempelkunst* and the Fulfilment of Wishes', *Art History*, vol. 19, no. 1 (March 1996), pp. 44-73, at p. 45.

7 See, for one example, Paul Friedman, *On Suicide: With Particular Reference to Suicide among Young Students. Discussions of the Vienna Psychoanalytic Society, 1910*, New York (International Universities Press) 1967.

8 Adolf Loos, *Trotzdem*, Innsbruck (Brenner Verlag) 1931, p. 124.

9 Willsdon 1996, passim.

10 Marian Bisanz-Prakken, *Gustav Klimt, der Beethovenfries: Geschichte, Funktion und Bedeutung*, Munich (Deutscher Taschenbuch Verlag) 1980, p. 52; cited in Willsdon 1996, p. 50.

11 'Radical implications' meaning both 'fundamental' and 'extreme'.

12 In her text *Egon Schiele: A Self in Creation: A Psychoanalytic Study of the Artist's Self-Portraits*, London (Associated University Presses) 1993, p. 95, psychoanalyst Danielle Knafo persuasively opines that "Schiele's fascination with sickness and death, especially as concerned babies, was most certainly related to the deaths of his [siblings]. During the years 1910 and 1911, Schiele became fixated on the fact that his mother's pregnant state had repeatedly led to dead babies .... Schiele's sense of himself included the notion that he too should be dead .... Repeatedly returning to the birth experience, Schiele confronted the survivor's dilemma. On the one hand, he is the special child, the 'genius' who makes it but, on the other hand, he is ridden with guilt and feels that he too must die."

13 Cecile Nebel, *The Dark Side of Creativity: Blocks, Unfinished Works and the Urge to Destroy*, Troy (Whitston Publishing) 1988, p. 1.

14 *The Gay Science*, §110, 'Origin of knowledge' (Nietzsche 1974).

15 *Thus Spoke Zarathustra*, Part One, 'On the despisers of the body' (*The Portable Nietzsche*, New York [Penguin], pp. 146-47).

16 Nebehay 1979, p. 102, cited in Stephanie Auer, 'Egon Schiele's Image of Woman: Between Saint and Whore?', in Agnes Husslein-Arco and Jane Kallir (eds.), *Egon Schiele: Self-Portraits and Portraits*, Munich/London/New York (Prestel) 2011, p. 49.

17 For example in his poem *Tannenwald* (Fir Woods), translated into English in Egon Schiele, *I, Eternal Child: Paintings and Poems*, translated by Anselm Hollo, afterword by Elfriede Friesenbiller, New York (Grove Press) 1985, p. 37.

18 Metropolitan Museum of Art, New York, Kallir D. 953.

19 *The Will to Power*, §21 (Friedrich Nietzsche, *The Will to Power*, New York [Vintage] 1967).

20 *The Will to Power*, §22, emphasis in original.

21 *The Will to Power*, §6, '"Reason" in Philosophy'.

22 *The Will to Power*, §811.

23 *The Gay Science*, §370, 'What is romanticism?', emphasis in original (Nietzsche 1974).

24 *The Will to Power*, §852 (Nietzsche 1967).

25 *The Will to Power*, §802.

26 *The Will to Power*, §802.

27 *The Will to Power*, §804.

28 *The Will to Power*, §307.

29 In Alessandra Comini, *Schiele in Prison*, New York (New York Graphic Society) 1973, p. 35.

30 *Beyond Good and Evil*, Part Two: 'The free spirit', §40 (Friedrich Nietzsche, *Beyond Good and Evil*, translated with an introduction and commentary by R.J. Hollingdale, London [Penguin] 1973).

31 *Beyond Good and Evil*, Part Nine: 'What is noble?', §270.

32 *Twilight of the Idols*, 'Expeditions of an untimely man', §38, 'My conception of freedom' (Friedrich Nietzsche, *Twilight of the Idols/ The Anti-Christ*, translated by R.J. Hollingdale, introduction by Michael Tanner, London [Penguin] 1990).

33 *Beyond Good and Evil*, Part Seven, §230, 'Our virtues' (Nietzsche 1973).

34 See, for example, the following passage, §232, where he says of woman: "her great art is the lie, her supreme concern is appearance and beauty".

35 Rudolf Leopold and Sandra Tretter (eds.), Egon Schiele: *Letters and Poems, 1910–1912, from the Leopold Collection*, Munich (Prestel) 2008, p. 127.

36 Leopold and Tretter 2008, p. 13.

37 Albertina, Vienna, Kallir D. 706.

38 Kallir 1998, p. 127.

39 For example in his poem *Ich, ewiges Kind* (I, eternal child), translated into English in Leopold and Tretter 2008, pp. 6, 8.

40 *The Gay Science*, §370, 'What is romanticism?' (Nietzsche 1974).

41 *The Gay Science*, §382, 'The great health'.

42 *The Will to Power*, §1052 (Nietzsche 1967).

43 *The Will to Power*, §1051.

44 Reinhard Steiner, *Egon Schiele: The Midnight Soul of the Artist*, Cologne (Benedikt Taschen Verlag) 2000, p. 12.

45 *The Gay Science*, §335, 'Long live physics!', emphasis in original (Nietzsche 1974).

46 *The Gay Science*, §371, 'We incomprehensible ones'.

47 *Ein Selbstbild* (A Self-Portrait), in Leopold and Tretter 2008, p. 53.

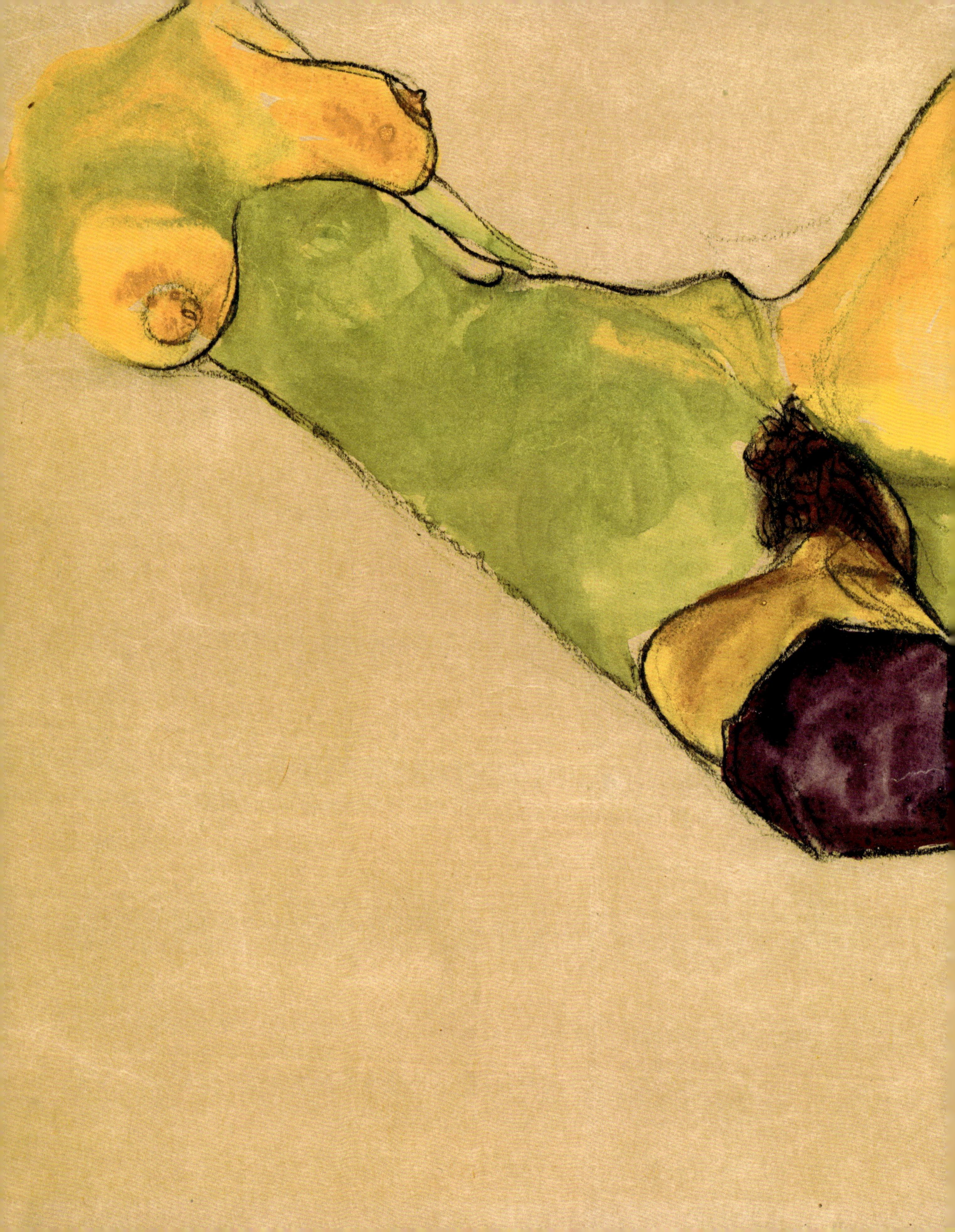

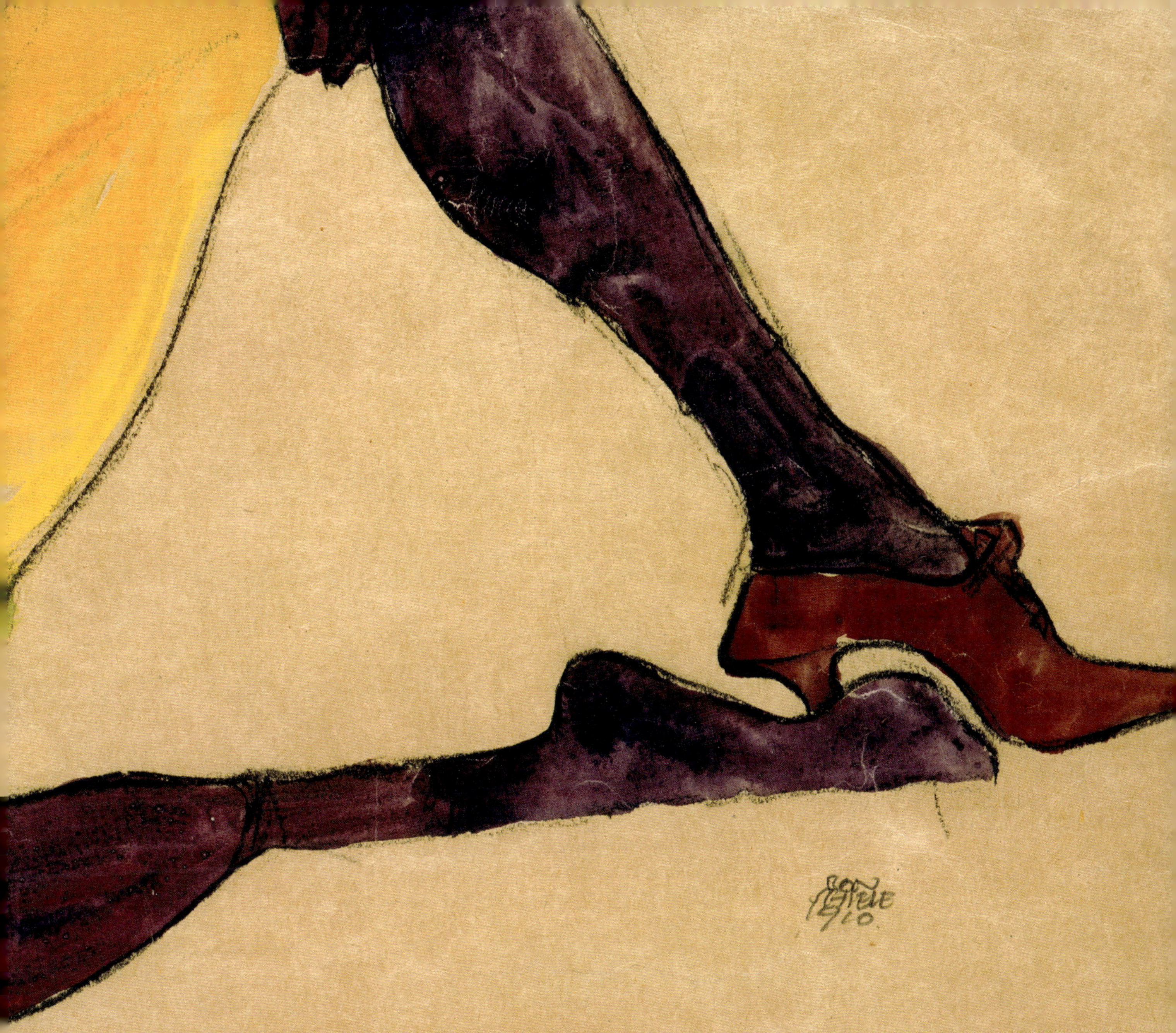

CATALOGUE

Peter Vergo

1

MALE NUDE CROUCHING, BACK VIEW

1909
Watercolour, ink and pencil, 31.4 x 31.5 cm
Leopold Museum – Privatstiftung, Vienna (Kallir D. 326)

The identity of the person portrayed in this work is unknown and even the gender appears uncertain, given that there are no obvious allusions to any defining sexual characteristics. With its long black hair, slender waist and wide hips, it would just as be easy to believe that the figure depicted was female rather than male, but for a certain resemblance between this and a small number of other drawings that show an unidentified, slender young man who sports a mass of jet black hair.[1] It was presumably on the basis of this resemblance that Jane Kallir assigned this drawing to the category of male nudes in her catalogue raisonné of the artist's works.

As Kallir remarks, during the years around 1909–10 that marked Schiele's 'breakthrough', the majority of his friends and patrons were male and he seems to have identified more readily with male models than females as subjects for depiction. This was also the period in which, in his treatment of the human figure, he started progressively to abandon internal modelling in favour of an emphasis on expressive, decorative outline.[2] Especially noticeable is the way the hair is represented as a largely undifferentiated mass, whose effect and even legibility owes much to the skilful manipulation of the outline within which the colour is contained. The gesture of one hand reaching over and clutching the opposite shoulder, as depicted here, also features in several of Schiele's own self-portraits of these years – an awkward position to hold, giving the pose struck by the nude figure a tense, somewhat edgy appearance.

1909 was the year of Schiele's debut at the Internationale Kunstschau exhibition in Vienna.[3] In this as in many of his drawings executed at that time, his debt to Klimt and to Art Nouveau is still apparent, not least in the decorative flatness that characterises his treatment of the figure and its placing on the page. On the other hand, *Male Nude Crouching* could not possibly be mistaken for a work by Klimt or any of the Secessionists. Although Schiele made a small number of designs for the Wiener Werkstätte (Vienna Workshops), the arts and crafts enterprise that was closely associated with the Secession during its early years, as Otto Benesch observed there was no real prospect of the artist's succumbing to their "sweet seductions". On the contrary, his attitude to colour and to the subject depicted had already begun to diverge markedly from anything that might "suit the WW's black and white interiors with their reflective display cases".[4] Although barely finished with his studies at the Academy, in his works of this period Schiele was already beginning to distance himself from the influences that helped to form his earlier style.

1 Compare Kallir D. 235-37 (1908) and D. 325 (1909).
2 Kallir 1998, p. 367.
3 See below, pp. 72-74.
4 Foreword to the catalogue of Schiele's exhibition at the Galerie Arnot, January 1915, quoted after Nebehay 1979, p. 317.

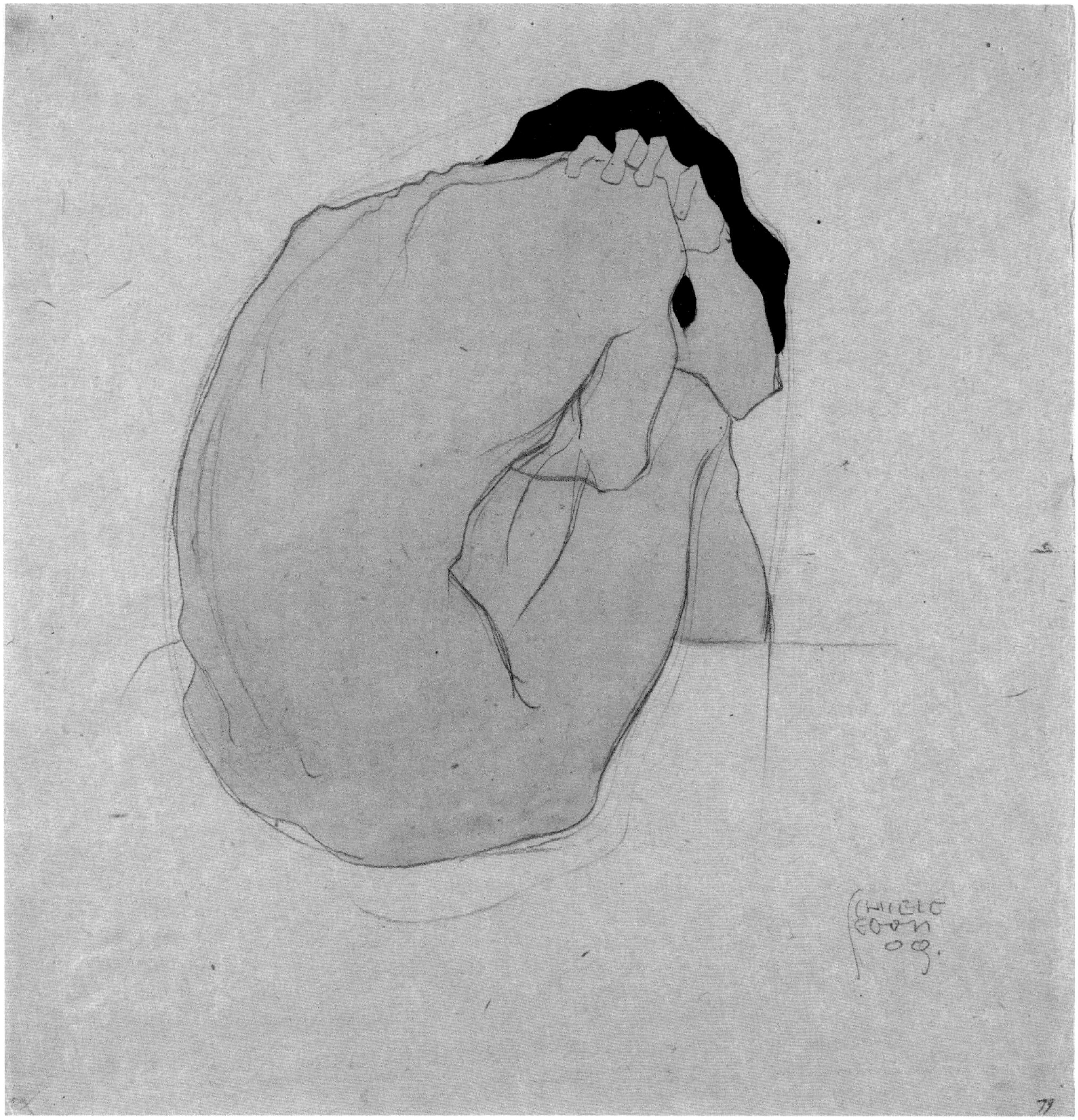
SCHIELE
EGON
09.

2

MALE NUDE

1910
Watercolour and charcoal, 44 x 31.5 cm
Private collection (Kallir D. 687)

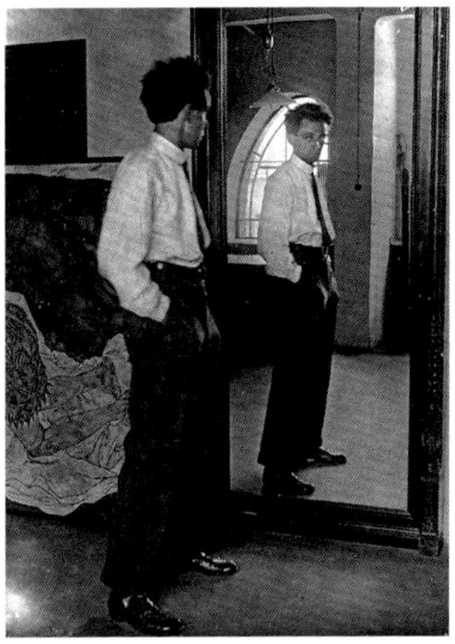

28
JOHANNES FISCHER (attr.)
Egon Schiele in front of a Mirror, 1915
Photograph
Egon Schiele Archive, Albertina, Vienna

Perhaps the oddest thing about this study of a male nude is the pose – angular, contorted, uncomfortable, the left arm thrown across the body, the legs seen in profile, while the back is twisted so far round that the spine is visible. One's first reaction is to ask what model could possibly have been asked to hold such a pose for any length of time. Our puzzlement is only slightly lessened when we realise that, like cat. 11 and 12, this too is likely to have been a self-portrait. This hypothesis is made almost a certainty by the glimpse of part of the face which, even though truncated, appears to bear the artist's own distinctive features.[1] In that case, such a view of his own body could only have been captured with the help of a mirror or, more probably, by artfully juxtaposing several mirrors. It is possible that what we are shown in this drawing is Schiele standing in front of the large picture mirror that appears in several photographs of his studio (compare fig. 28), twisting and craning his neck to see as much as possible of his own back. The tense neck muscles and protruding rib-cage, each rib clearly delineated, might be thought to argue for this suggestion; on Schiele's use of mirrors see also catalogue entry for cat. 28.

The drawing is undated but, if it is indeed a self-portrait, it can be firmly situated within the group of decidedly 'unbeautiful' depictions of himself which the artist completed early in 1910, a date that is also plausible on stylistic grounds. As several Schiele scholars have remarked, his own body is the subject that occurs most frequently in his nude studies of this period, alongside portraits of his sister Gerti and of close friends such as Erwin Osen, whom the artist also depicted nude (compare cat. 13, 14). Almost none of these portraits is flattering to the person portrayed, including Schiele himself, who appears intent on conveying not the beauty but the morbidity of human flesh, something his critics were quick to point out. This impression is produced above all by the colours, mostly unhealthy-looking greys and muddy browns, contrasting with a decidedly non-naturalistic green wash that covers part of the upper back. Our sense of revulsion on contemplating this seemingly gangrenous body is further heightened when we notice the abnormal discrepancy between the two arms, the right arm being almost twice the size of the left. Here, compositional factors, rather than anatomical accuracy, may well have played a decisive part, since the prominently jutting right elbow fulfils an important structural role in anchoring firmly on the page what might otherwise appear as a disconcertingly unstable figure, in constant danger of tipping sideways or falling flat on its face. At the same time, the deliberate interplay of angular lines creates an intriguing succession of rhythmic repetitions, which is unusual in such an early drawing, but is a distinguishing feature of many of the artist's later works.

1 This drawing is categorised as a self-portrait in Jane Kallir's catalogue raisonné of Schiele's works, albeit without further comment: see Kallir 1998, p. 425.

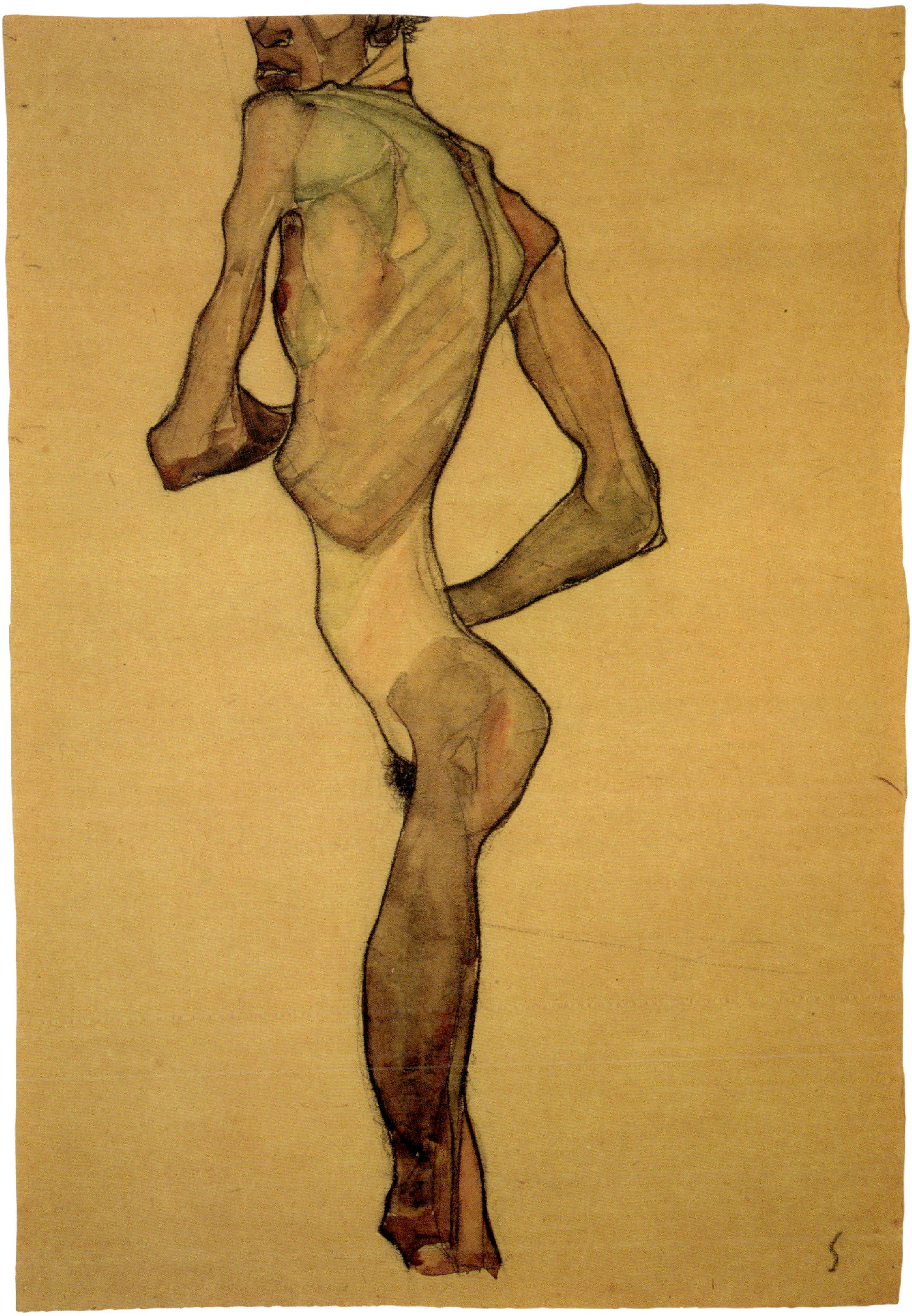

3

SEATED FEMALE NUDE WITH RAISED RIGHT ARM (GERTRUDE SCHIELE)

1910
Gouache, watercolour and black crayon, 45 x 31.5 cm
Wien Museum, Vienna (Kallir D. 518)
Inscribed lower left (in German) by the architect Otto Wagner: "Original design by Egon Schiele for the panel shown at the Hunting Exhibition in Vienna 1910 purchased in the coffee house by colleagues of Professor Jos. Hoffman [sic]"

At first sight, the inscription added to this work by the Viennese architect Otto Wagner, who posed for Schiele at about this time, might appear puzzling since it is far from clear what (if anything) a painting based on this study might have had to do with a hunting exhibition. In fact, the *Internationale Jagdausstellung*, held in Vienna's Prater in the spring of 1910, included several spaces in which works both by avant-garde artists and by more conservative painters belonging to established societies such as the Vienna Künstlerhaus were displayed. The exhibition catalogue illustrates Schiele's now vanished painting – very similar in appearance to the present watercolour only much bigger – hanging at the far end of one of these spaces. To judge by the old and rather indistinct photograph, it appears to have been a large oil, similar in format to *Seated Nude (Self-Portrait)* of the same year (fig. 23), to which it was probably a pendant.[1] Both paintings may, as Jane Kallir suggests, have belonged to a group of five large nude portraits – three of Schiele and two of Gerti – done in the early part of 1910, some (or all?) of which were acquired by the industrialist Carl Reininghaus.[2] However, Schiele's friend the gynaecologist Dr. Erwin von Graff was unimpressed by the way the pictures were hung, remarking that the 'commercial' ones (presumably those by members of the Künstlerhaus) could just as well have been relegated to the walls of the hunting lodges and cafés that were a feature of the exhibition. In his opinion, works by Schiele produced a far more powerful impression when viewed in the artist's studio than when placed in such unsuitable surroundings.[3]

In her landmark study of Schiele's portraits, American art-historian Alessandra Comini described the relationship between Schiele and his younger sister Gertrude ('Gerti'), four years his junior, as "intense" and "not without erotic overtones". Evidently she was not the first person to have harboured suspicions of this kind. According to Comini's account, Schiele's father once broke open a locked door in their apartment in order to find out what Egon and Gerti were up to, only to discover the two of them closeted together in the dark, innocently developing photographs. But on other, seemingly less innocent occasions, Gerti was "easily persuaded to pose in the nude for her brother, and this led to other secrets which they kept from their mother".[4] Among those secrets may have been the fact that, in 1907 at the age of seventeen, the artist took his then thirteen-year-old sister off to Trieste, where they shared a room in the same hotel their parents had stayed in on their honeymoon.[5] (As children of an employee of the Austrian State Railways, Egon and Gerti were entitled to free train travel, probably the only thing that made such an escapade possible.) What might or might not have happened after that, again behind locked doors, has – not surprisingly – been a matter for sometimes lurid speculation.

What appears certain is that, during the years around 1909–10, Gerti was Schiele's preferred female model. Significantly, her portrait was one of only three oil paintings he exhibited in Vienna at

1 The photograph is reproduced in Kallir 1998, p. 294.
2 Kallir 1998, entry for P. 170. *Seated Male Nude* (Kallir P. 172) appears to be the only survivor of this group of five paintings.
3 Nebehay 1979, p. 131, doc. 102; on Schiele's friendship with Graff, see also cat. 5.
4 Comini 1974, p. 14. Interviewed in 1963, Schiele's elder sister Melanie described his affection for Gerti as "unnatural" (Comini 1974, p. 192, note 14); see also the more recent article by Comini, 'Pilgrimage to Schiele's Past: Forgotten Sites, Still-Living Sitters and Early Collectors', in Schiele 2005, pp. 73-101, esp. pp. 76ff.
5 Leopold 1973, p. 12. Comini maintains that the visit to Trieste took place when Egon was sixteen and Gerti twelve, which would put it in 1906 rather than 1907.

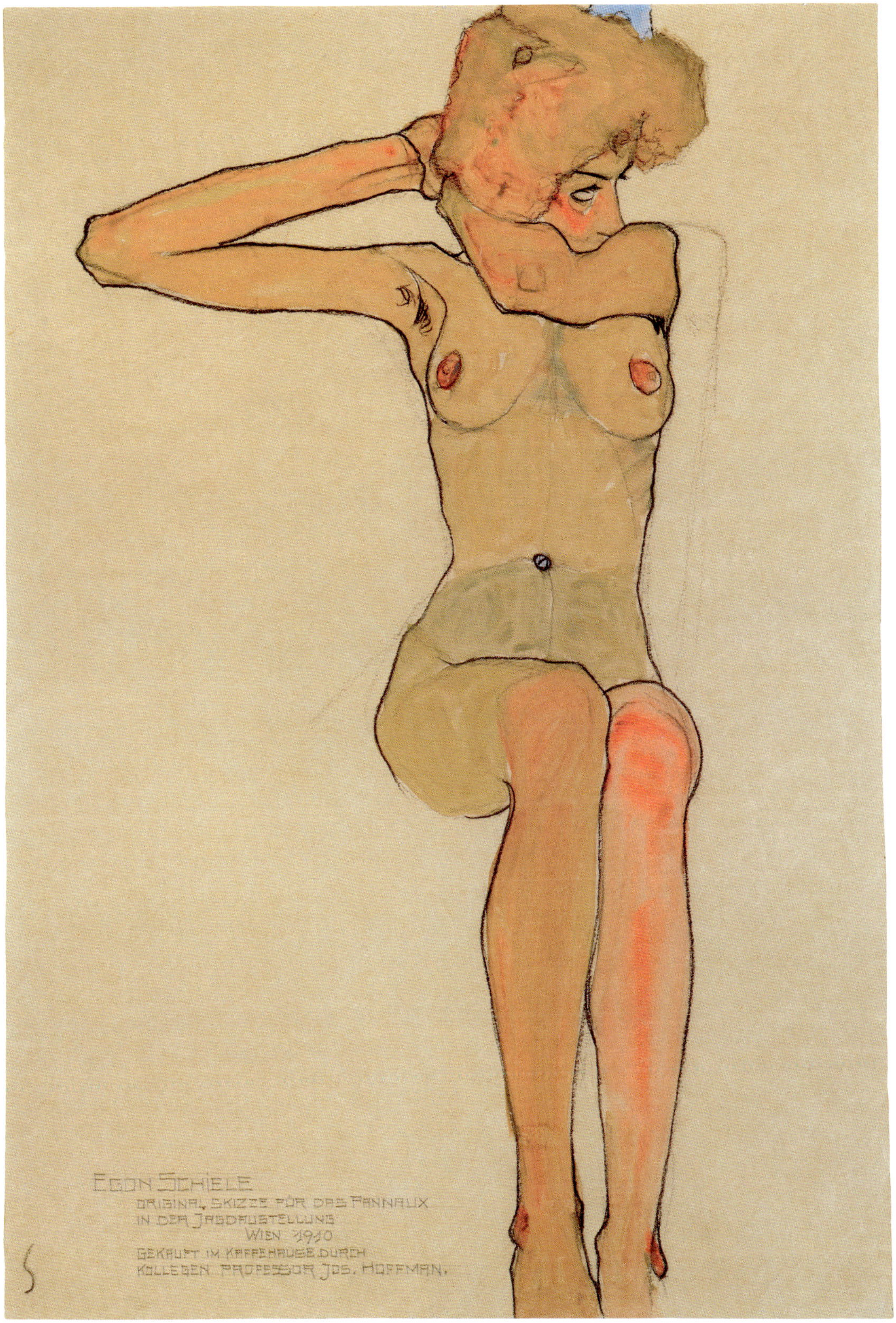
EGON SCHIELE
ORIGINAL, SKIZZE FÜR DAS PANNAUX
IN DER JAGDAUSTELLUNG
WIEN 1910
GEKAUFT IM KAFFEHAUSE DURCH
KOLLEGEN PROFESSOR JOS. HOFFMAN.

29
EGON SCHIELE
Female Nude with Folded Arms (Gertrude Schiele), 1910
Watercolour and black chalk, 48.8 x 28 cm
Albertina Museum, Vienna
(Kallir D. 516)

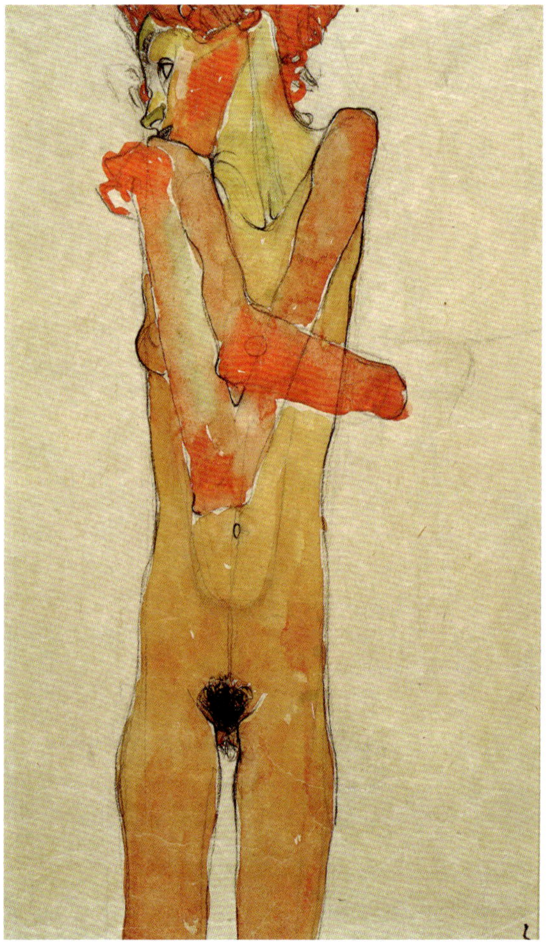

the Internationale Kunstschau in 1909, the others being portraits of fellow-painters Anton Peschka and Hans Massmann.[6] From many of his drawings and watercolours including cat. 3, it seems obvious that he took a close, even excited interest in the onset of puberty and in his sister's rapidly blossoming sexuality. In other nude studies of Gerti – for example, his 1910 watercolour *Nude Girl with Folded Arms* (fig. 29) – Schiele is at pains to emphasise, sometimes in startling detail, his sister's luxuriant pubic hair, which contrasts somewhat disconcertingly with her still only half-developed body. *Seated Female Nude* is somewhat less extreme in this regard but is still likely to strike the viewer as unashamedly erotic in intent.

The sitter's pose appears to be a curious mixture of the natural and the contrived. On the one hand, the artist seems determined to capture a chance, fleeting movement as Gerti rapidly adjusts her hair. On the other, the position of her right arm recalls other carefully studied 'expressive' gestures similar to those found in Schiele's nude studies of Osen (see cat. 13, 14). We may also detect faint echoes of the life-drawing classes the artist had attended, albeit unwillingly, at the Academy of Fine Arts only a couple of years earlier, where studies of contrived (and difficult-to-hold) poses such as these would still have been the norm.[7]

6 See Kallir P. 149, P. 150 and P. 155.
7 See above, pp. 17-18.

4

RECLINING MALE NUDE

1910
Watercolour and charcoal, 32.1 x 44.8 cm
Private collection (Kallir D. 662)

One cannot travel any distance in the history of Western painting without stumbling across reclining female nudes. They occur everywhere and in every period, from Titian's *Venus of Urbino* via Goya's *Maja Desnuda* to Manet's *Olympia* and beyond. By contrast, reclining male nudes are somewhat rarer, at least until the late nineteenth century. When they do occur, it is often in the form of academic exercises, as studies for figures depicted clothed in subsequent paintings, and sometimes in the finished painting itself, perhaps in the guise of injured warriors or men stricken by illness, shipwreck or other disaster. They may also be given a role to play in representations of mythological or religious subjects such as *The Garden of Earthly Delights*, while Michelangelo's portrayal of Adam in his famous fresco of *The Creation of Man* provides another memorable instance. To this roll-call of horizontal males we should add a few further images that might be characterised one way or another by homo-erotic intent: for example, depictions of the beautiful (but mythical) youth Ganymede or studies of real-life male bathers such as those created by the American painter and photographer Thomas Eakins or the English artist Henry Scott Tuke.

However, none of these categories seems adequately to describe the present watercolour which, at least at first sight, appears bereft of any obvious narrative content. Rather, it is surely the product of Schiele's already-remarked fascination with his own image – more precisely, that of his own naked body. That this is, once again, a self-portrait is highly probable, even if, as so often with Schiele, it can be considered a portrait only in a rather unusual sense. We may experience a sense of pity (or disgust?) on contemplating this alarmingly emaciated figure, but we can guess next to nothing about the personality or thoughts of the person depicted – only, perhaps, that he is in pain or distress or possibly in the grip of some violent emotion. Equally tantalising is the fact that the artist has initialled the sheet twice: once, in close proximity to the left heel, as if the image were meant to be read horizontally, a second time in the area of the right foot, where the characteristic undulating initial 'S' that appears in many of his drawings of this period reads the other way, as if the figure had been conceived vertically. Nor is the title 'Reclining Male Nude' much help in solving this riddle since, apart from those cases where Schiele has added his own inscription, most of 'his' titles were, in reality, invented by gallery owners or exhibition curators. Whether he himself considered

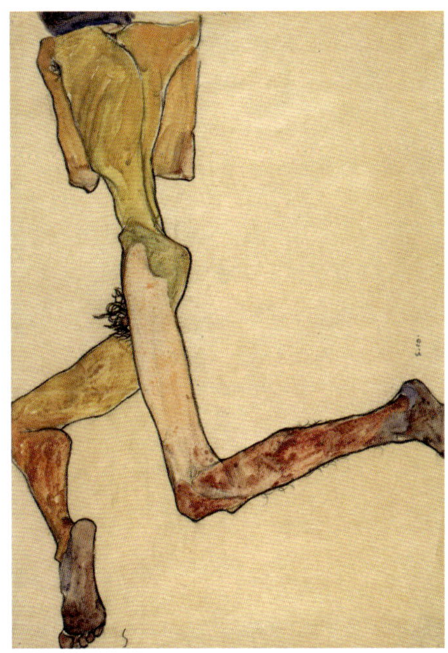

Cat. 4 rotated

this figure to be 'reclining' remains, therefore, open to question.

Inevitably, drawings signed or initialled in this way – and there are quite a few other, similar examples to be found in Schiele's oeuvre – pose a conundrum as to which way they should be displayed: horizontally or vertically.[1] The two signatures in different orientations seem to imply that either solution would be acceptable, although in this instance it is easier to accept the notion that the figure is meant to be horizontal, with one leg hanging off the edge of a bed or couch, despite the fact that no such support is visible. Turn the sheet the other way so that it becomes a standing figure, and we quickly realise that neither the artist nor anyone else could possibly have held such a pose; the figure must surely have been drawn in a recumbent posture, even if intended to be viewed otherwise. On the other hand, when placed upright it exhibits an uncanny resemblance to *Male Nude* (cat. 2), with mottled legs, prominent rib-cage and twisted spine. Viewed in this way, one drawing appears almost as if intended as a companion piece to the other. However, in the case of the present work the figure looks slightly less uncomfortable when positioned horizontally, and has therefore been displayed this way in the exhibition and also reproduced in this catalogue.

1 Compare entry for cat. 37.

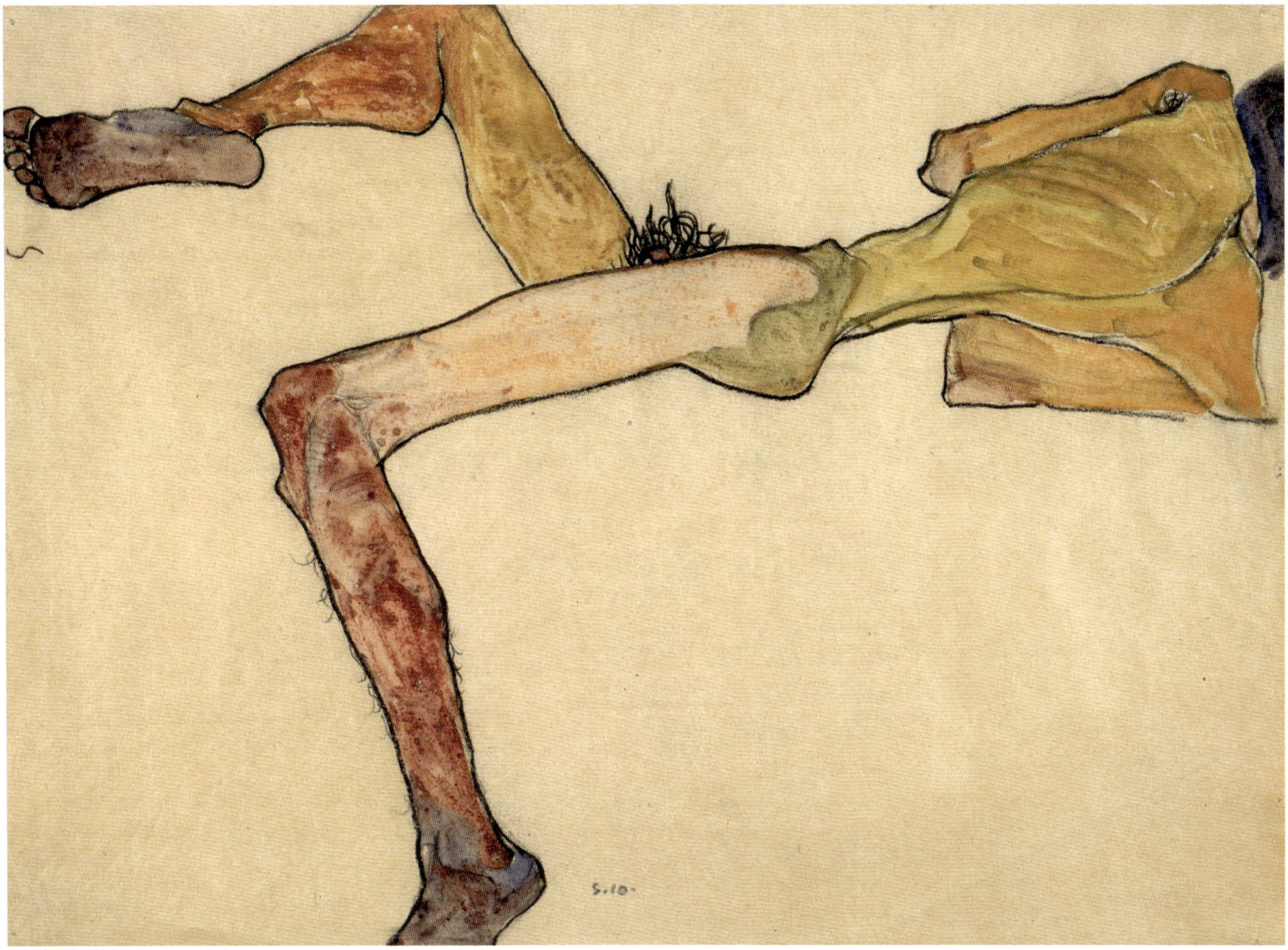
S.10.

5

NUDE PREGNANT WOMAN RECLINING

1910
Gouache and black chalk, 43 x 30.7 cm
Leopold Museum – Privatstiftung, Vienna (Kallir D. 528)

6

NEWBORN BABY

1910
Watercolour and pencil, 44.6 x 31.4 cm
Private collection, courtesy of Richard Nagy Ltd, London
(Kallir D. 386)

Early in 1910, Schiele painted a portrait of the gynaecologist Dr. Erwin von Graff, to whom he had been introduced by their mutual friend the collector Carl Reininghaus.[1] Graff was one of a number of medical men in Vienna at that time who took a keen interest in contemporary art. Evidently, he also got to know Schiele's companion Erwin Osen, another founder-member of the Vienna-based Neukunstgruppe, established the preceding year. In a letter dated 18 May 1910, the doctor asked Schiele about Osen and enquired when the two of them would be returning to Vienna.[2] Osen, we know, later made a sequence of studies of mental patients undergoing treatment at the psychiatric hospital 'Am Steinhof', just outside Vienna. These studies were used as illustrations for a lecture by another medical practitioner, Dr. Kronberg, whose name appears twice in a sketchbook used by Schiele during 1913–15.[3] As Gemma Blackshaw has noted, these scattered but important details provide crucial background to Schiele's treatment of the theme of the pathological body; they also add at least something to our knowledge of Osen and his career as an artist, many details of which remain tantalisingly obscure.[4]

Whether Graff allowed other artists access to the maternity ward at Vienna University's women's clinic is not known, but Schiele was certainly permitted for a time to draw and sketch there. During the course of 1910, he made a series of studies of new-born babies and also women and girls in an advanced stage of pregnancy or who had just given birth. To judge by the above-mentioned letter from Graff to Schiele, a young woman who visited the clinic, known to us only by her initials, may have been one of the artist's former models; the implication contained in the letter ("She seems very unhappy about your infidelity – probably better that way, both for you and for her") is that Schiele may have been the father.[5]

As others have pointed out, Schiele had so far drawn and painted relatively few female nudes other than his sister Gerti (see cat. 3).[6] Access to Graff's clinic afforded him a welcome opportunity to do so since, at that date, his finances were far too stretched to allow him regularly to employ professional models. However, on the evidence of the drawings themselves, Schiele's attitude to the women he encountered in this way appears somewhat peculiar. Despite his undoubted voyeuristic tendencies, he betrays no interest whatever – either erotic or of any other kind – in them as individuals. Instead of being seen as living creatures of flesh and blood, they are treated as "depersonalised vehicles for formal experimentation", whose facial features are sometimes obliterated or omitted entirely, or else, as in the present watercolour, reduced to an expressionless, mask-like shell.[7] Even odder is the way the face is completely separated from the trunk, almost as if it had been added as an afterthought, while the deliberate massing of flat, block-like forms and tendency to decorative pattern-making also emphasises the artist's lack of interest in the personality of the woman portrayed or the nature of her condition.

This seemingly detached, even dispassionate attitude to his subject-matter is in striking contrast to the more convincing and engaged manner in which his mentor (and role model) Klimt had treated both the allegorical and the emotive implications of pregnancy in his paintings *Hope I* of 1903 and its successor, *Hope II* (1907–08). Schiele would certainly have known both these works, shown at the second Kunstschau exhibition in summer 1909, when he himself made his debut before

1 Kallir P. 161.
2 Nebehay 1979, p. 131, doc. 102.
3 Blackshaw 2007, p. 392.
4 For more on Osen see cat. 13, 14.
5 Nebehay 1979, p. 131, doc. 102.
6 See, for example, the article by Stephanie Auer, 'Egon Schiele's Image of Woman: Between Saint and Whore?', in Husslein-Arco and Kallir 2011, pp. 48-49.
7 Auer in Husslein-Arco and Kallir 2011.

the Viennese public.[8] Themes of fertility and pregnancy (as well as mortality) had also played an important role in Klimt's University Paintings, especially the second of these, *Medicine*, exhibited at the Secession in 1901 and again at the Klimt retrospective exhibition held two years later (18th Secession exhibition, 1903). Even if he did not know the University Paintings in the original, Schiele may well have seen some of the drawings related to these pictures in Klimt's studio, which he began frequenting around the time of the Kunstschau exhibition.

By contrast, Schiele's attitude to babies appears far more personal and engaged. Notwithstanding the often exploitative strategies he employed with regard to many of his adolescent and pre-pubescent models, he seems to have been genuinely fond of children, even very small ones. A vivid sense of empathy and insight into their little lives characterises his series of studies of his nephew Anton Peschka Jr, born in December 1914.[9] (His favourite sister Gerti had married Schiele's friend and fellow-painter Anton Peschka, another founder-member of the Neukunstgruppe, in November that year.)[10] Something of the same alert interest and close involvement is evident in his earlier studies of new-born babies dating from the weeks and months he spent observing the patients' comings and goings in Vienna University's Frauenklinik (Women's Clinic). Not only does Schiele succeed in capturing the awkward, uncoordinated movements of very young infants and the improbable positions in which, to their consternation, parents often find their babies, even when left alone for just a couple of minutes. These studies also convey a vivid sense of the miniature adult, so small and helpless, yet seemingly aware and watchful, sometimes appearing to stare fixedly at the spectator. In cat. 6, the emphasis placed on the male sexual organs only serves to reinforce our slightly uncomfortable feeling that what we are looking at is indeed the 'man within the child', as in several other works by Schiele – for example, his painting *The Birth of Genius* (fig. 19).

8 See the essay by Walther K. Lang, 'Der mönchische Tod – Todesmotive bei Egon Schiele', which also explores the relationship between the themes of pregnancy and mortality, in Müller-Tamm 1995, esp. pp. 113ff.
9 For example, Kallir D. 1702-06, D. 1813-15.
10 For more on Schiele's relationship with his sister see cat. 3.

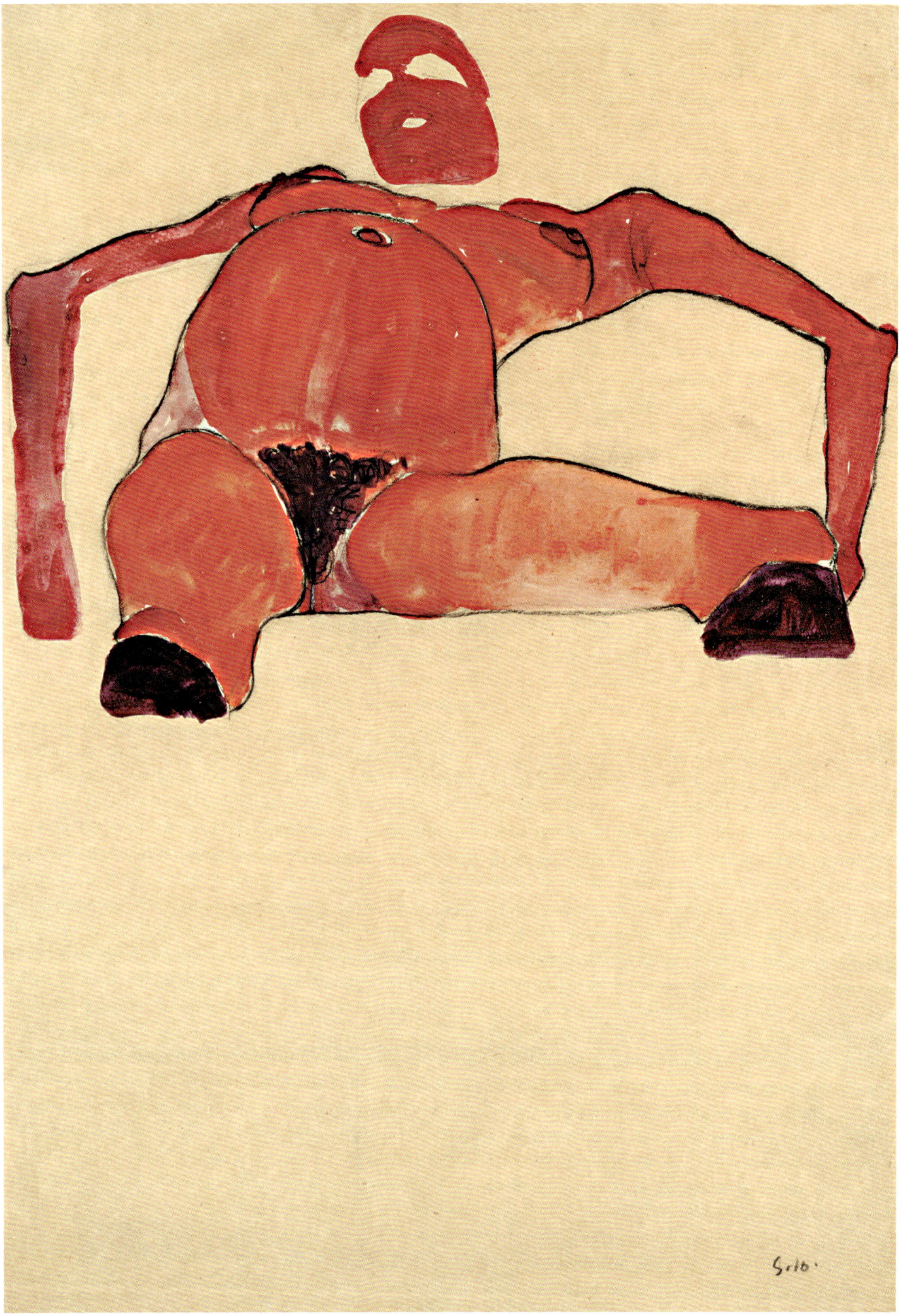

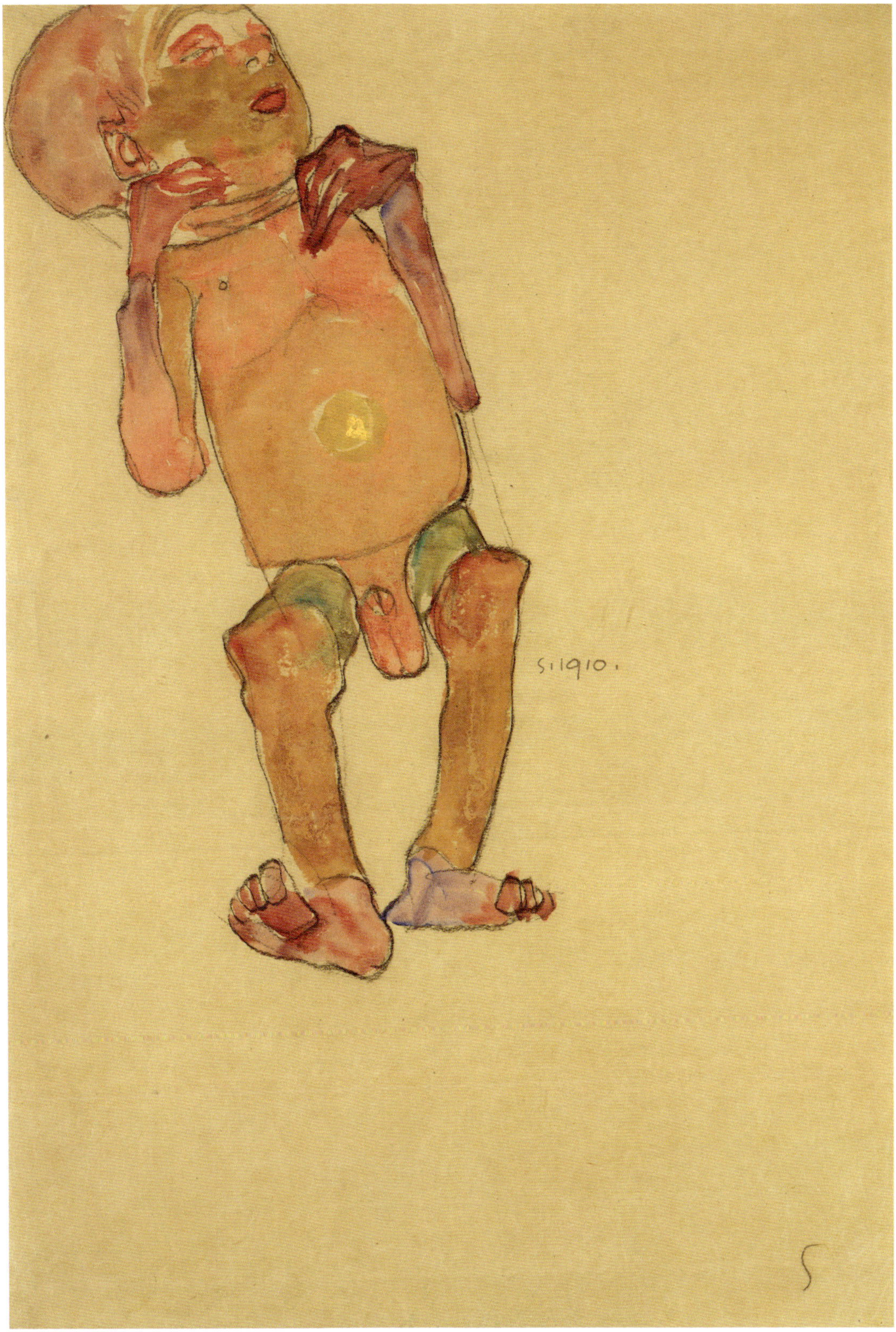
S.1910.

7

MOTHER AND CHILD (WOMAN WITH HOMUNCULUS)

1910
Gouache, watercolour and pencil, 55.6 x 36.5 cm
Private collection, courtesy of Richard Nagy Ltd, London (Kallir D. 396)

Mother and Child is one of Schiele's most accomplished and striking watercolours of 1910, that *annus mirabilis* which saw the astonishingly rapid development of his art, now increasingly independent of Klimt's influence or that of any other artist. As regards its subject, this study of what one presumes to be a young mother with her baby may belong to that group of drawings and watercolours based on observations he made in the Frauenklinik of Vienna University (compare cat. 5 and 6). It is, however, very different in both style and technique. Many of those watercolours are painted in flat, block-like colours, as in the case of cat. 5, and the women depicted often seem devoid of character or personality, showing to the world only blank, expressionless faces. By contrast, *Mother and Child* appears far more personal in character. Moreover, Schiele's depiction of the naked body of the young woman carries a powerful erotic charge, conveyed not only by anatomical details such as the pulsating red of the left nipple but also by the woman's seemingly sly, sideways glance directed at the artist and hence, by implication, at the viewer.

This obviously greater degree of personal involvement on Schiele's part has given rise to a number of speculations. For example, it has been proposed that the young woman depicted here could be the same 'dark-haired girl' who appears in several of his other drawings and watercolours of this period, for whom Schiele allegedly displayed a particular preference.[1] However, the facial features, especially the nose with its prominent bridge, are quite unlike those of the snub-nosed *Seated Nude Girl with Pigtails*, also tentatively identified as the 'dark-haired girl' (see cat. 9). Nor can it be the same young woman who appears in the drawing *Sleeping Girl* of 1911, who has Gerti Schiele's distinctive retroussé nose (compare *Gerti Schiele Sleeping*, executed the same year).[2] On the other hand, it clearly is the same model, with luxuriant dark hair and alluring, almond-shaped eyes, who appears in the watercolour *Two Girls Embracing*, again of 1911.[3] However, her actual identity remains, as in so many other cases, uncertain.

It has also been suggested that the woman depicted here could be the otherwise unidentified "L. A." mentioned in a letter to Schiele written by the gynaecologist Dr. Erwin von Graff.[4] Graff's letter (see cat. 5 and 6) states that the girl was unhappy about Schiele's alleged infidelity and implies that she had come to his clinic carrying the artist's unborn child.[5] This hypothesis seems unlikely. Unless Schiele painted this watercolour entirely from his imagination, contrary to his usual practice, why should he go to Graff's clinic (or visit the woman's lodgings) intent on creating a visual record of the evidence of his alleged infidelity, only to be met with the inevitable reproaches regarding his feckless behaviour? More plausible is the idea that, aside from any factual narrative, what this work reflects is just as importantly a state of mind. Thus Lloyd, for example, observes that the young woman looks as if she is pulling away in horror from the seemingly hydrocephalitic "child-monster" (or is it a still-birth?) attached to her back. If that is the case, Schiele is here exploring what would become a recurrent theme in his work, the relationship between pregnancy and childbirth on the one hand and disease, deformity and death on the other. A succession of his paintings from this period deal with preoccupations of this kind, including *Dead Mother* and *The Birth of Genius* (see fig. 19) [6] As has often been remarked, the prevalence of this kind of subject-matter in Schiele's art may have much to do with childhood experiences which, as we know, in later life preyed on his mind – his

1 Lloyd 2011, n. p. [p. 4]. In her recent study *Egon Schiele's Women*, Jane Kallir suggests that there may have been several 'dark haired girls' and claims that a series of drawings of couples make it plain that the artist had sex with at least one of them: see Kallir 2012, p. 91.
2 Kallir D. 897, D. 864.
3 Kallir D. 885.
4 Lloyd 2011.
5 Nebehay 1979, p. 131, doc. 102.
6 Kallir P. 177 and P. 195.

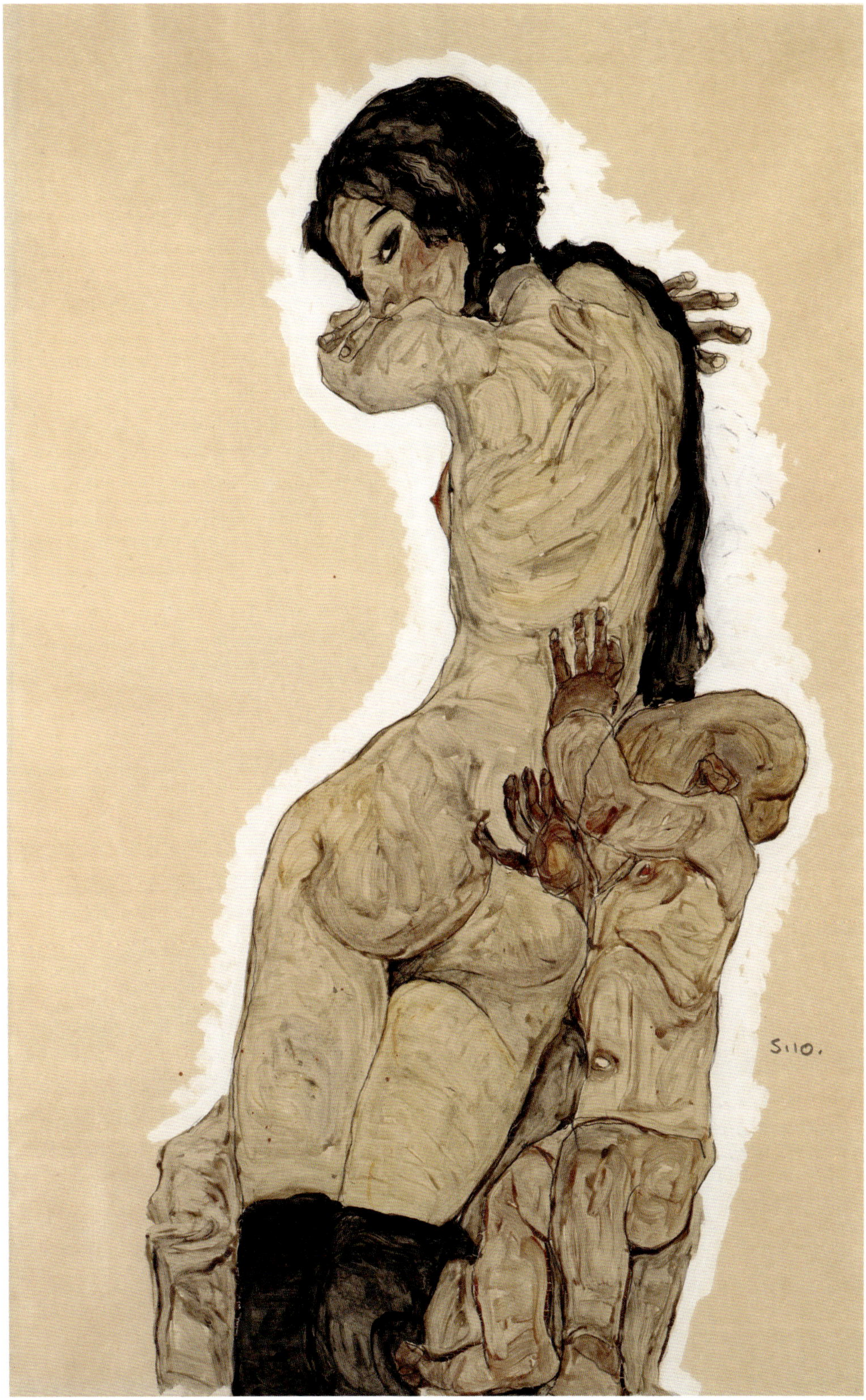

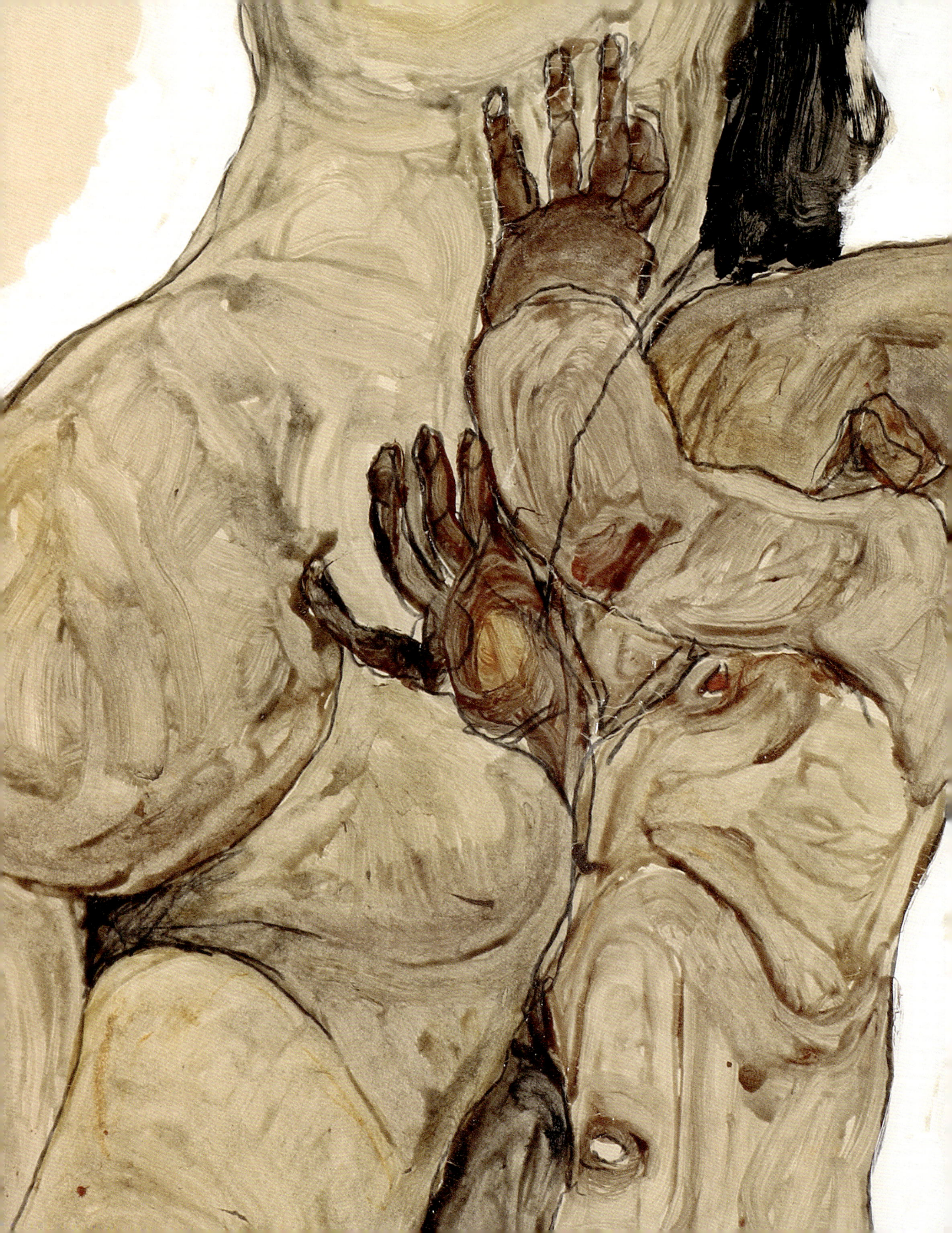

father's death from untreated syphilis, the death of his elder sister Elvira and the repeated still-births (again, probably the consequence of acquired syphilis) that his mother Marie had to endure.

However, Schiele did occasionally portray the relationship between adults and children in a somewhat more cheerful manner. Some of his depictions of children have a touching intimacy about them – for example, his drawings of Paul Erdmann, his wife's Edith's nephew, who appears sometimes on his own, sometimes together with Edith. Schiele evidently felt a profound sympathy with children: not for nothing did he allude to himself as an "eternal child".[7] But these drawings, too, can have disturbing implications; as Kallir points out, in some cases we are uncertain whether it is Egon or Paul who is locked in a seemingly erotic embrace with Edith.[8] In other cases, where it is clearly Paul whose features appear in the drawing, the relationship between aunt and nephew appears, in Kallir's words, "eerily sexual".[9] Not infrequently, we find ourselves compelled to insert the further term 'sexuality' into the equation 'pregnancy – adulthood – mortality', as in the case of the present work, whose erotic undertones are undeniable.

7 For example, in his poem that begins 'Ich, ewiges Kind', published in Nebehay 1979, p. 504; for a discussion of the Nietzschean overtones that characterise Schiele's poem see Kathryn Simpson's essay in this catalogue, p. 61.
8 Kallir 1998, p. 546.
9 Kallir 2003, p. 323.

8

SICK GIRL

1910
Black chalk and gouache, 44.9 x 31.3 cm
Leopold Museum – Privatstiftung, Vienna (Kallir D. 427)

Some of our encounters with Schiele's early work leave us pondering the exact nature of the relationship between his art and that of Edvard Munch, even if we can find no proof of direct influence nor any specific response to the example set by the great Norwegian artist. By 1910, there can be no doubt that Munch was very well known in Vienna, as he was throughout the German-speaking world. Several of his paintings had been exhibited at the Secession, and in 1909 drawings by Munch were included in the second Internationale Kunstschau exhibition. As noted elsewhere in this catalogue, Schiele himself was represented by three paintings at that exhibition, his first important showing before the Viennese public.[1] Thus, it appears unthinkable that he did not become acquainted with the Norwegian's work on that occasion, if not earlier.

Like Munch, in this drawing Schiele tackles a theme common in late Romantic painting and literature, that of the sick or dying child. The subject was probably drawn from life, although we know nothing about the circumstances in which the work was created; it may have been done at the same time as his studies of infants and pregnant women made in the Frauenklinik of Vienna University (compare cat. 5 and 6). Munch had treated the same theme in several painted versions showing a pale-faced girl propped up in bed, her flowing locks contrasting with the pallor of her skin and the white of the pillow. *The Sick Child* was also one of the best known of all his lithographs, versions of which circulated widely in a bewildering succession of different states and variants.

More significant is the obvious visual similarity between Schiele's drawing and another equally famous work by Munch, his painting *Puberty*, whose subject-matter was closely related to that of his well-known cycle of pictures on the theme of love and death entitled *The Frieze of Life*.[2] At the time it was painted, and ever since, commentators on that picture have remarked on the sense of eerie foreboding that Munch manages to instil into what is, in essence, a very straightforward composition. This effect is produced largely by the ominous shadow that plays above and behind the naked figure of a young girl, seated apprehensively on the edge of a bed. This shadow has often been interpreted as signifying death; at the same time, the girl's fear of what might be about to befall her and intimations of her impending sexual awakening are almost palpable.

In *Sick Girl*, the means Schiele employs are even simpler. There is no indication of any bed or chair, nor any visual clue as to the spatial setting or context in which the figure is located. A smear of what looks like white heightening across her abdomen merely serves to accentuate the skinny body, with knock knees and clenched hands, drawn almost entirely without internal modelling. Here, the artist relies above all on outline to capture the corporeality of this waif-like child. The sickly yellowish tinge of her face is picked up again only in the small patch of the same colour that draws attention to her pudenda, noticeably devoid of pubic hair – further evidence of the artist's obsession with observing the genitals of the child models who featured frequently in his drawings of 1910–11.

1 See above, pp. 72-74.

2 As so often with Munch, there are several versions of this painting. Among the earliest and most famous are two oils, both with the same title – one of 1893 owned by the Munch-museet, Oslo, and another dated 1894-95 in the collection of the Nasjonalgalleriet, Oslo; on their relationship to Munch's *Frieze of Life* see the exhibition catalogue edited by Klaus Albrecht Schröder and Antonia Hoerschelmann, *Edvard Munch, Thema und Variation*, Albertina, Vienna, 2003, esp. pp. 133ff.

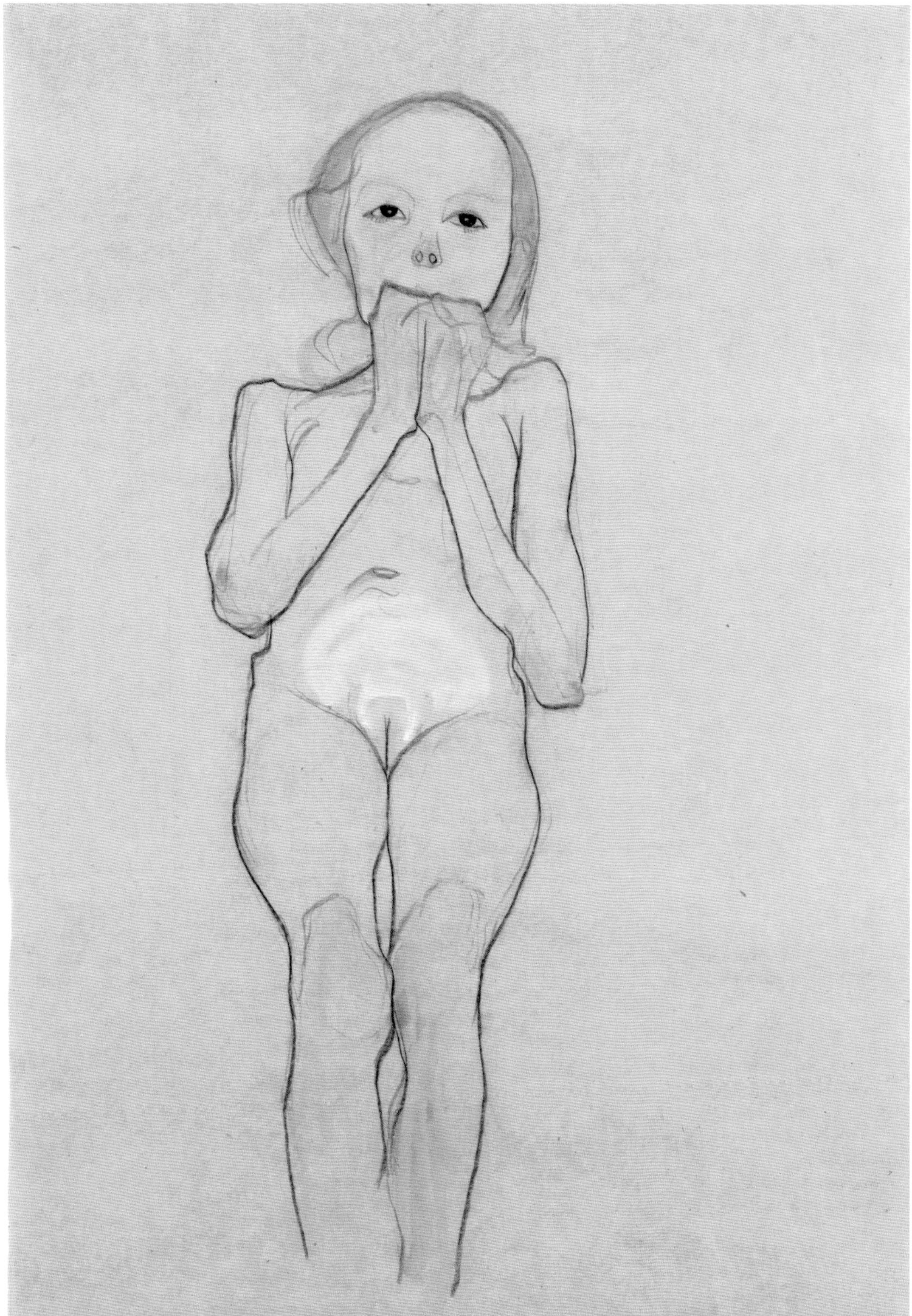

9

SEATED NUDE GIRL WITH PIGTAILS

1910
Gouache, watercolour and pencil, 56 x 35.5 cm
Private collection, courtesy of Richard Nagy Ltd, London (Kallir D. 571a)

Schiele has frequently been taken to task for his use of under-age models, although his contemporaries seem to have cared rather less about this issue than later generations. As Jane Kallir, Jill Lloyd and other writers have pointed out, in pre-First World War Vienna child prostitution was rife; Lloyd even claims that many of the adolescent models Schiele depicted "undoubtedly doubled as prostitutes and entered into casual sexual relationships with the artist".[1] However, caution is needed when describing these girls as 'under age' since, in many cases, we cannot know for certain how old a particular model was.[2] Some of them may have looked younger than they really were or Schiele may have purposely made them look younger – skinnier, more waif-like, a type that evidently appealed to him and which may have fuelled his fantasies about the compelling nature of infantile sexuality.[3]

Nor, with very few exceptions, do we know who these 'child' models were. The girl with pigtails portrayed in this drawing has been tentatively identified with the 'dark-haired girl' who appears in a number of the artist's works of this period, although the snub-nosed features depicted here look rather different from those of the pubescent black-haired girl pictured in his famous drawing now in the Albertina (fig. 30). But even if it is the same model, her identity remains unknown. Nor does Schiele seem very interested in trying to convey anything much about her personality or character. He appears more concerned to capture details such as the disturbingly emaciated arms and claw-like hands with their "scrofulous finger joints".[4] No less interesting to the artist are the girl's pubic hair and also her nipples, deliberately accentuated by a lurid red, among the few touches of vivid colour in an otherwise largely sombre drawing.

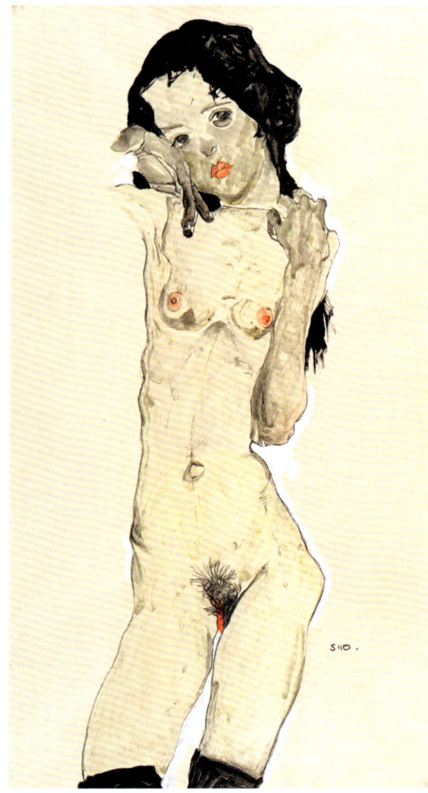

30
EGON SCHIELE
Nude Black-Haired Girl, 1910
Watercolour and pencil with white heightening, 54.3 x 30.7 cm
Albertina Museum, Vienna
(Kallir D. 575)

1 Lloyd 2011, n. p. [p. 4].
2 As noted in the introduction to this catalogue, in Austria at that time the age of consent was fourteen; see above, p. 29, note 47.
3 In his so-called 'Prison Diary', Schiele allegedly wrote: "Have adults forgotten how corrupted they themselves were as children – that is, how incited and aroused they were by the promptings of sex? And, while they were still children, what terrible passion burned within them and tormented them? I have not forgotten, for I suffered dreadfully from it"; quoted from Roessler 1922, p. 33.
4 For the review of Schiele's work by Arthur Roessler in which this striking phrase occurs see above, p. 21.

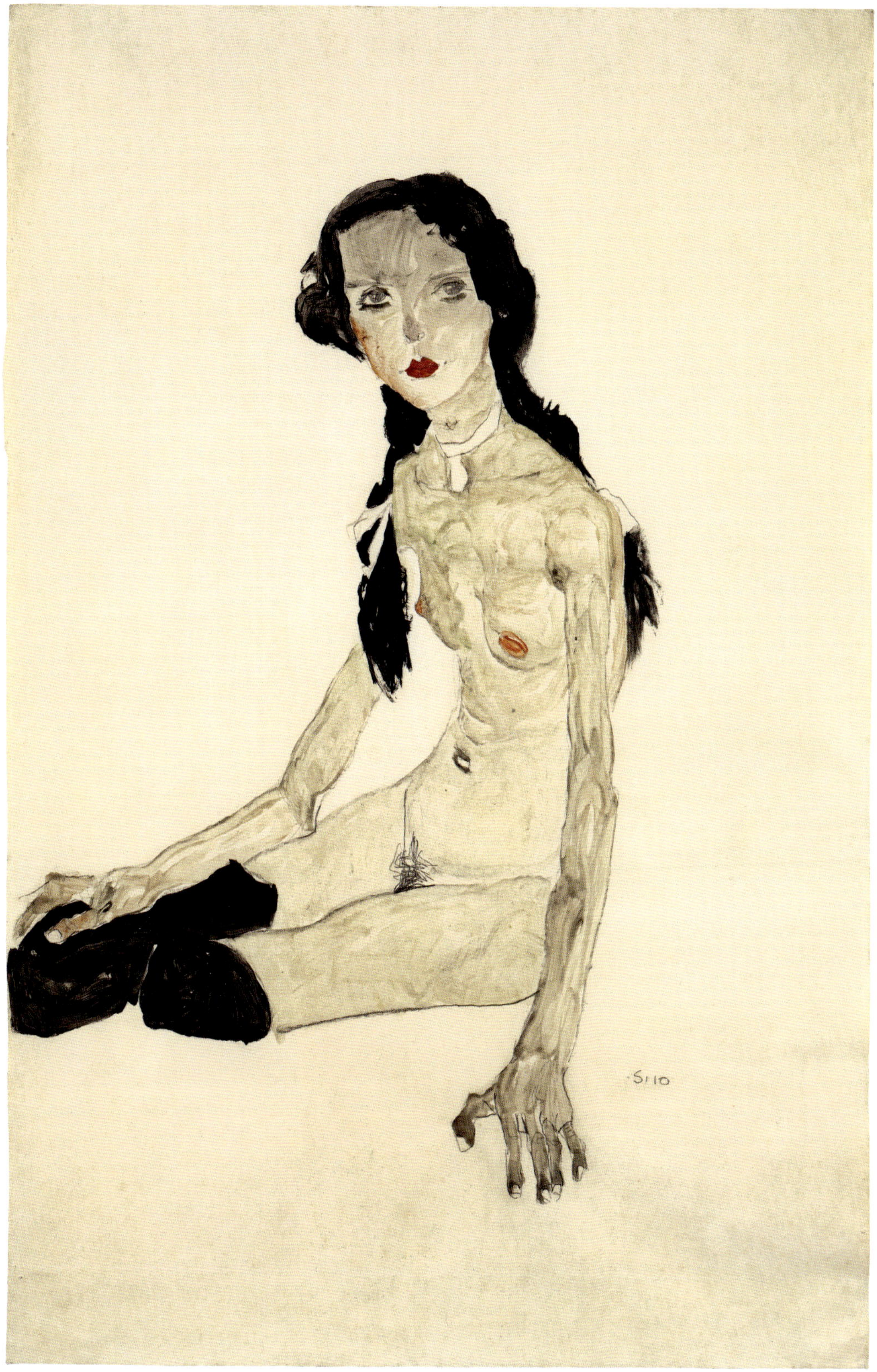
S10

Seated Nude Girl with Pigtails shares many of the defining characteristics of Schiele's nude figure studies of 1910–11, in particular his increasingly radical treatment of the human figure. Especially striking is the way the artist studiously ignores many details that he evidently considers unimportant. As so often, limbs – in this case, the girl's legs – are truncated, cut off by the edge of the paper as if unfinished or perhaps even amputated. Equally radical is the absence of any spatial reference points, the figure simply being set against the void created by the blank page, without any indication of background or setting. Only occasionally does Schiele add a degree of emphasis to his figure studies by using white heightening to create a kind of 'halo', as in the case of cat. 15 and 16; even then, the rest of the paper remains blank.

This featureless empty space, sometimes characterised as a 'psychological void', has intrigued any number of art historians, some of whom have hastened to contrast this aspect of Schiele's art with the *horror vacui* evident in so many of Klimt's paintings, with their elaborately decorated backgrounds. The comparison is not entirely apt: in his drawings (as opposed to his paintings), Klimt was just as likely to set the nude figure against the simple white of the page. The more telling difference is that, whereas Klimt was able to afford top-quality paper that significantly enhanced the delicate lines of his drawing, Schiele's financial situation during the years 1910–12 grew increasingly precarious following the rift with his guardian, his uncle Leopold Czihaczek, who until then had provided him with a measure of support. Even when he did have a little money, he was apt to squander it on trips to the cinema or meals out – a frequent bone of contention between him and his mother, Marie Schiele. Thus, he was dependent on whatever paper he could afford or, in some cases, scrounge, even resorting on occasion to drawing on both sides of the sheet (compare cat. 26 and 27). On inspection, it appears that many of his early drawings were done on something not much better than cheap brown wrapping paper; only after 1914, when growing success brought with it a greater degree of prosperity, was he gradually able to afford better-quality materials.

10

KNEELING MALE NUDE WITH RAISED HAND (SELF-PORTRAIT)

1910
Gouache and black chalk, 62.1 x 44.1 cm
Leopold Museum – Privatstiftung, Vienna (Kallir D. 692)

It has become something of an art historical cliché to point out that the impoverished artist, unable or unwilling to pay for professional models, will often have recourse to what Shearer West calls "the cheapest and most accessible model", available at all hours of the day and night and demanding no payment, namely himself.[1] However, confronted with Schiele's numerous self-portraits, it is immediately obvious that he had other, more compelling agendas in mind than mere convenience or saving money. On the one hand, nude self-portraiture was one method of exploring the to him constantly fascinating subject of his own sexuality. In some of his drawings and watercolours, he exposes himself while fondling his genitals or blatantly masturbating. In others, he deliberately draws attention to the body's erogenous zones, principally his nipples and penis, by using exaggerated colour, in most cases a lurid red. The same device is also found in his more explicitly erotic depictions of female models, especially children and adolescents.

On the other hand, in other drawings and watercolours including the present work, it was the expressive potential of the human body, seen in more general terms, that was evidently the principal focus of his attention. Schiele heightens the expressive impact of the nude figure in several ways. By 1910 he was already an accomplished master of the provocative *mise-en-page*, ruthlessly omitting anything – for example, parts of the anatomy such as hands, feet or even the trunk – that might distract from the impact produced by the unconventional positioning of the figure on the paper or canvas (compare cat. 19 and fig. 23). He also uses disconcertingly contorted poses to imply intense emotions seemingly undergone by the figure portrayed. At the same time we, as viewers, often find ourselves intrigued and puzzled by the expressive but enigmatic hand gestures such as those found in Schiele's portraits of the mime artist Erwin Osen (compare cat. 13 and 14), as well as in the present watercolour. Similar hand movements also characterise many later photographs of Schiele, especially those dating from c.1914–15 (see, for example, fig. 1), leading one to suppose that these gestures were not only carefully studied but also conceived as deliberate signals of some kind. Their precise meaning has, however, so far eluded art historians and commentators on Schiele's art.

The unusual pose of the half-kneeling figure has been linked with that of the central figure of the boy depicted on the title page of Oskar Kokoschka's illustrated poetry book *Die Träumenden Knaben* (The Dreaming Youths) of 1908 (fig. 31).[2] The suggestion is all the more plausible given the intense rivalry between these two *enfants terribles*,

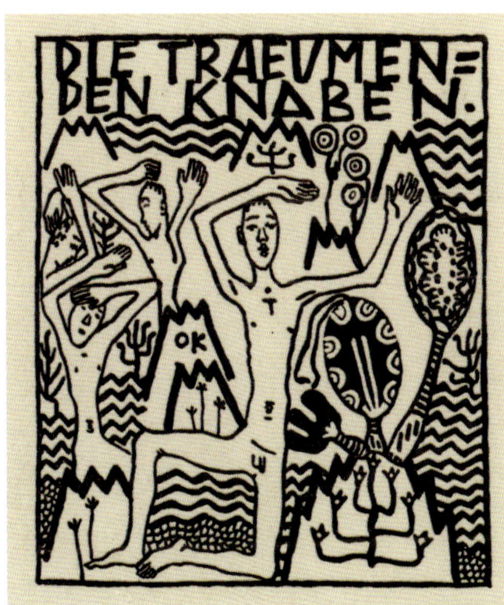

31
OSKAR KOKOSCHKA
Frontispiece for *Die Träumenden Knaben* (The Dreaming Youths), 1907 (published 1908/17), 24 x 29 cm
The Courtauld Gallery, London (Samuel Courtauld Trust, Princes Gate Bequest ,1978)

1 Shearer West, *Portraiture*, Oxford 2004, p. 174.
2 Leopold 1973, p. 90.

who inflicted themselves upon the Viennese public at much the same time, around 1908–09. The two artists shared a penchant for depicting youthful, preternaturally thin, at times even emaciated figures. In this regard, their common source of inspiration may have been the work of the Belgian sculptor Georges Minne, a favourite among the artists of the Vienna Secession: Minne's work had featured prominently at the second Kunstschau exhibition in Vienna in 1909, organised by Klimt and members of his circle, at which Schiele was represented by three important early canvases.[3] Kokoschka later recalled that the Belgian artist's work had produced an even deeper impression on him than paintings by Gauguin, Van Gogh and the Fauves, shown at the same exhibition.[4] As Kallir remarks, Minne's "gaunt, hermaphroditic adolescents" must have looked like "counterparts in the round" to Kokoschka's *Träumenden Knaben*, shown at the first Kunstschau exhibition the preceding summer.[5]

3 The three canvases in question were all portraits; for details see above, pp. 72-74 and cat. 11.

4 Oskar Kokoschka, *My Life*, London (Thames & Hudson) 1974, p. 21.

5 Kallir 1998, p. 55.

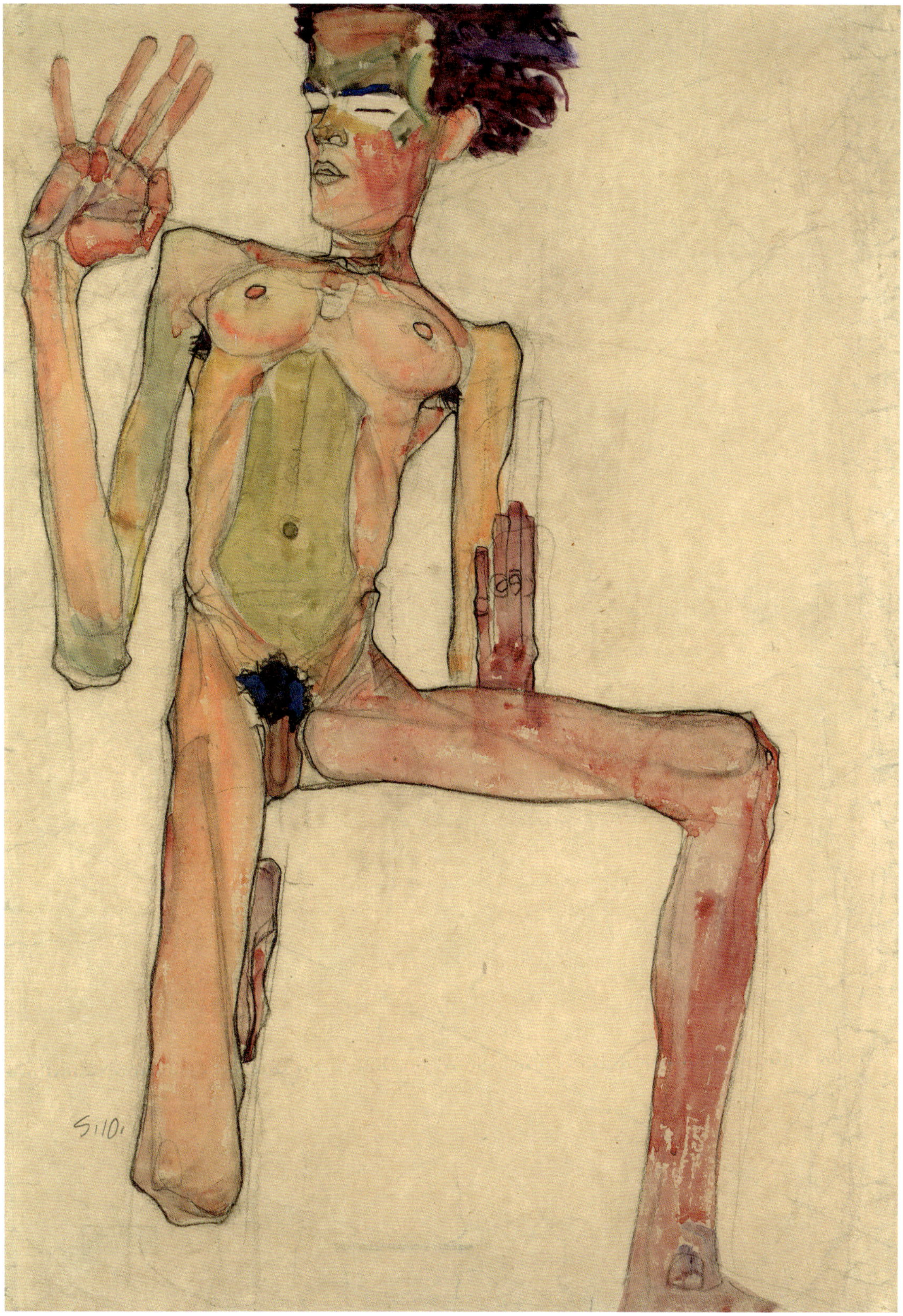
S.10.

11

STANDING MALE NUDE WITH ARM RAISED, BACK VIEW

1910
Watercolour and charcoal, 44.8 x 31.4 cm
Museum of Modern Art, New York (Kallir D. 650)

12

STANDING MALE NUDE WITH LEGS SPREAD, BACK VIEW

1910
Gouache, watercolour and pencil, 45 x 32 cm
Private collection, courtesy of Richard Nagy Ltd, London (Kallir D. 655)

So similar are these two drawings in their colouring, their handling of form and the expressive body language of the figure depicted that they were probably created within a very short time-span. Given Schiele's prodigious rapidity of working, on which many of his contemporaries remarked (and which he himself emphasised, contrasting his fluency in drawing with the time it took him to fashion an acceptable print), they may even have been completed on the same day. They are also, almost certainly, self-portraits, even though no facial features or other distinguishing physical characteristics can be confidently identified. But the unsparing depiction of the seemingly emaciated figure, with its unhealthy-looking and, for the most part, non-naturalistic flesh tones, coupled with the contorted posture as of someone convulsed by pain or grief or some other violent emotion – all this so strongly recalls other works in which Schiele portrayed himself in a similarly 'unlovely' fashion that the identification of these drawings as self-portraits appears unquestionable.

Even in these still relatively early figure studies Schiele is already defining the basic markers that will characterise both his style and his technique in his works on paper over the following two or three years. Watercolour (often combined with gouache) and either pencil or charcoal for the outlines are, in most cases, his preferred media. There is little by way of internal modelling, at least of any conventional kind. It is colour, above all, that is tasked with conveying the solidity of flesh and bone as well as, on occasion, the semi-transparency of tightly stretched skin. Usually, despite occasional distortions and abbreviations, these representations of the human figure are anatomically correct or, at the very least, convincing – one consequence, perhaps, of the tedious life-drawing classes the artist had attended during his time as a student at the Vienna Academy. By contrast, his use of heightened and in many places non-naturalistic colour, the vivid reds and bright oranges suggestive of inflammation or violent exertion, exhibit a formal logic of their own, one that has little to do with any kind of realistic depiction. As in some of his landscape studies, in these drawings Schiele appears to be treating colour largely as an autonomous element, devoid of any narrative purpose. Thus they are likely to strike the viewer not so much as faithful depictions of the world of appearances but rather as abstract colour compositions in their own right.

However, if these two drawings are really self-portraits, they can plausibly be considered as such only in a rather peculiar sense. Almost none of the aims of traditional portraiture are here achieved, least of all any intimation of the sitter's personality or psyche. As pointed out elsewhere in this catalogue, in portraying both himself and others Schiele appears far more interested in role play, fictive identities and histrionics generally than in trying to reveal the 'truth' about a particular person. The contrast with Kokoschka, who repeatedly claimed that his aim in portraiture was to lay bare the 'inner life' of his sitters, could not be greater. Only very occasionally – for example, in Schiele's magisterial double portrait of Heinrich and Otto Benesch (fig. 8) or his touching depictions of his father-in-law Johann Harms – does something of the character and personality of his sitters emerge, largely as the result of a carefully considered combination of pose, gesture and facial expression.

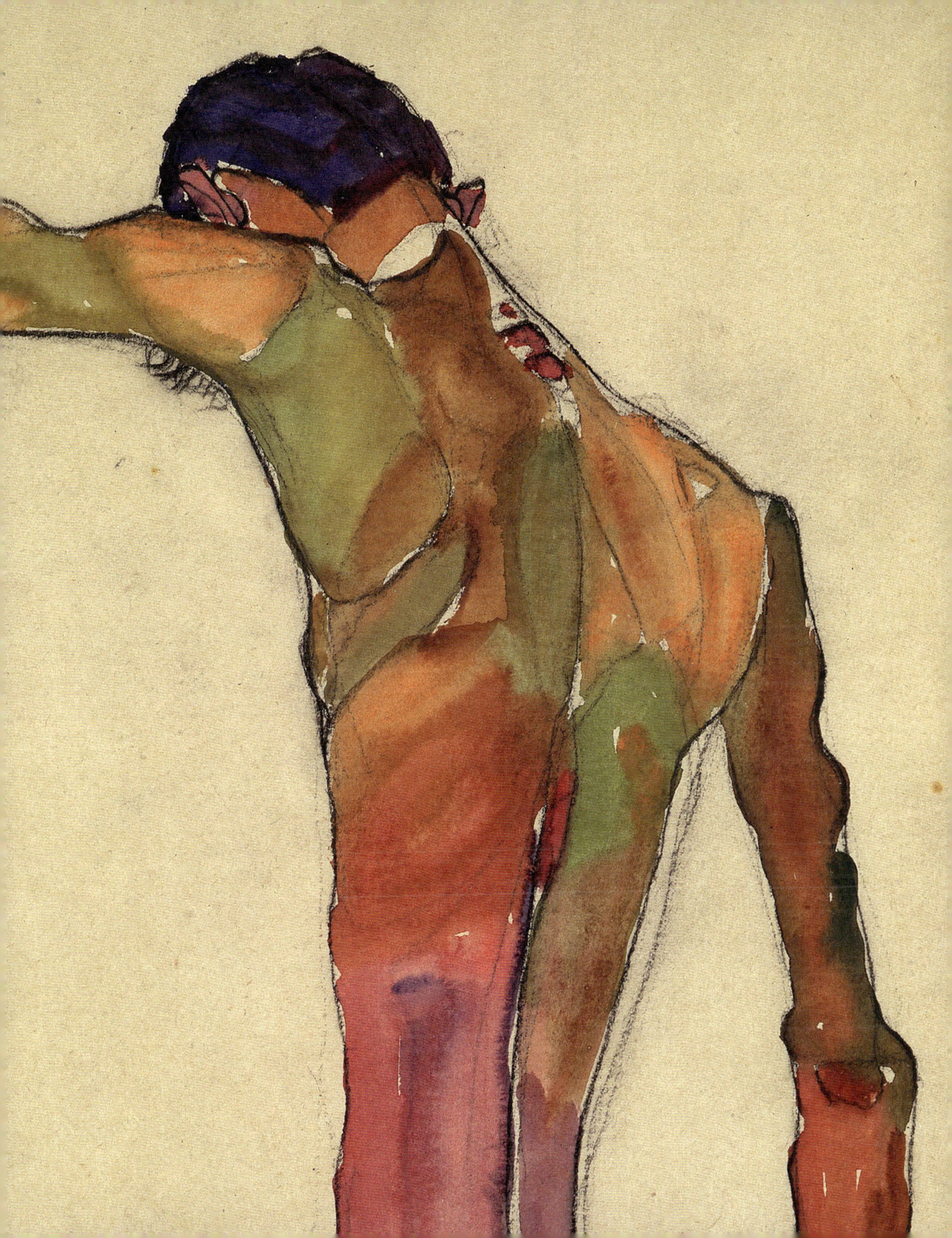

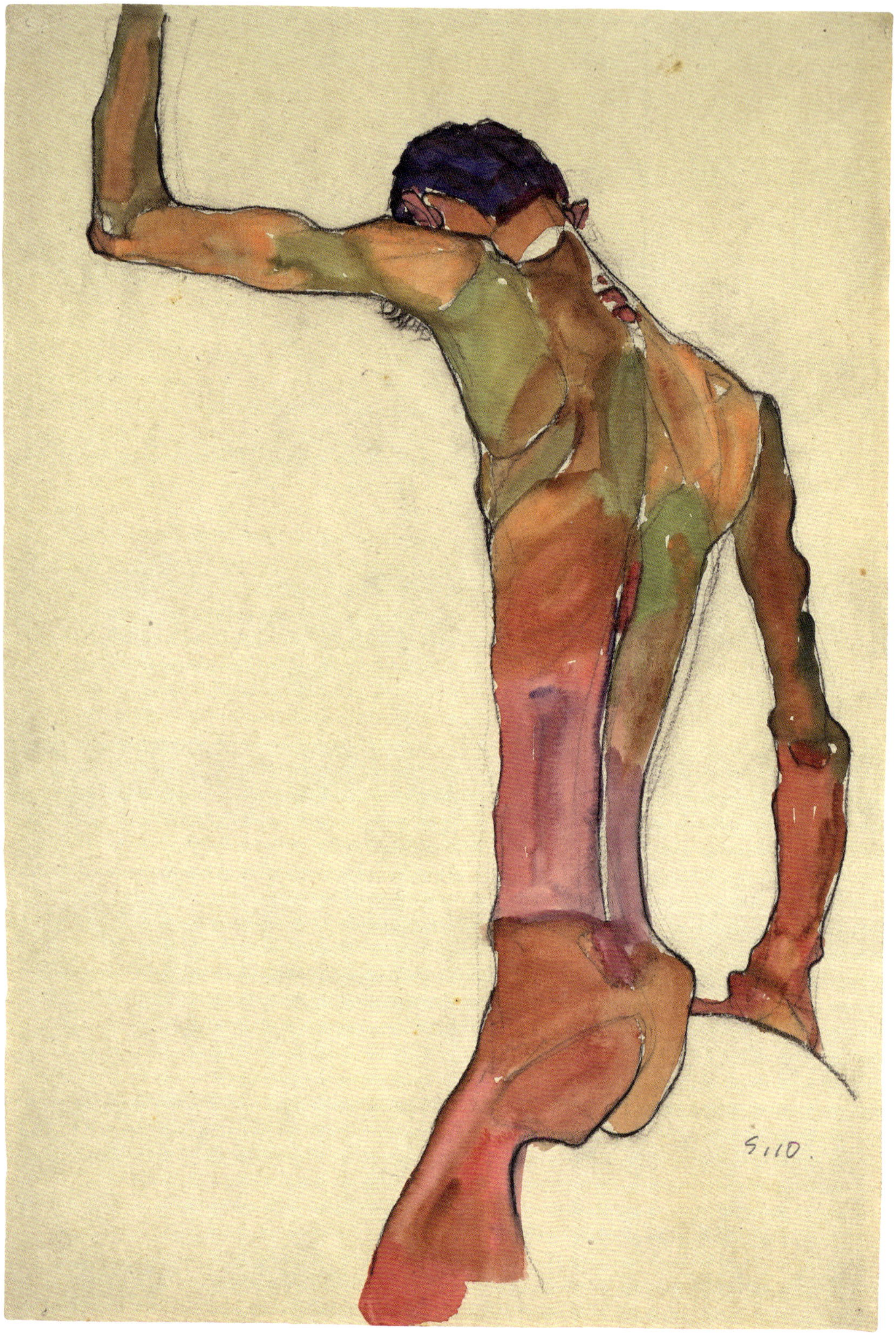
S.10.

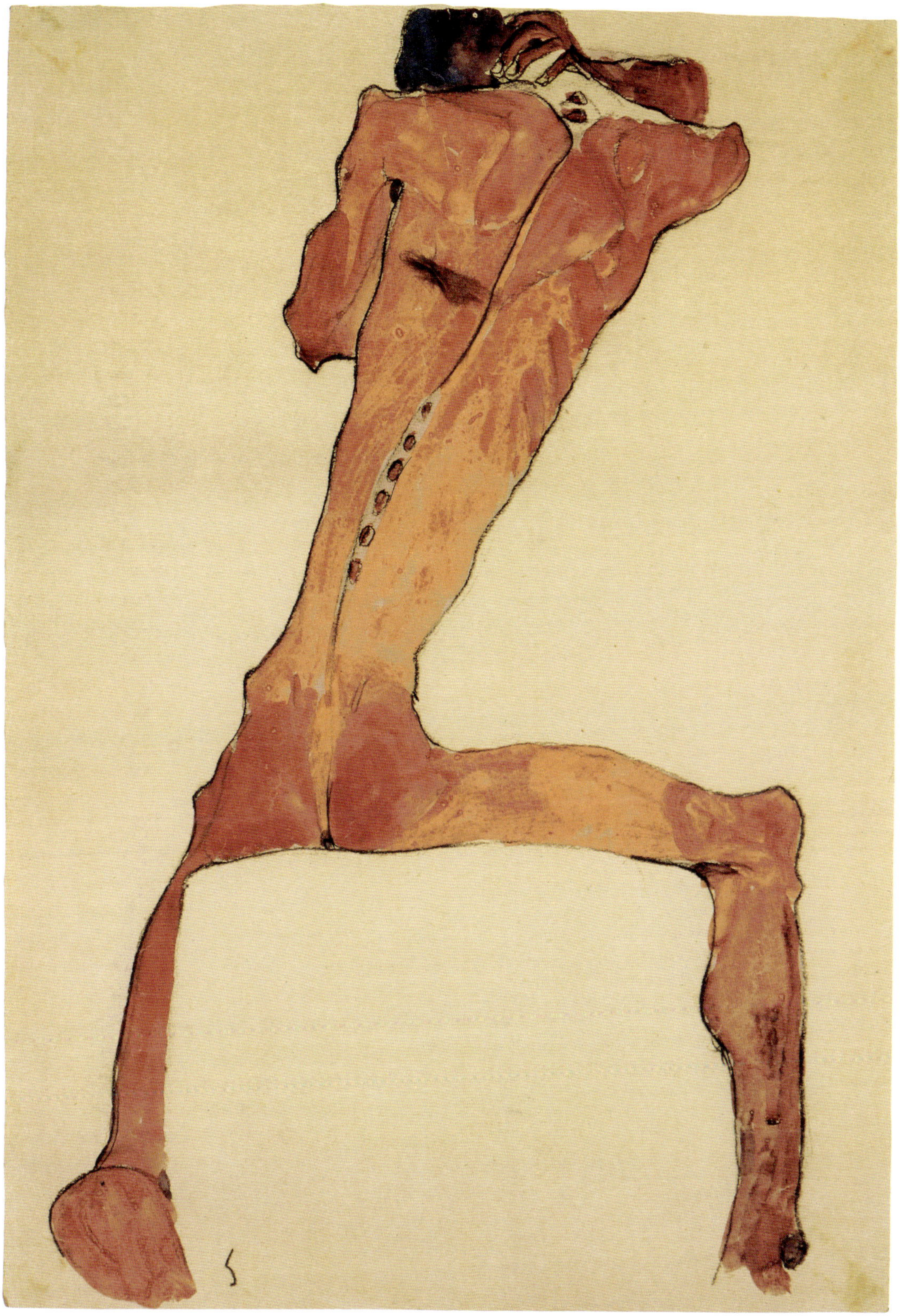

13

ERWIN DOMINIK OSEN

1910
Gouache, watercolour and black chalk, 44.4 x 30.5 cm
Leopold Museum – Privatstiftung, Vienna (Kallir D. 598)

14

MIME VAN OSEN

1910
Gouache and black chalk, 37.9 x 30 cm
Leopold Museum – Privatstiftung, Vienna (Kallir D. 600)

In 1910, Schiele created a masterly series of expressive nude portraits of the artist Erwin Osen, also known as 'Erwin Dominik Osen' or 'Mime van Osen', who played an important if somewhat dubious part in Schiele's life during the years c. 1909–13. Among them are these two works, which depict Osen in exaggerated poses executing theatrical hand gestures that strongly resemble those evident in photographs of Schiele himself and in many of his self-portraits. These gestures may be partly explained by the fact that, among other occupations, Osen allegedly earned a living as a mime artist.[1] When performing in Viennese cabarets, he was sometimes joined by his companion, the dancer Moa, likewise repeatedly depicted by Schiele.[2] An early photograph (fig. 5) shows Osen and Moa in what appears to be theatrical costume, presumably in the course of such a performance.

Osen's relationship with Schiele and the former's erratic life-style are documented by a sporadic exchange of letters and postcards between them and by references to him in Schiele's correspondence with other people, including his patrons and collectors. Like Schiele, in June 1909 Osen signed a document committing himself to contribute at least six pictures to the exhibition of the Neukunstgruppe (New Art Group: see p. 17), held in Vienna at the Kunstsalon Pisko in December that year.[3] Seemingly, at some point in his career he had received professional training as a theatre artist; he may have been a pupil and/or collaborator of the celebrated Anton Brioschi who, over a period of many years, created innumerable sets and costumes for the Vienna Opera.[4] Osen apparently provided the designs for the first performance of Richard Wagner's opera *Parsifal* to be given at the Neues Deutsches Theater (New German Theatre) in Prague, which premiered on New Year's Day 1914. A letter of December 1913 that Osen sent to Schiele from Prague not only alludes to this project but also documents his presence there.[5]

Apart from this, we would know next to nothing about Osen were it not for the recollections of Schiele's friend and patron, the critic and collector Arthur Roessler. Roessler describes Osen as "tall and thin, with the pale, beardless face of a 'fallen angel'", and implies that this unwonted apparition exerted an extraordinary (and perhaps unhealthy) fascination on Schiele.[6] According to Roessler's account, the artist never told him more or in greater detail about any other person than about Osen, thus underlining the extent of the spell the latter evidently succeeded in casting upon the young and impressionable painter. In his published recollections of Schiele, Roessler further characterised Osen as a charlatan, a liar and a thief who could imitate not only Schiele's drawing style but also his signature, and accused him of having created a number of out-and-out forgeries of the artist's work, using materials purloined from Schiele's studio.[7] This unflattering account, which feebly attempted to disguise its object of attack under the all-too-transparent pseudonym 'Mr Neso', prompted Osen to conduct a successful lawsuit against its author, as a result of which a later edition of Roessler's 'Recollections' had to be withdrawn from sale.[8]

As Patrick Werkner has observed, an eerie, disquieting exaggeration in Schiele's manner of representing the human body links his depictions of Osen with his own, often disturbingly contorted self-image as captured in many of his nude self-portraits (compare cat. 10, 17).[9] Equally noticeable are the similarities between the appearance of Osen's pliant but emaciated torso (Roessler, who

1 Comini 1974, p. 204, n. 68.
2 See, for example, Kallir D. 906-08, D. 910.
3 Agreement dated 17 June 1909: Albertina, Egon-Schiele-Archiv, inv. no. 0441.
4 Nebehay 1979, p. 551; compare Kallir 1998, p. 87. In signing the June 1909 Salon Pisko agreement, Osen described himself as "*Maler für Theaterkunst*" (painter of theatre-art).
5 Nebehay 1979, p. 276, doc. 616. The catalogue in question relates to an exhibition of Osen's work held in Vienna in 1947 in the premises of the Wiener Kulturreferat. Here, Osen claims inter alia, quite implausibly, to have been Klimt's only pupil; see Nebehay 1979, p. 551.
6 Roessler 1921, p. 73.
7 On the broader topic of Schiele forgeries generally, an extensive article by Johann Thomas Ambrózy entitled 'Der Forschungsstand zu Fälschungen nach Egon Schiele und Methodisches zur Fälschungsforschung anhand einiger Beispiele' will appear in vol. IV of the *Egon Schiele Jahrbuch* (2014). The article is based on a paper delivered at the 2nd International Egon Schiele Research Symposium held on 29 June 2013 in Neulengbach, Austria.

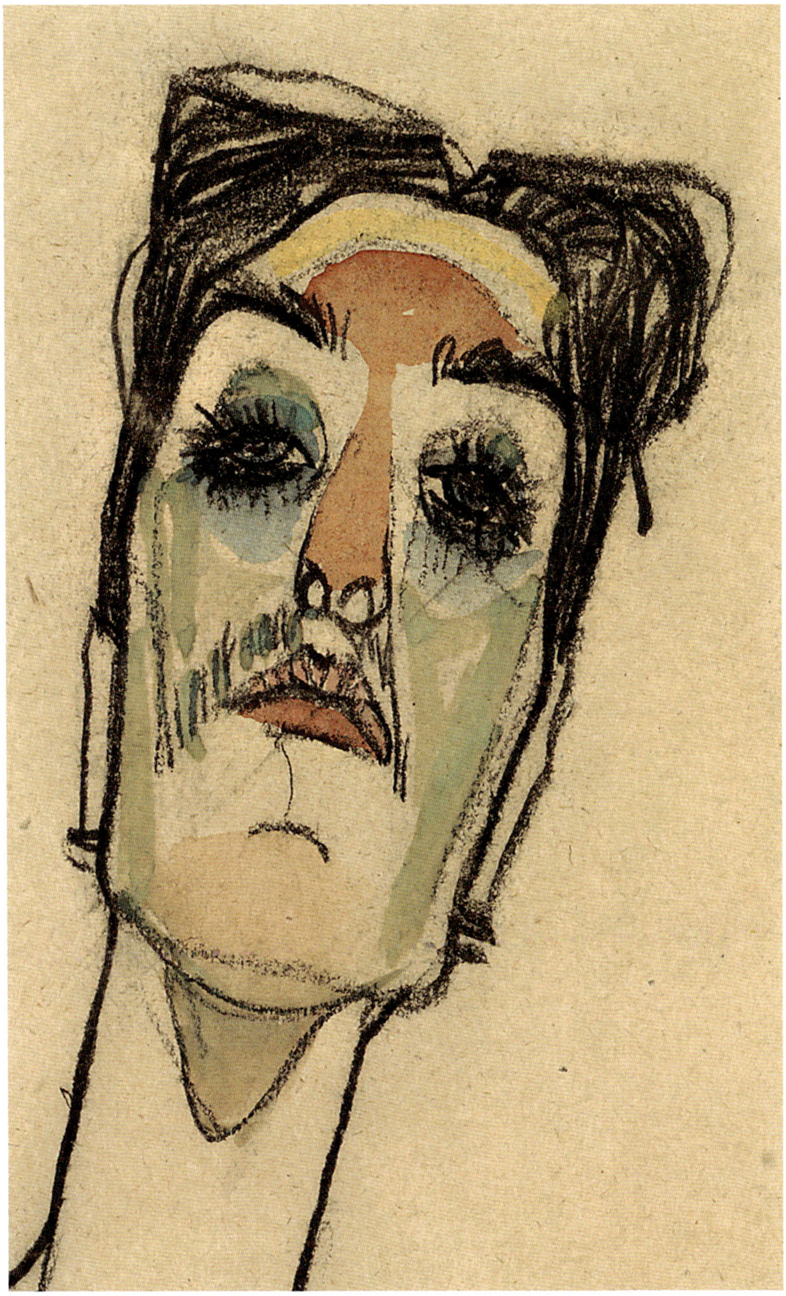

evidently knew him quite well, described him as "scrawny as an Arab") and the way the artist depicted his own bony rib cage and skeletal limbs, not only in drawings and watercolours but also in paintings such as *Seated Nude*, 1910 (fig. 23).[10] Given Roessler's statement that Osen had succeeded in "bewitching" Schiele and filling his mind with largely fabricated traveller's tales, it seems likely that this succession of portraits, in addition to their artistic qualities, demonstrates a degree of identification between the artist and his sitter. Osen's striking facial features and penetrating gaze further suggest the almost hypnotic fascination this older and supposedly more experienced 'adventurer' exerted upon the younger artist.[11]

8 Schiele himself gave an account of these thefts and forgeries in a letter to Roessler dated 3 July 1912, but did not specifically name Osen; see Nebehay 1979, p. 224, doc. 370. In his 'Recollections', Roessler published this letter verbatim and identified Osen as the culprit: see Karpfen 1921, pp. 79-80.

9 'The Child-Woman and Hysteria: Images of the Female Body in the Art of Schiele, in Viennese Modernism, and Today', in Werkner 1994, p. 59.

10 Kallir likewise suggests that Osen's "supple body movements and attenuated gestures" may have served as a "particular inspiration" for Schiele: Kallir 1998., p. 86.

11 The chapter of Roessler's 'Recollections' that deals with Osen is entitled 'Encounter with the Adventurer'; see Karpfen 1921, pp. 73-80.

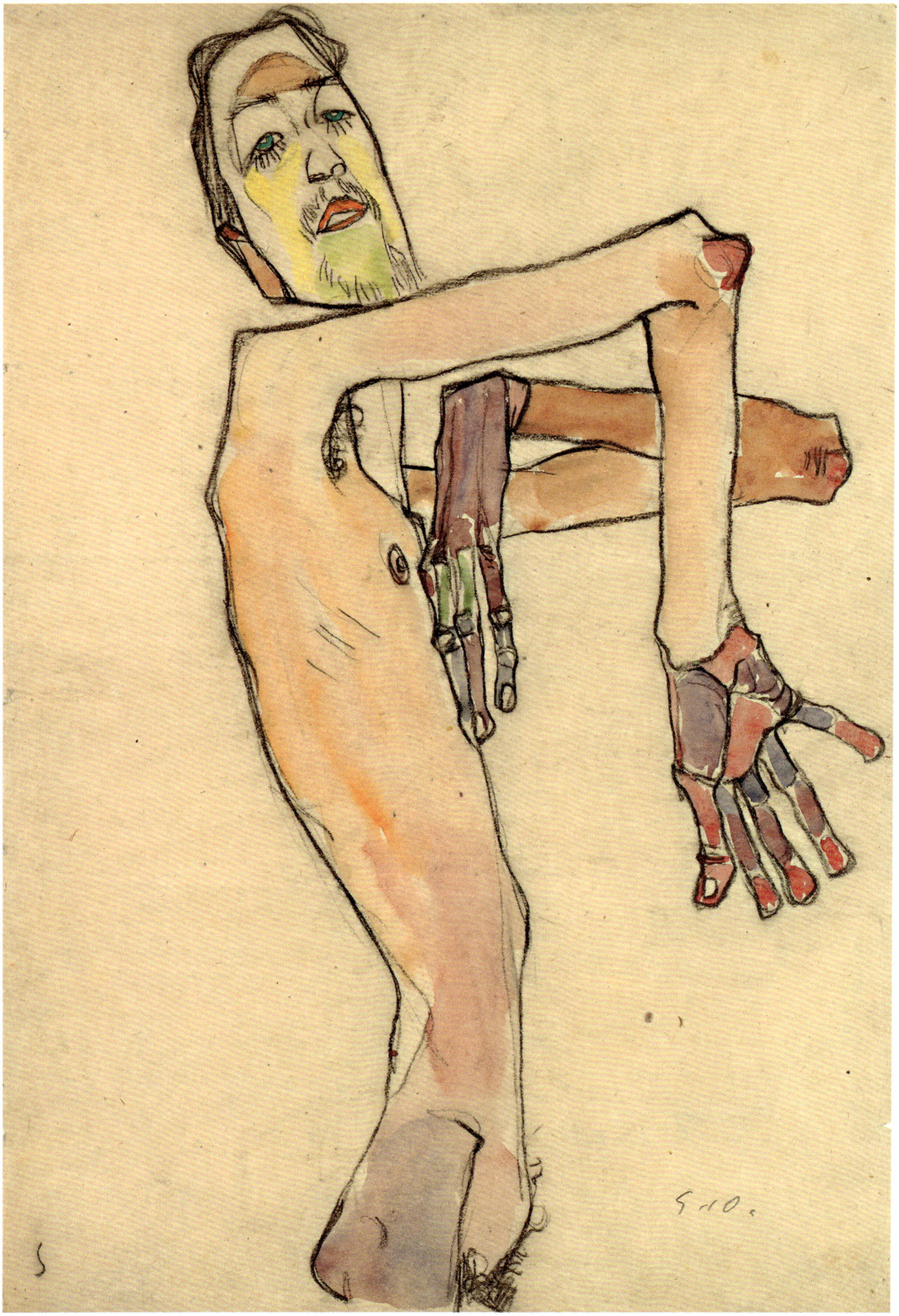

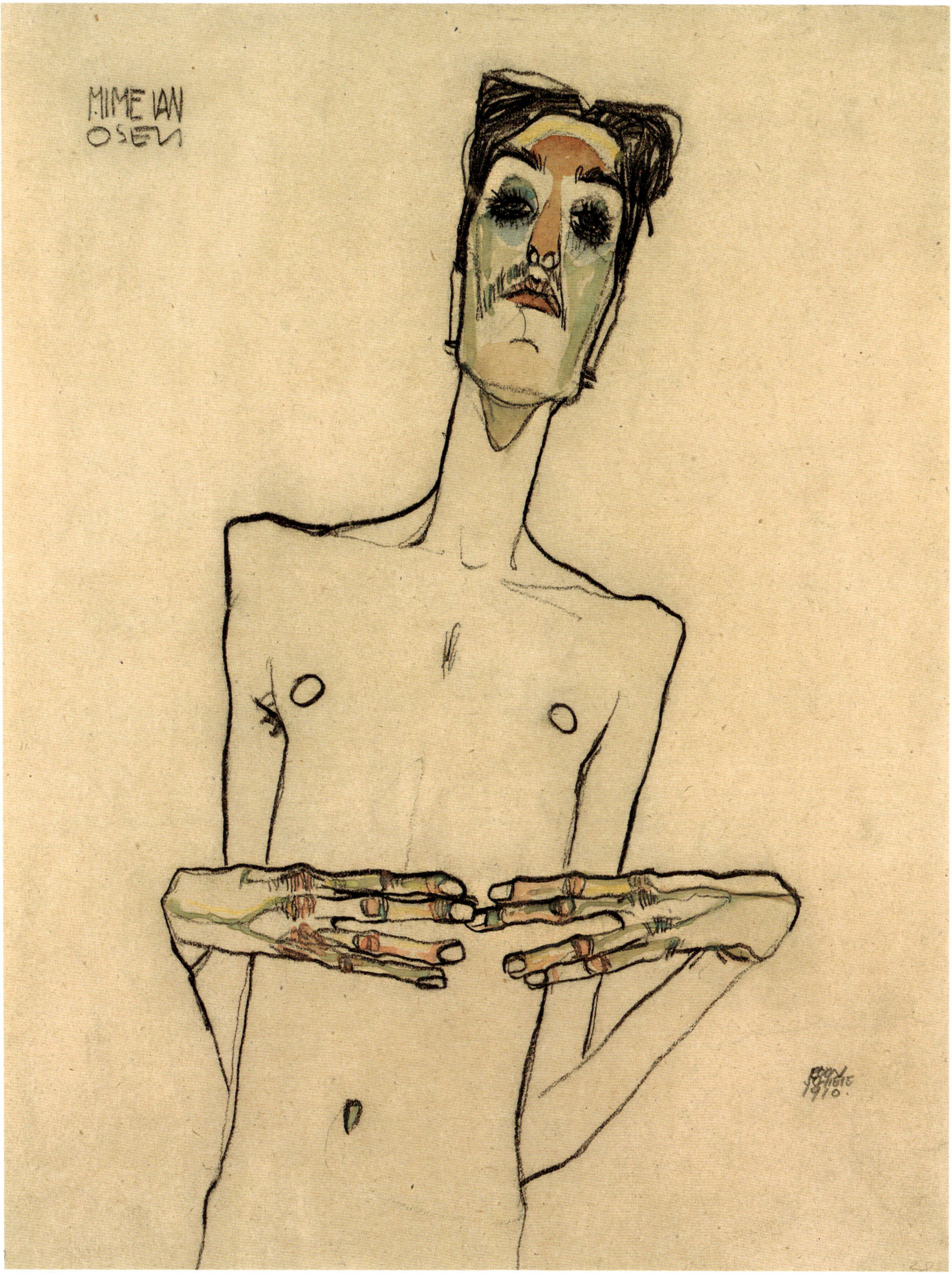
MIME VAN
OSEN
EGON
SCHIELE
1910.

15

SNEERING WOMAN (GERTRUDE SCHIELE)

1910
Gouache, watercolour and charcoal with white heightening, 45 x 31.4 cm
Wien Museum, Vienna (Kallir D. 546)

Several sources describe Schiele's younger sister Gertrude ('Gerti', born 1894) as "*bildhübsch*" – 'pretty as a picture'. Why the artist might have wished to depict such a pretty girl pulling an ugly face, as in *Sneering Woman*,[1] might, therefore, pose something of a conundrum – or it would, but for the fact that we already know a good deal about his passion for role-play and theatricality generally. As an adolescent, he is said to have been inseparable from Gerti and emotionally very attached to her. He was also inclined to boss her around. One can only conclude that, in posing for this portrait, she had been compelled to assume a fictive persona, just as Schiele himself was wont to do in many of his self-portraits of this period. That it is nonetheless an image of Gerti can be proved in a number of ways, not least by taking into account the over-sized hat, which appears in other paintings and drawings executed at this time, several of which the sitter later acknowledged as portraits of herself.[2]

This frequently reproduced watercolour has given rise to a number of conflicting interpretations. Among them, one widespread but misleading notion is that the work reflects Schiele's preoccupation with 'proletarian' subjects, a topic mentioned by numerous writers even during the artist's lifetime and continuing right up to the present day. Thus Otto Benesch, for example, allowed himself the curious observation that this "fashion model" pulls a defiant face out of "proletarian feelings of inferiority and contempt for her environment".[3] The designation 'fashion model' is not so wide of the mark: Gerti had a weakness for fine clothes and elegant hats, luxuries she could ill afford. With her slender figure and pretty face, plus a bit of help from her brother, she soon got a job modelling clothes for the Wiener Werkstätte, the Viennese craft group for whom Schiele provided a small number of designs during the years around 1909–10. Thereafter she was apparently able to earn quite a respectable living as a mannequin.

But while Schiele's family fell upon hard times following his father's death at the end of 1904, whatever else they might have been, they were certainly not proletarian. Rather, they were unrepentantly middle-class. Nor were they without pretensions. Schiele's parents regularly dismissed their maids for trifling misdemeanours , and years afterwards local people still recalled the family's snobbish attitude towards their neighbours. Equally telling are photographs of Adolf Schiele resplendent in his full-dress uniform as an official of the Austrian Imperial State Railways, complete with sword.[4] Nevertheless, as late as 1973, while well aware that the sitter in this watercolour was Gerti, Rudolf Leopold still wrote that Schiele had here "succeeded in illustrating a type to which he constantly alluded ... that of the suburban working-class girl".[5] Whether the artist might have specifically asked his sister to play the role of a working-class girl (which is an entirely different matter) is not known, although it is perfectly possible.

Schiele has sometimes been called an 'Expressionist' or, with perhaps slightly greater precision, an 'Austrian Expressionist'. One important characteristic of Expressionism is thought to have been a determination to expose the 'inner', that 'internal' element being equated sometimes with the inner aspect of the world, sometimes with the artist's own emotional life. It has also been suggested that one defining aspect of Expressionist portraiture is a desire to probe beyond the physical appearance, the external façade, of the sitter in order to lay bare psychological truths. But none of this really applies to Schiele, and certainly not to a

1 In much of the literature in English on Schiele, this watercolour, called *Die Hämische* in German, has been given the title *Scornful Woman*. However, a literal translation of the phrase '*ein hämisches Gesicht*' would be 'a sneer', whereas the word for 'scornful' is '*verächtlich*' or '*spöttisch*', hence the more accurate title *Sneering Woman* adopted here.
2 Nebehay 1979, note 32 on p. 22.
3 'Egon Schiele' [1958], quoted after Benesch 1973, p. 183.
4 See Christian Bauer, 'Egon Schiele: Der Anfang', in Bauer 2013, esp. pp. 159ff.
5 Leopold 1973, p. 118.

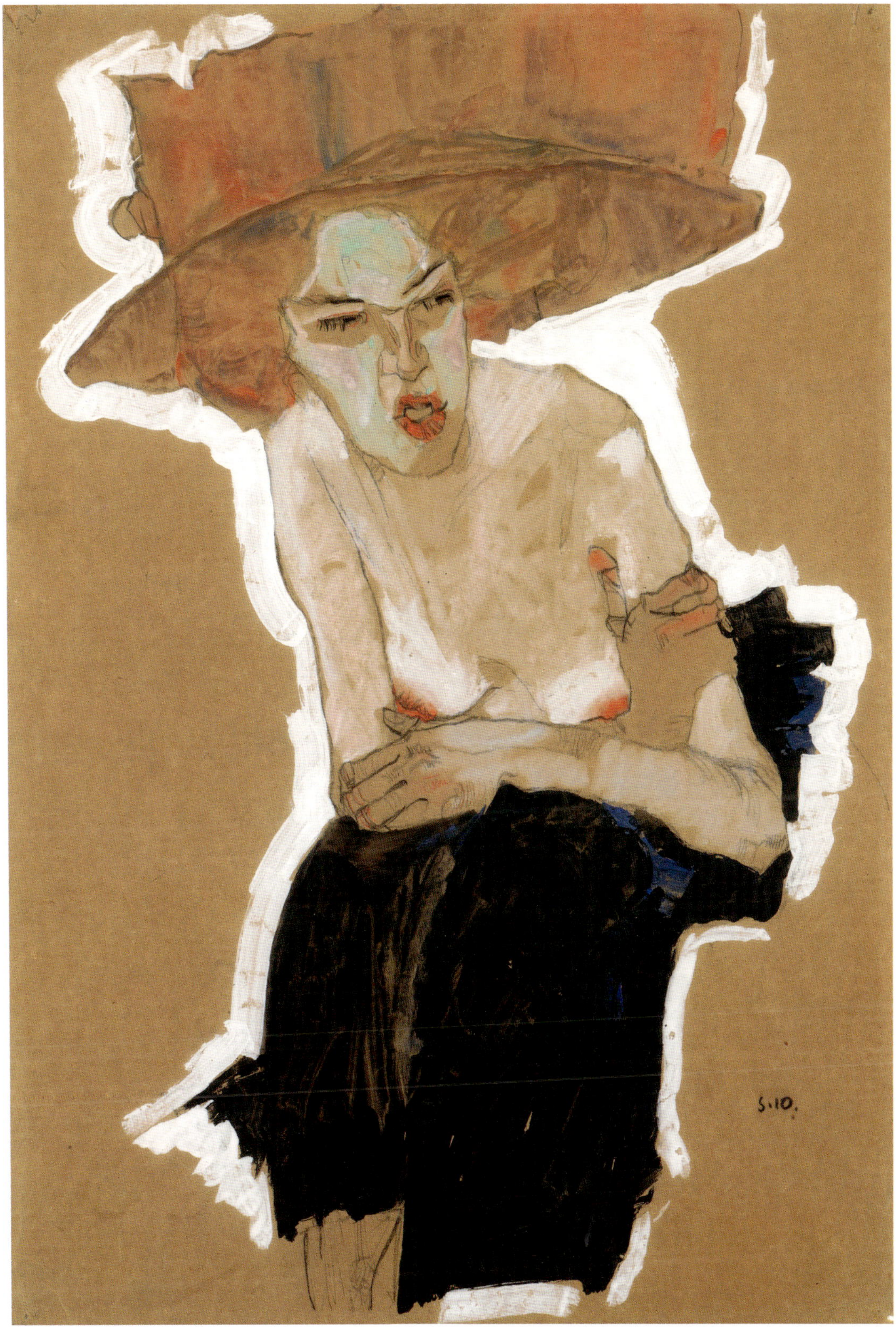
S.10.

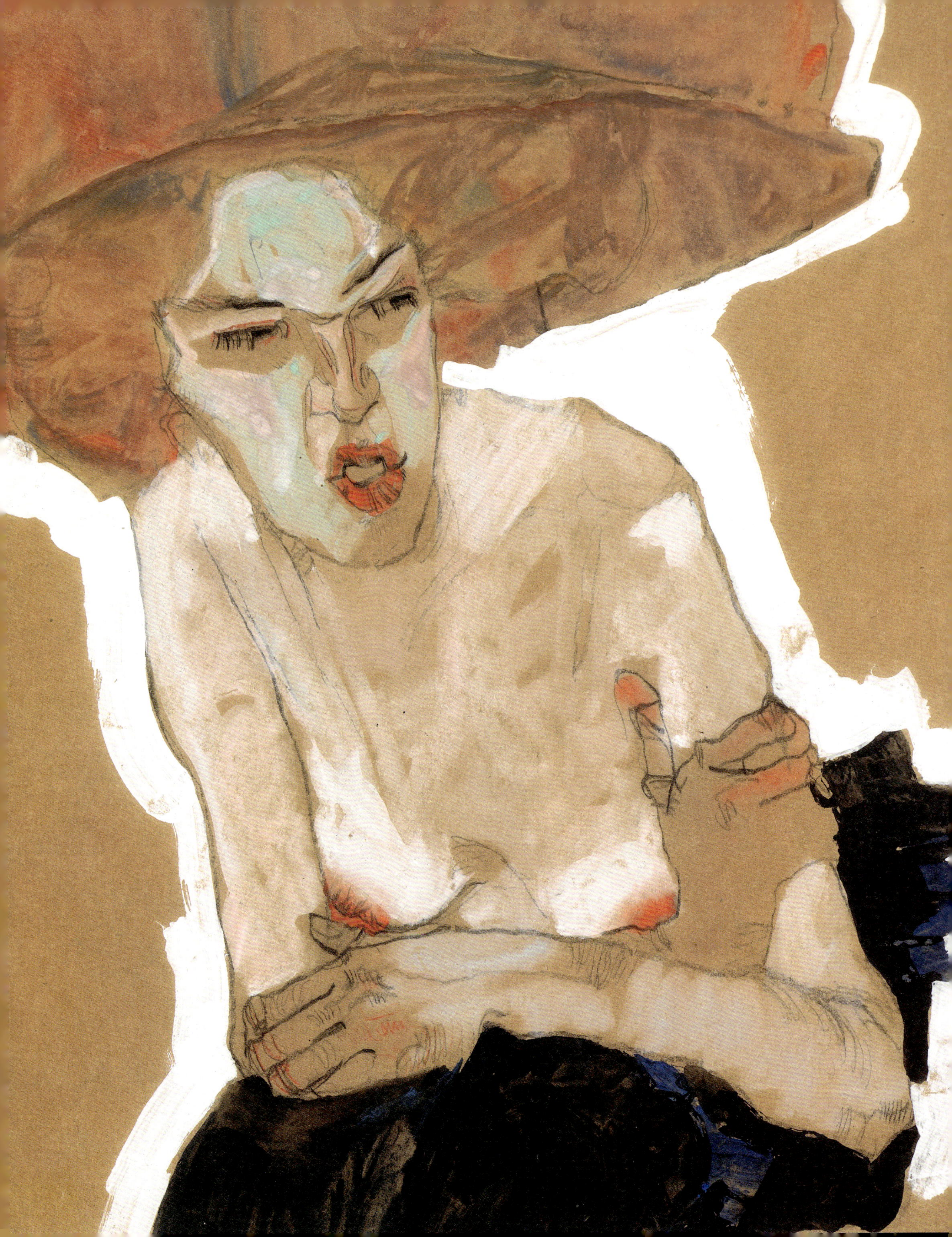

work such as *Sneering Woman*. One contemporary reviewer alluded to the tendency, evident in much of Schiele's portraiture, for facial characterisation to become simply a grimace.[6] However, as Klaus Albrecht Schröder has observed, the grimace reveals little of the true personality of the sitter; rather, it rejects the artist's or the viewer's gaze, blocking any possibility of emotional engagement, let alone any kind of psychological penetration. "The grimace is a mask, which screens out the physiognomy that has become inseparably interwoven with character and personality ... the utopian ideal of achieved communication that is evoked by eye-contact is shattered by a grimace .... By definition, the well-brought-up middle-class person does not pull faces."[7]

As for what artistic influences might have impelled Schiele to fashion this unappealing image of his sister, Otto Benesch pointed to the importance of the major exhibition of works by Toulouse-Lautrec shown in Vienna at the Galerie Miethke the preceding year, 1909.[8] Certainly, there are obvious points of resemblance between *Sneering Woman* and some of the great French artist's depictions of the Parisian *demi-monde* that he frequented, and whose denizens he subjected to sardonic, even parodistic scrutiny. All the Viennese artists, including Klimt, took a close interest in Lautrec's work. Benesch, however, in writing about cat. 15, was at pains to emphasise the distance that separated Klimt's "music of intoxicating sweetness and lyrical magic" from Schiele's "demonic visions ... his shrill, piercing dissonances and cruel tearing-open of the abyss".[9] This observation seems equally applicable to many of the artist's self-portraits (compare, for example, cat. 16 and 17). Schiele may also have been influenced by the famous sculpted heads created by the eighteenth-century Baroque artist Franz Xaver Messerschmidt, which likewise depict a range of 'unlovely' facial expressions including frowning, sneering and grimacing.

6 *Neue Freie Presse*, 8 January 1915.
7 Schröder 1995, p. 64.
8 Benesch 1973, p. 183; see also Nebehay 1979, p. 18.
9 Benesch 1973, p. 183.

16

NUDE SELF-PORTRAIT IN GREY WITH OPEN MOUTH

1910
Gouache and black chalk, 43.8 x 30 cm
Leopold Museum – Privatstiftung, Vienna (Kallir D. 696)

17

SELF-PORTRAIT, NUDE

1910
Gouache and black chalk with white heightening, 44.5 x 31 cm
Leopold Museum – Privatstiftung, Vienna (Kallir D. 708)

As already noted, self-portraiture occupies an exceptionally important place among Schiele's works of 1910 and 1911, which include a succession of nude self-portraits. For much of the time, the artist seems to have been deliberately experimenting with this genre as a way of trying out a variety of assumed identities or quasi-theatrical roles. It is, however, noticeable how rarely he presents us with a seemingly 'beautiful' self-image. Whereas many of his watercolours from this same period depend on vivid, even lurid colours for their effect (compare cat. 20), in these two self-portraits it is striking how far he has reduced his palette to dark and even muddy tones, predominantly greys, rust browns and ochres. In the foreword to the catalogue of the exhibition shown at Vienna's Galerie Arnot in January 1915, the earliest of his many appreciations of Schiele's work, Otto Benesch singled out this restricted colour range for particular comment, alluding to the way in which the artist's "joyful, sensuous colours" were "transformed into the drab, unappealing hues of decay".[1]

Equally unappealing is the image of himself that Schiele chooses to project. We know from descriptions and photographs that he was tall and good-looking, albeit of slender build. But the torso depicted in both these drawings appears positively emaciated, the flesh fallen away, the rib-cage protruding, each individual rib clearly delineated. Several commentators have pointed out that the face confronting us in *Self-Portrait with Open Mouth* bears a passing resemblance to that of the principal character in Munch's *The Scream*, a work that Schiele may possibly have known, if only in reproduction. Even leaving such comparisons aside, the figure's contorted facial features and open mouth seem to speak plainly of horror or despair. As Rudolf Leopold has remarked, from our standpoint of more than a century later this image of a seemingly starved, mutilated and traumatised human being conjures up disturbing memories of victims of the concentration camps and other atrocities.[2] Our feelings of discomfiture and alienation are intensified by the spectacle of the brutally truncated limbs, a recurrent feature of Schiele's representations of the human body in the years around 1910. Such abbreviations are clearly deliberate. Not only does the artist simply choose to ignore what he has decided he does not need – what Benesch called "Schiele's ... highly sophisticated art of omitting".[3] But it is also evident that these omissions have been calculated with an eye to the effect created by the placing of the figure on the page, the size and format of the sheet of paper and the compositional logic of the drawing as an autonomous creation in its own right.

Why the artist should have chosen to depict himself in this way is a question that has occupied the minds of many Schiele specialists and art historians more generally. In her essay 'Klimt, Schiele and Schönberg: Self Portraits', Gemma Blackshaw stresses, as does the introduction to the present catalogue, the theatricality that characterises so much of Schiele's work, describing his representations of his own naked body with its "histrionic distortions and convulsions" as being every bit "as theatrical, as staged" as Klimt's ornately costumed bodies.[4] Viewing the same question from a different angle, Kathryn Simpson has pointed to the way in which, after Klimt, the Viennese avant-garde implicitly rejected the classical association between beauty and truth. Instead, they believed that "the most truthful pictures were ones that showed their subjects naked, diseased, painfully exposed, angry, and

1 Quoted after Nebehay 1979, p. 317.
2 Leopold 2009, p. 70.
3 Otto Benesch, 'Egon Schiele as a Draughtsman' [1950], in Benesch 1973, p. 197.
4 In Blackshaw 2013, p. 130.

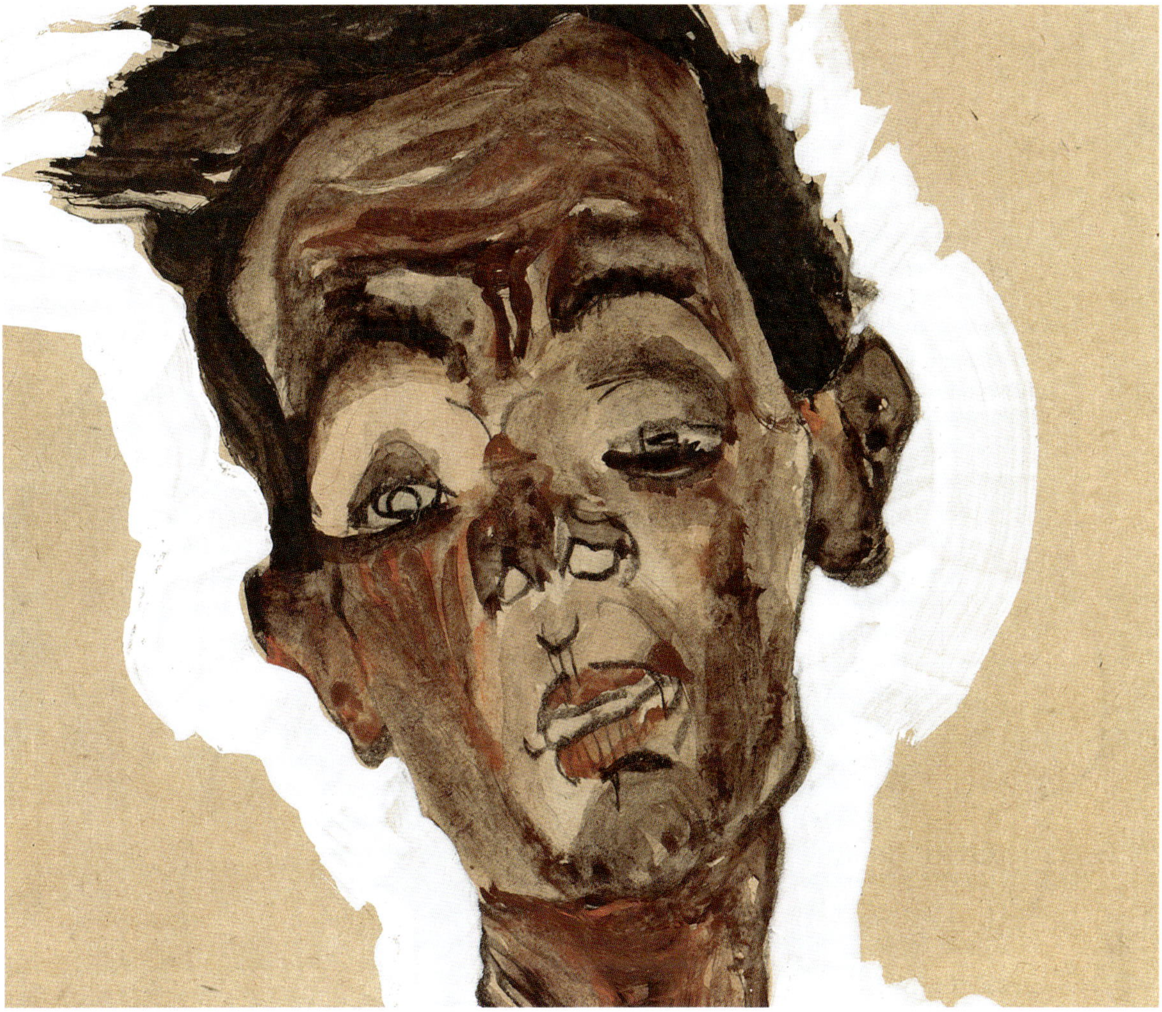

deformed", an observation as applicable to many of Kokoschka's works of this period as it is to Schiele's.[5] By contrast, Klaus Albrecht Schröder has questioned whether Schiele's self-portraits have the capacity – or were ever intended – to convey any kind of 'truth' or 'reality', drawing attention to the sheer range of different personae reflected in the artist's elaborately constructed images of himself, to the way in which, at times, he depicts himself as "wrathful, with a look of spiritual vacancy", at other times "as if wracked by a severe spasm of hysteria; or arrogantly looking down his nose, with head tossed back; or apprehensively or naively peering out of the picture", and poses the question: "Which Schiele is the real Schiele?"[6] We may find ourselves asking the same question.

5 Simpson 2010, p. 1; compare the same author's 'I'm Ugly Because You Hate Me: Ugliness and Negative Empathy in Oskar Kokoschka's Early Self-Portraiture', in *Ugliness: The Non-Beautiful in Art and Theory*, edited by Andrei Pop and Mechtild Widrich, London/New York (I. B. Tauris) 2013, pp. 122-40.

6 Schröder 1995, p. 50.

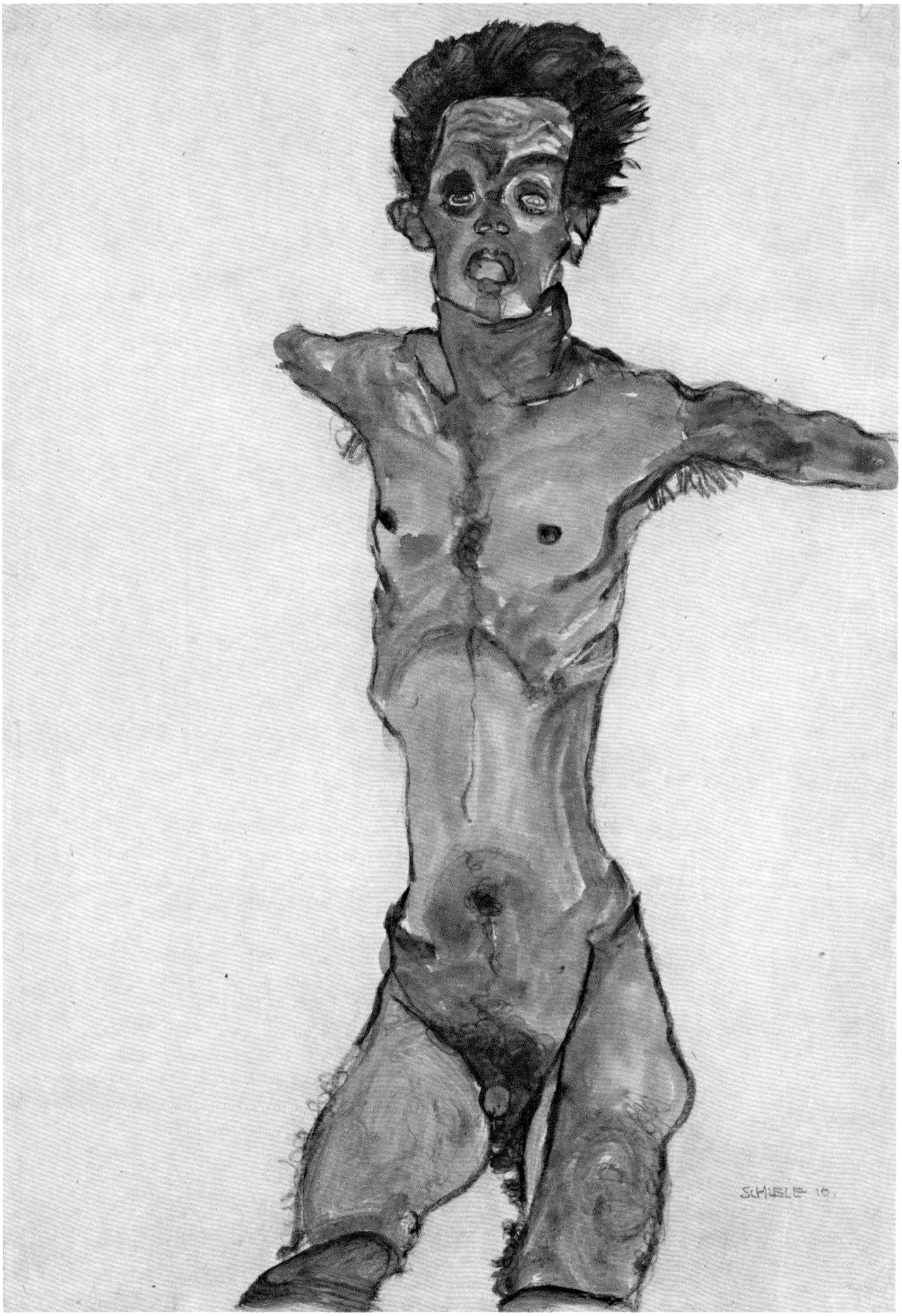
SCHIELE 10.

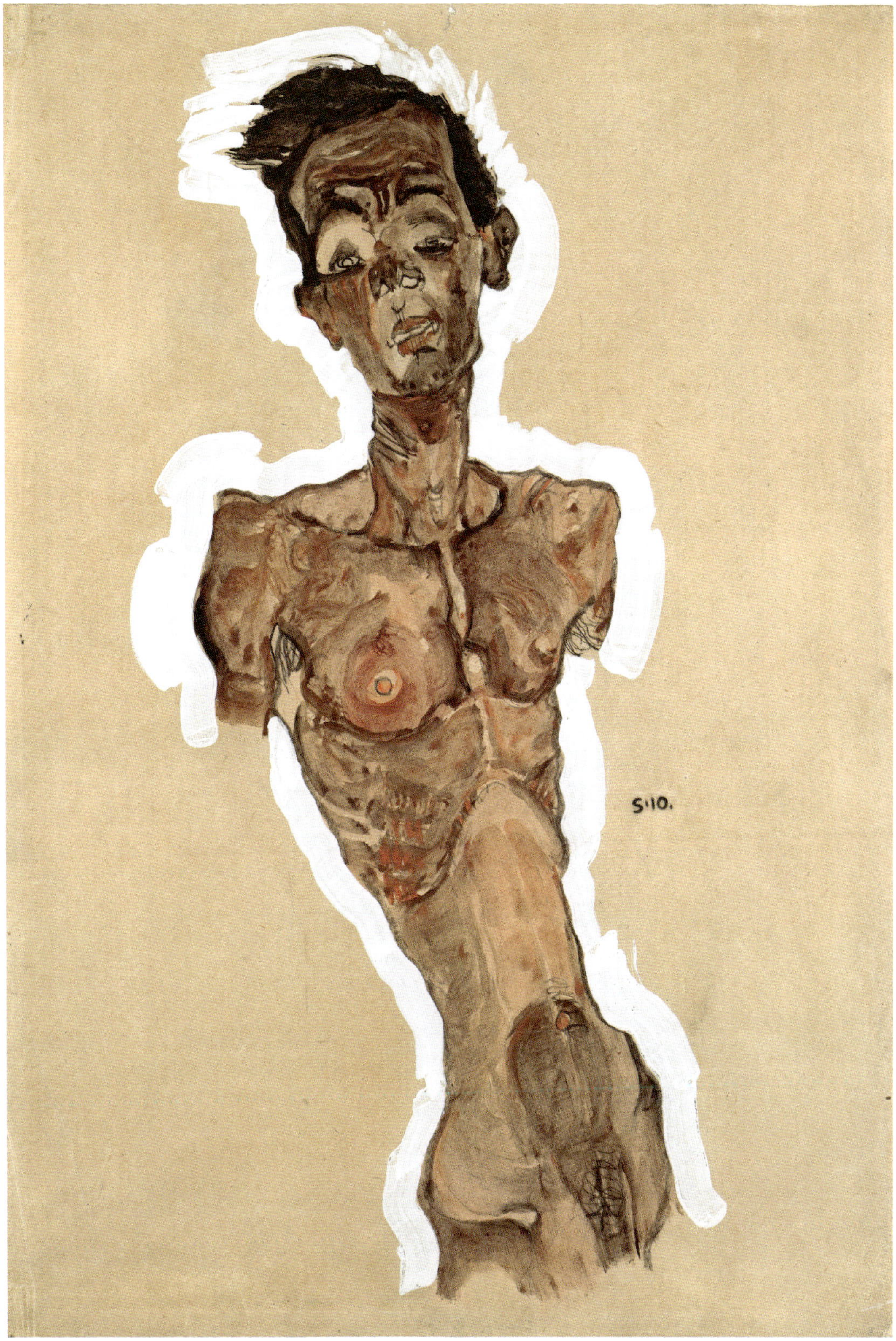
S.10.

18

SQUATTING FEMALE NUDE

1910
Gouache and black chalk with white heightening, 44.7 x 31 cm
Leopold Museum – Privatstiftung, Vienna (Kallir D. 556)

The model depicted here may, once again, be the artist's sister Gerti. For much of 1910, female models were in short supply, other than the pregnant women and newly delivered mothers he had the opportunity of studying in Dr. Erwin von Graff's Frauenklinik (see cat. 5). This watercolour can therefore plausibly be assigned to a group of works depicting a similar-looking model, probably his sister in each case, which includes *Sneering Woman* (cat. 15) as well as a number of other nude studies. These are linked by Schiele's dramatic use of white heightening, which defines and isolates the figure from the brownish tint of the cheap wrapping paper he often used for drawings at this time. This eye-catching swathe of brilliant white now has a somewhat greater emphasis than it did originally, as the paper has darkened to some extent, but it was clearly always intended to stand out. In this work, especially, its effect is to project the figure forwards, almost as if she has suddenly appeared from nowhere. This device serves to emphasise not only Schiele's assertiveness as an artist but also the model's nakedness as a subject.

Colouristically, this is one of the boldest of Schiele's early drawings, even if it does not exhibit quite the same lurid, non-naturalistic colours as *Reclining Female Torso, Nude* (cat. 20). The girl's hair is shown as a dense, complex mass of interwoven red, magenta and lilac against an orange forehead, while her legs and torso, for the most part captured in browns and ochres, are partly modelled by further touches of green and yellow. Apart from the hair, the most striking colour accents are, however, the bright red of the nipples and the small touch of the same red that defines the navel, close to the centre of the composition.

In his *Self-Portrait* of 1910 (cat. 17), Schiele explored the idea of treating the human body as a fragmentary or dismembered form. In the present work, he develops this further by having the model tuck in her legs and stretch her arms behind her so as to eliminate them from the composition. In so doing, not only does he compel the viewer to confront her torso as the main subject of the watercolour, he also creates an intriguing reversal of the deliberate, expressive use of arm and hand gestures found in other works of this period – for example, his nude portrait *Erwin Dominik Osen* (cat. 13). In creating such a 'cropped' depiction of the figure, Schiele may have had in mind the academic tradition of drawing from fragments of classical sculptures, often with their heads, arms and legs lost to history. His treatment of this particular 'Venus', with her sexually charged attitude, might thus be seen as a further challenge to this venerable artistic tradition.

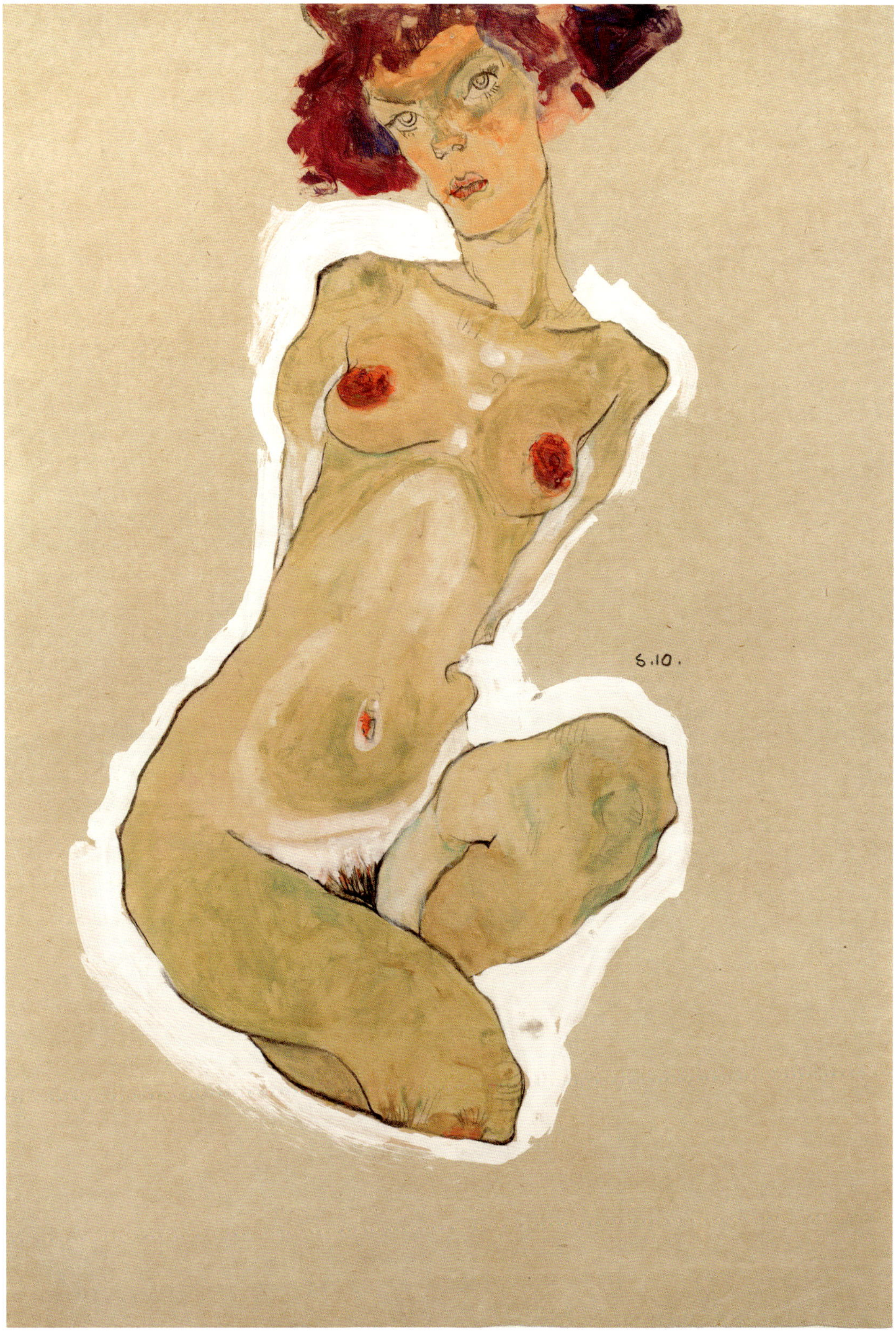
S.10.

19

MALE LOWER TORSO

1910
Gouache and black chalk, 44.4 x 27.6 cm
Leopold Museum – Privatstiftung, Vienna (Kallir D. 675)

When representing the human figure, Schiele was inclined to treat his own body even less kindly than those of other people. No matter where he was working, a large, full-length mirror such as appears in a 1915 photograph (fig. 28) was an indispensable feature of his studio. It is easy to imagine that this highly unusual view of the body was, in fact, his own lower half seen in the mirror including, importantly, his genitals as well as his dangling finger-tips. Interestingly, a teenager named Willy Lidl, who got to know Schiele in Krumau during this same year 1910 and evidently developed a schoolboy crush on him, later wrote a somewhat rambling appreciation of the artist, perhaps hoping that it might see the light of publication in Arthur Roessler's newly established magazine *Bildende Künstler*. For all its patent immaturity, this draft article contains the striking and highly relevant observation that, in Lidl's opinion (and Lidl was clearly very close to the artist during that summer in Krumau), all Schiele's works were ultimately nothing other than a form of self-portraiture.[1] This passing remark springs hauntingly to mind in contemplating this seemingly gruesome image.

As regards the purely visual qualities of the present work, it is easy to be distracted by the spectacle of what Rudolf Leopold called this "miserable figure", the right foot manifestly larger than the left, with its seemingly putrescent flesh, its "deeply curved spine and pendulous buttocks".[2] Only after prolonged inspection do we become aware of the many subtleties of the composition: the carefully calculated *mise-en-page*, the elaborate play of curving lines – for example, the knees and buttocks – which seem to echo one another like musical phrases and, above all, the use of contrasting colours to conjure up a palpable human form that straddles a deeply satisfying albeit illusory three-dimensional space at odds with the flat, off-white surface of the paper. These qualities were recognised even in Schiele's own lifetime – and not only by his admirers but even by predictably hostile reviewers such as Adalbert Franz Seligmann, the art critic of Vienna's leading liberal newspaper, the *Neue Freie Presse*, and self-appointed scourge of the avant-garde. Reviewing the Galerie Arnot exhibition of January 1915, Seligmann took marked exception to the seeming cruelty, even sadism of Schiele's depictions of the human figure, observing that his art leaned so strongly towards the pathological that it was more likely to interest the psychoanalyst than the art lover, "unless the art lover also happens to be a psychoanalyst, as happens from time to time – especially at the present time". Even so, he was perfectly willing to acknowledge the artist's technical mastery and unparallelled command of his chosen medium; in the same review, he described Schiele as possessing "far and away the greatest talent and the greatest ability" among what he called the "ultra-moderns" – "a truly magisterial draughtsman with a distinctive feeling for colour, likewise his technical competence, his treatment of the surface, his application of pigment".[3]

1 A copy of the typescript of Lidl's article is preserved in the archives of the Leopold Museum, Vienna; on Lidl himself and his relationship with Schiele see also Nebehay 1979, p. 541. On 21 October 1910 the boy wrote a passionate love letter to Schiele that says a good deal about the strength of his feelings: "I love you so much ... if you stay with me, I shall become strong but if you desert me, it will mean the death of me"; see Nebehay 1979, p. 116, doc. 131.
2 Leopold 2009, p. 46.
3 'Kunstaustellungen', *Neue Freie Presse*, 8 January 1915; Nebehay 1979, p. 332.

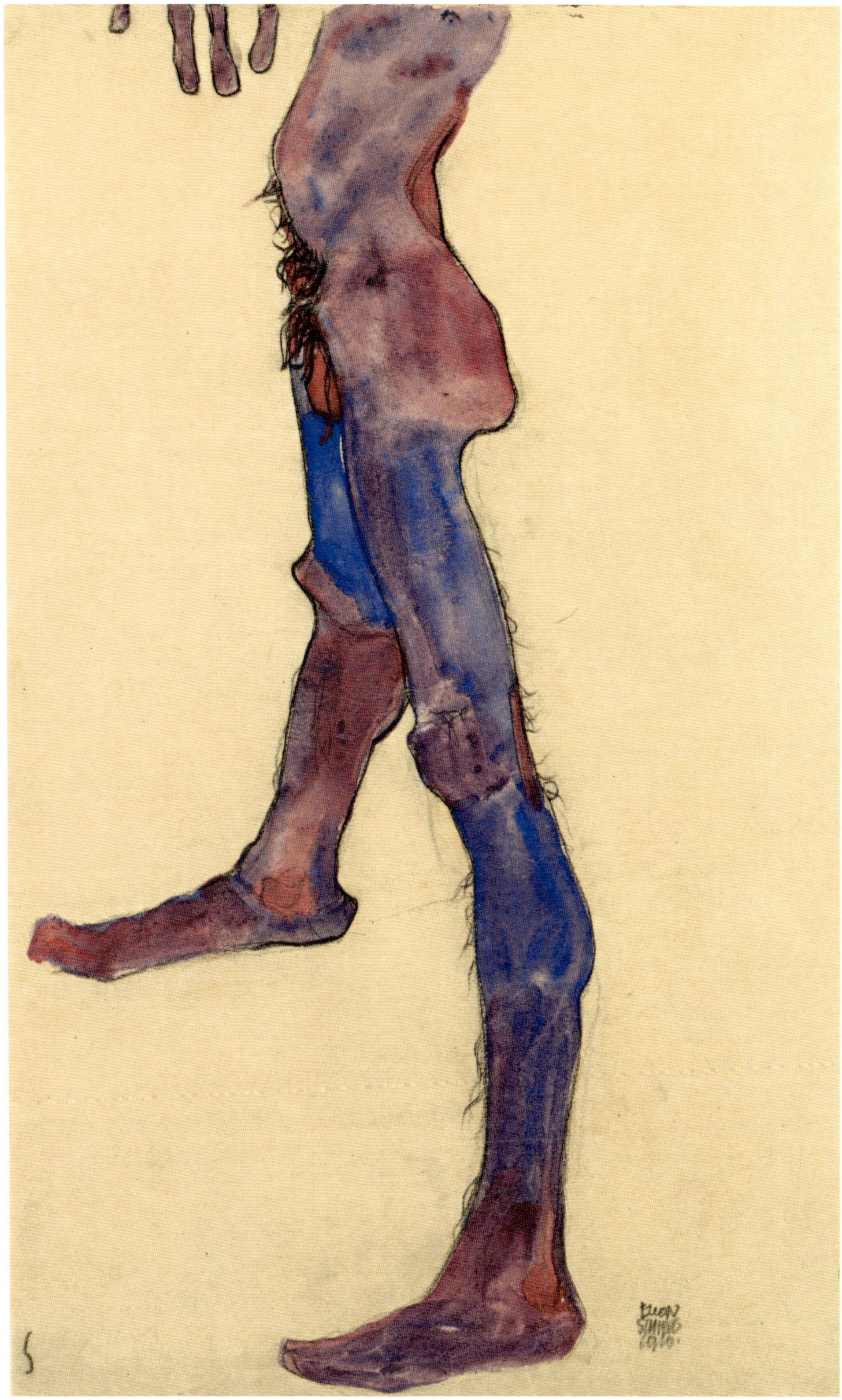

20

RECLINING FEMALE TORSO, NUDE

1910

Gouache, watercolour and black crayon, 31.6 x 44.9 cm

Private collection, courtesy of Richard Nagy Ltd, London (Kallir D. 524)

As was the case with Klimt, Schiele's detractors repeatedly accused him of being a pornographer. This celebrated drawing is the type of work they might have had in mind, as it so directly challenges conventions of the nude. We are left in little doubt as to where the viewer's focus of attention is meant to be, given the degree of detail lavished on this seemingly decapitated woman's pubic hair and exposed genitals, which occupy the centre of the composition.[1] Our initial impression, namely that the artist is here preoccupied with female sexuality and little else, is underlined by the way in which the naked woman looks almost as if she has been flung carelessly down upon the blank sheet of paper, her legs parted. As in other instances, the model depicted is not set against an identifiable background but is isolated in a disconcerting, featureless void. The startlingly exhibitionist pose suggests someone eagerly anticipating or, perhaps more likely, having just enjoyed sex. However, this study, although undoubtedly done from life, provides few other clues as to the circumstances under which it was created.

Perhaps because of its exaggerated, non-naturalistic colours, this work has sometimes been singled out as an example of the 'Expressionist' tendency that supposedly characterised Schiele's art of the years 1910–11. However, as noted elsewhere, it is questionable whether the term 'Expressionism' can properly be applied to any of his work, for a variety of reasons.[2] At that date, the word itself had scarcely been invented, nor had it been widely used to identify those German artists – Kirchner, Heckel, Pechstein and others – now considered to have been 'Expressionists'.[3] Although he was certainly exposed to many of the same influences that affected the painters of the Brücke group – for example, that of Van Gogh – it seems improbable that, at any point before 1911, he had much idea about the latest art being produced in Dresden, let alone Paris. More likely is that the strident colours seen in this 1910 nude study are his own invention, in part a reaction against his Viennese academic training, based largely upon traditional representations of the classicising nude.

Equally probable is that Schiele, who at this point in his career seems to have quite enjoyed his self-appointed role as *enfant terrible*, was determined to heighten still further the sense of provocation engendered by this flagrant display of female sexuality through the addition of outrageously lurid colours: breasts and legs painted in acidic, sulphurous yellows, the abdomen, rib cage and part of one buttock all rendered in an unhealthy-looking green, accentuated by the clearly deliberate contrast with the purple stockings. Also striking is the fact that this drawing exhibits several characteristics commonly associated with fetishistic pornography, including stock-in-trade appurtenances such as thigh-length stockings and high-heeled shoes, one shoe here casually discarded and hidden from view, the other prominently displayed on the model's left foot. Similarly lewd images, many of which took the form of clandestine photographs, circulated widely in Vienna at that time, and would certainly have been known both to the artist and to many of his patrons, some of whom evidently encouraged him to produce ever more explicit drawings for their private gratification. But, like Courbet's painting *The Origin of the World*, the power of this drawing lies in its ability to provoke us to reconsider the boundaries and possibilities of the nude.[4]

1 Schiele himself is alleged to have rejected any accusation of having fabricated pornography, remarking bitterly on one occasion that he "certainly didn't feel erotic" when he made his erotic drawings; see Grete Helfgott, 'Egon Schiele, zu seinem 30. Todestag', *Arbeiter-Zeitung*, 31 October 1948. Supposedly, he also insisted that "no work of erotic art is filthy, provided that it is artistically significant; it is only turned into filth by the viewer, if he himself is filthy". However, in this instance what we are hearing is not Schiele's own voice but Roessler's, in what the writer claimed was a transcription of the artist's so-called Prison Diary (see above, p. 13); here quoted after Roessler 1922, p. 33.

2 See above, p. 102.

3 Although the term itself is occasionally found in earlier journal articles and exhibition reviews, the first serious study of Expressionism by Paul Fechter did not appear until 1914, under the imprint of R. Piper Verlag, Munich, with a cover illustration by Max Pechstein. Fechter identified Pechstein and Kandinsky as the two opposite poles of Expressionism; he also included in his account other artists such as Max Beckmann and Oskar Kokoschka, whom he likewise regarded as representatives of this new movement. Nowhere in his book is there any mention of Schiele.

4 Musée d'Orsay, Paris.

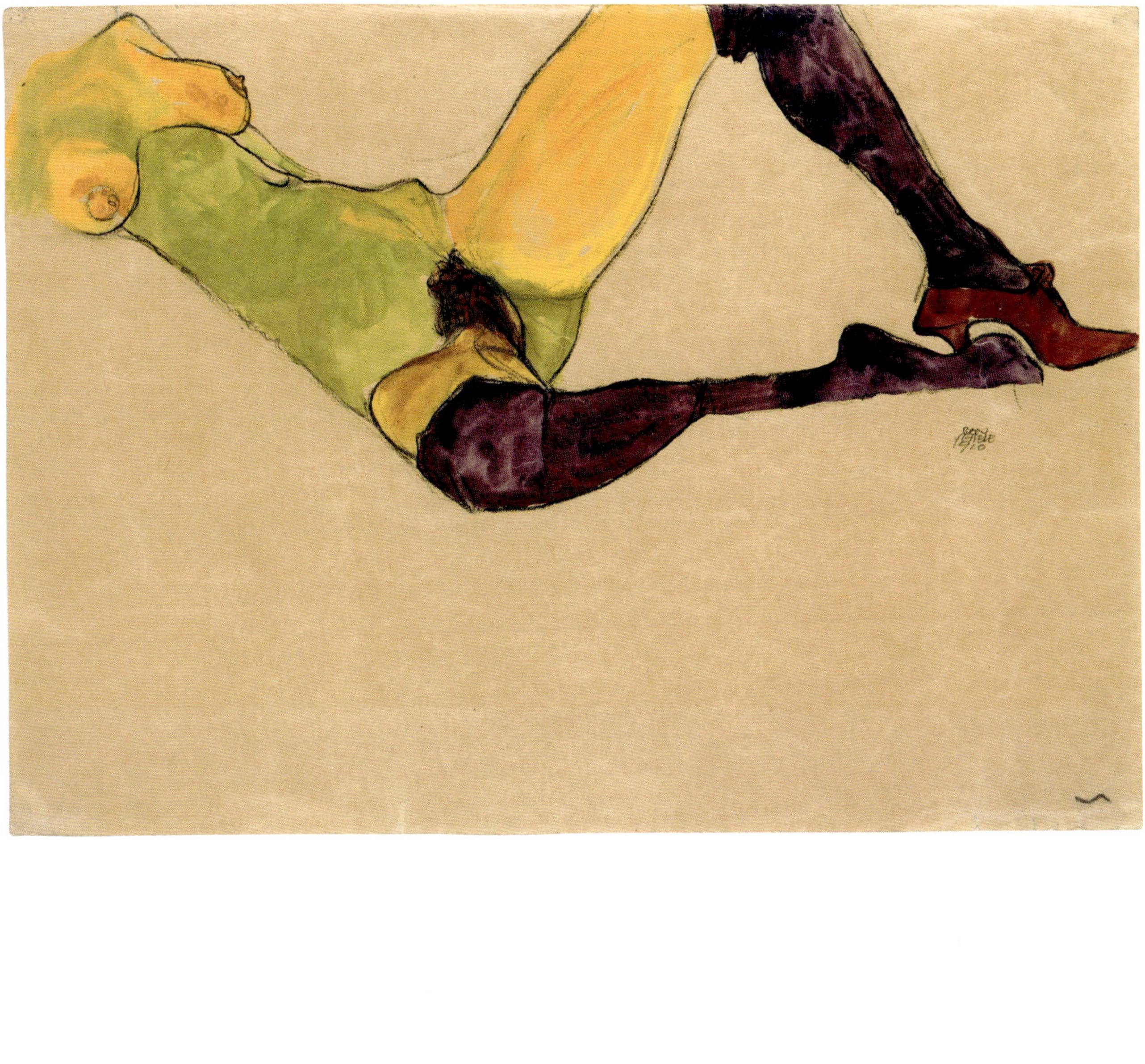

21

FEMALE NUDE

1911
Pencil, 48 x 38.1 cm
Private collection (Kallir D. 921a)

The success of this drawing in conveying a realistic impression of the female figure depends almost entirely on Schiele's mastery of line. Internal modelling, often used to suggest the solidity of flesh or muscle or bone, is almost entirely absent. Only in one or two places did he add a few pencil strokes to indicate the slight swelling of the abdomen immediately below the navel or the protruding right hip and muscles of the upper thigh. Otherwise, the flowing pencil line seems to caress the contours of the figure in an almost unbroken movement, as in many of Rodin's drawings. Indeed, Rodin may well have been a dominant influence on Schiele's early drawing style. Already chafing at the limitations of his academic training, with its uninspiring approach to the human figure, he would surely have looked closely and with lively interest at the exhibition of the French artist's work shown at the Galerie Hugo Heller in Vienna in 1908. Probably, the uncompromising eroticism of Rodin's treatment of the female nude also left a lasting impression on Schiele, then still little more than an adolescent.

Represented here is seemingly a fully grown, mature woman, at a time when Schiele often preferred to use children or young teenagers as models, a practice which came to an abrupt halt following his arrest and imprisonment in the spring of 1912. Especially noticeable is the close attention paid to the woman's erogenous zones, for example the pert (or erect?) nipples, which are depicted in almost fetishistic detail. More detailed still is the microscopic rendering of every smallest part of her sexual organs, to such an extent that this representation of the female vulva might almost serve as an illustration for a medical textbook. This preoccupation with anatomical accuracy may strike us as more than a little disconcerting, especially given the summary treatment of the rest of the figure.

Whereas many of the nudes depicted in his drawings of this period look as if they have been simply thrown down on an otherwise blank sheet of paper, as in the case of cat. 20, in this instance Schiele spares a few precious pencil strokes to indicate, albeit in an abbreviated fashion, the bed or couch or other support on which this female nude seems to be propping herself up with unseen hands. However, the drawing does not provide nearly enough detail to allow us to come to any firm conclusions regarding the context or spatial environment in which the figure is located.

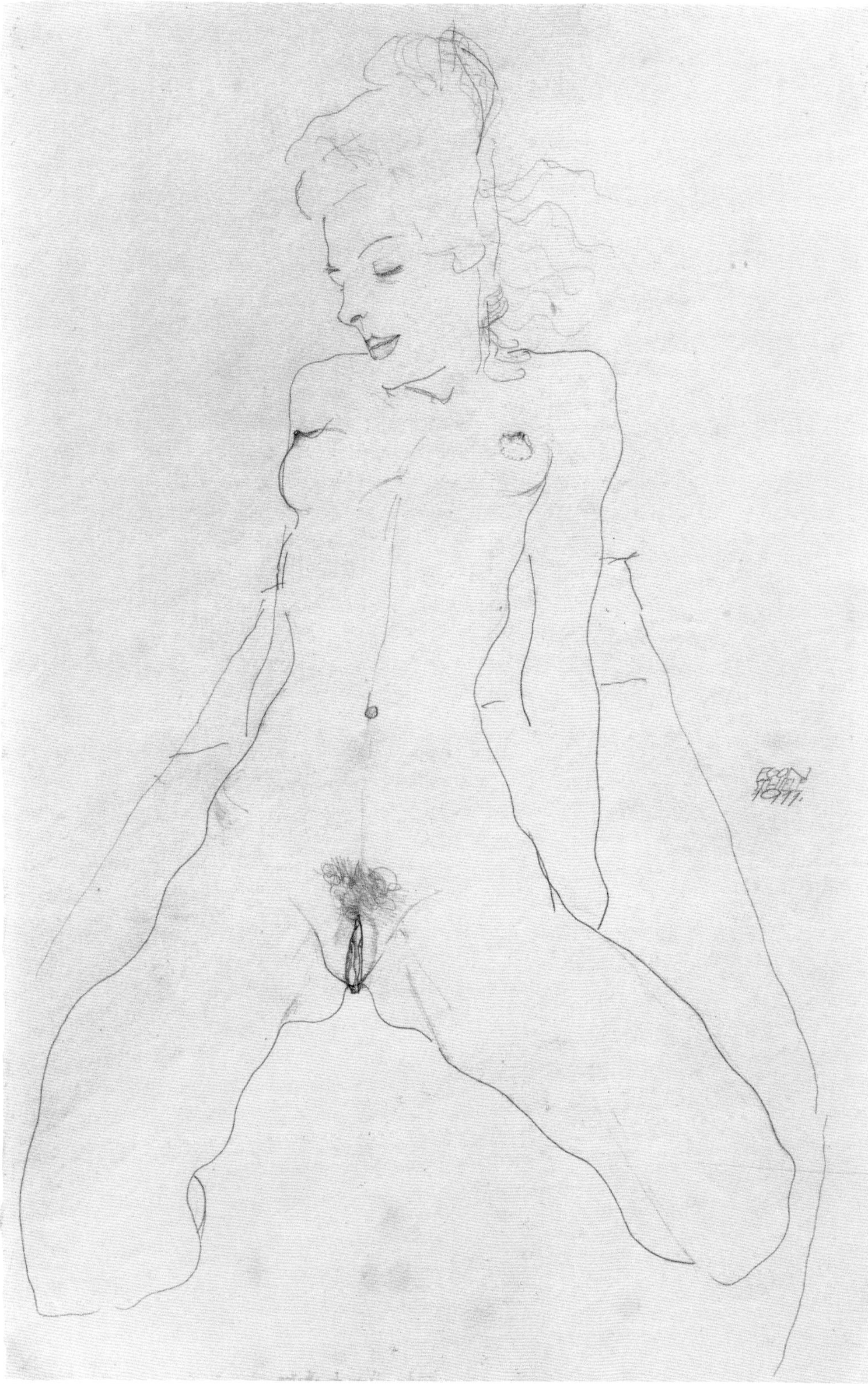

22

TWO GIRLS

1911
Watercolour and pencil, 51.3 x 37.7 cm
Private collection, courtesy of Richard Nagy Ltd, London (Kallir D. 857)

This watercolour, painted at a time when sexually explicit subjects account for by far the greater number of Schiele's works on paper, is among the most unsettling of his depictions of young girls. Presumably at the artist's behest, both girls have their dresses pulled up to reveal their sex. Their actions appear to be both calculated and deliberate. While many sexually explicit works by Schiele cast the male viewer in the role of voyeur, someone who takes a sly peep at models purportedly unaware of the presence of any spectator, in this instance both girls directly engage us with an uncompromising stare. Nor is their facial expression neutral: on the contrary, they look as if they might be prostitutes eyeing up a prospective client, their self-exposure serving merely to underline the nature of the services they are willing to offer.

One peculiar aspect of the way the model in the red dress is portrayed is what she is doing with her right hand, which projects above the neckline in a way that suggests that she has thrust her arm up inside her clothes until her hand meets her mouth. Not only that: the splayed fingers make almost exactly the same gesture that Schiele performs in several of his own self-depictions – for example *Self-Portrait with Black Clay Vase and Spread Fingers* (fig. 32), painted in the same year.[1] However, as noted elsewhere in this catalogue, the exact meaning of these gestures, frequently encountered in his works of this period, remains unexplained.[2]

As regards its compositional structure, this watercolour depends for its effect far more on colour than on line. Apart from the hair and stockings of the two models, the main colour accents are the vivid red of one girl's dress and the darker, greyish-blue of the other. However, the fact that Schiele here conjures up bodily form out of the blank paper means that the left arm of the girl to our left lies across the red of her dress in a way that seems to create a void between two distinct areas of colour. At the same time, a further patch of red extends beyond the body of the right-hand figure, as if one girl is lying on the other's dress, spread out so that it extends beyond and beneath her. In similar fashion, a largish area of grey-blue appears to be somehow propping up the girl in red, although in this case it might conceivably denote the sleeve of the garment worn by her companion. It is clear in any case that representational accuracy was not the artist's main concern when he created this drawing. Apart from its overtly sexual content, there is another, more complex agenda reflected here, one that has to do with abstract pattern-making and the consequent balance and disposition of forms and colours in such a way as to create a visually satisfying composition.

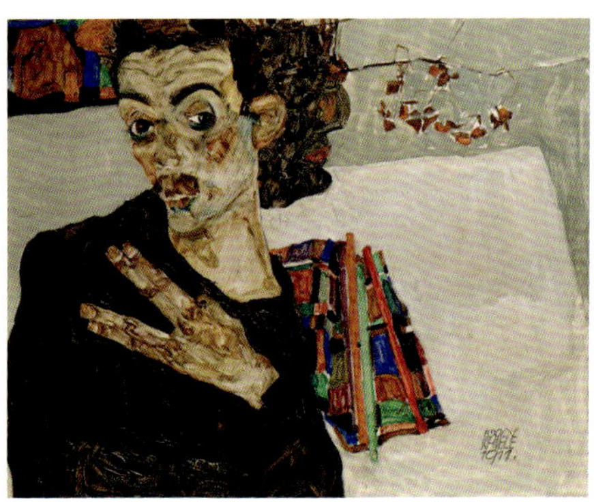

32
EGON SCHIELE
Self-Portrait with Black Clay Vase and Spread Fingers, 1911
Oil on panel, 27.5 x 34 cm
Wien Museum, Vienna (Kallir P. 204)

1 Compare also *Self-Portrait with Hand to Cheek* of 1910 (Albertina Museum, Vienna: Kallir D. 706).
2 See above, p. 91.

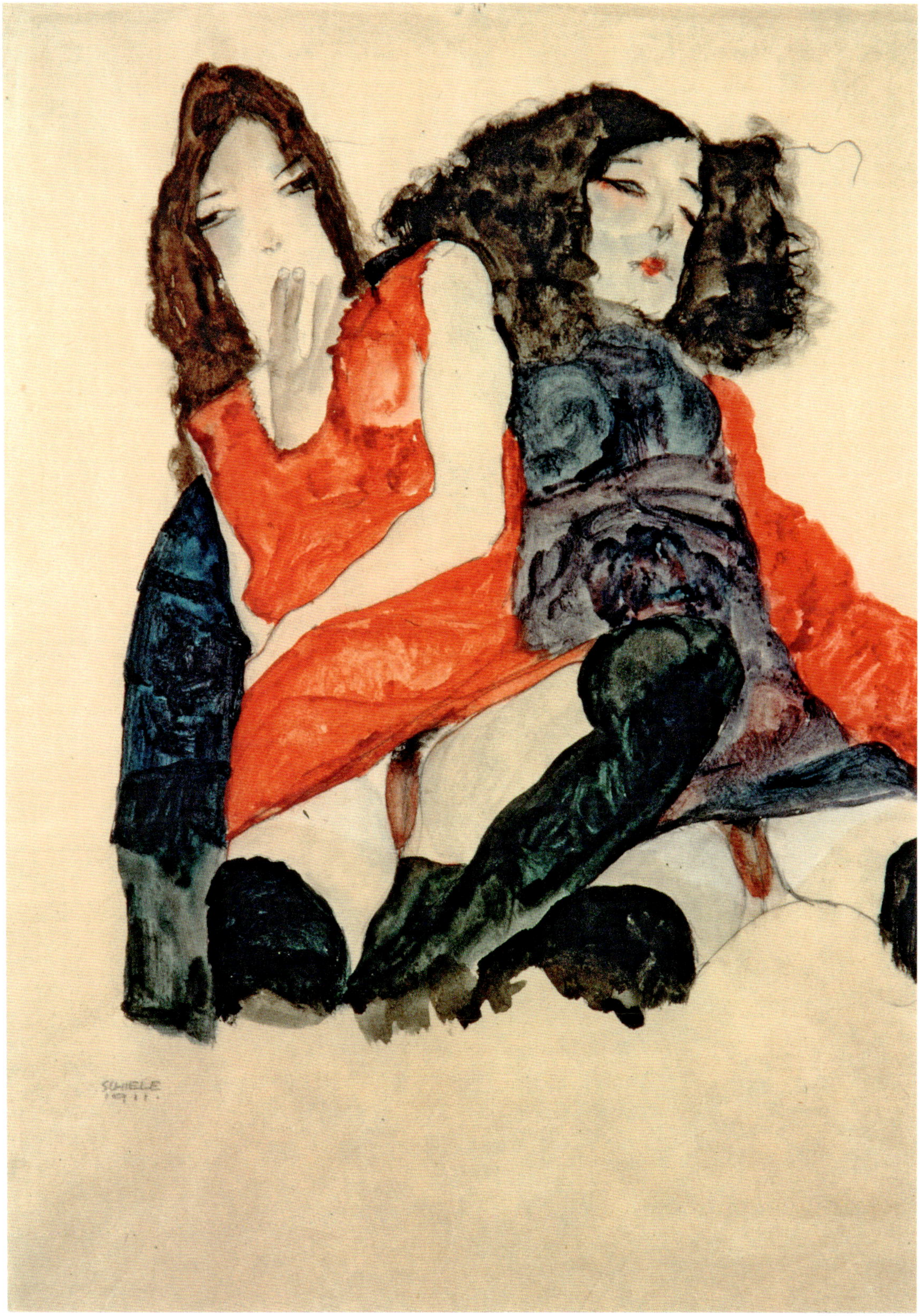
SCHIELE

23

WOMAN WITH BLACK STOCKINGS (WOMAN IN RED GARTERS)

1913
Gouache, watercolour and pencil, 48.3 x 31.8 cm
Private collection, courtesy of Richard Nagy Ltd, London (Kallir D. 1245)

The young woman depicted here is thought to be Wally Neuzil, Schiele's loyal companion throughout his ordeal of 1912, whom he would eventually abandon for a more socially acceptable bride. Wally had been modelling for him since 1911, when the couple spent part of the summer together in Krumau, and she stood by him through thick and thin. Her widely spaced eyes, generous mouth and piled-up auburn hair are recognisable in this and several similar drawings, in one of which she wears the same black stockings and likewise exposes her sex.[1] In other respects, however, this depiction of her body is strikingly incomplete: we are allowed to see barely three-quarters of her head, next to nothing of her right arm and just the upper part of her legs, although these are no longer the seemingly amputated limbs that feature in several of Schiele's earlier nude studies, including some of his nude self-portraits (compare cat. 16, 17). Instead, the unconventional *mise-en-page* seems to imply that the figure extends beyond the edges of the paper, as if the artist had originally drawn it on a larger sheet which he subsequently trimmed or cropped. In reality, of course, he did nothing of the kind. Rather, his aim appears to have been two-fold: to present a startlingly abbreviated view of the model seen close-up as if through a lens, a device that also characterises many erotic photographs created at that time, and to anchor firmly on the page what might otherwise be an asymmetrical and fundamentally unstable composition by situating the figure not in any plausible, fictive space but only in relation to the edges of the paper.

Some of Schiele's earlier images of Wally are imbued with a certain wistful tenderness – for example, the small oil portrait of her (fig. 33) that he executed as a pendant to his *Self-Portrait with Chinese Lantern Plant*, perhaps in the immediate aftermath of his release from prison.[2] Since those two paintings were evidently conceived as a pair, they might be considered proof of a certain degree of emotional commitment or perhaps gratitude for her loyalty. In the present work, by contrast, he treats her just as he might treat any other model. There is no obvious attempt to capture the sitter's mood or personality, and the drawing betrays little if anything by way of emotional involvement on Schiele's part. Nor does he spare Wally's blushes: instead, in an exaggerated and perhaps even brutal way, he deliberately places her exposed sex at the exact centre of the composition.[3]

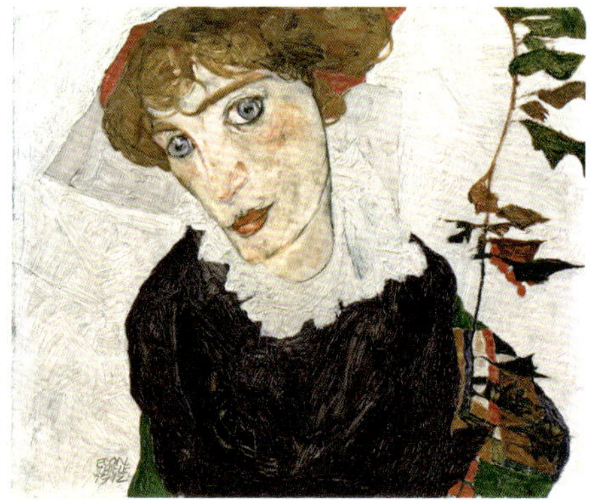

33
EGON SCHIELE
Portrait of Wally Neuzil, 1912
Oil on panel, 32 x 40 cm
Leopold Museum – Privatstiftung, Vienna (Kallir P. 234)

1 Kallir D. 1240.
2 Kallir P. 233, 234.
3 As Blackshaw points out elsewhere in this catalogue, Schiele sometimes obliged Wally to peddle his explicitly sexual images of herself by taking them to show to potentially interested clients, much to her chagrin; see above, esp. p. 46. The present work may well have been one of those drawings.

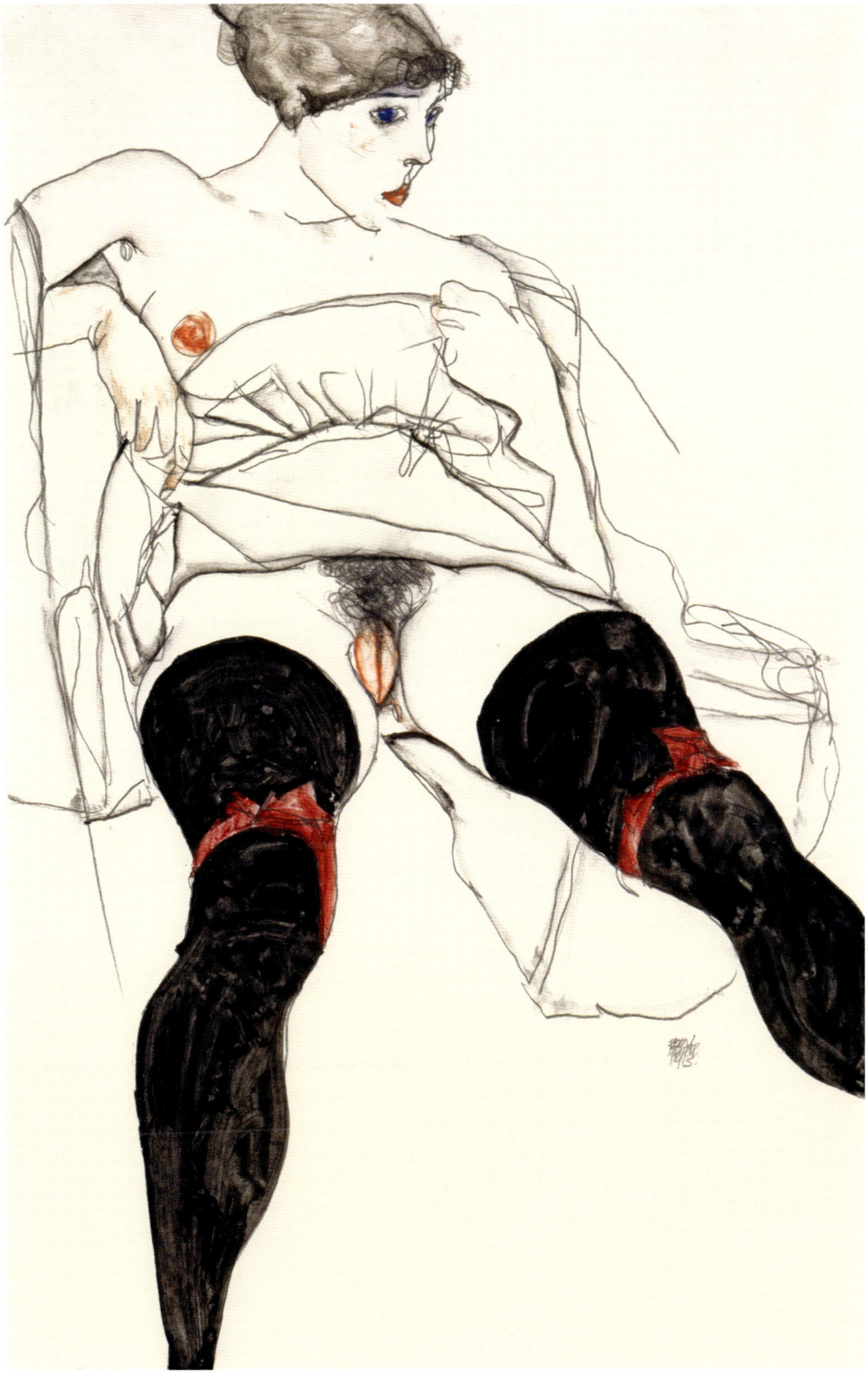

24

STANDING NUDE IN RED JACKET

1913

Gouache, watercolour and pencil, 41.9 x 28 cm

Private collection, courtesy of Richard Nagy Ltd, London (Kallir D. 1370)

Probably as a result of his traumatic experiences at Neulengbach and Sankt Pölten, which included arrest, imprisonment and trial, after 1912 Schiele abruptly stopped depicting children and young adolescents.[1] Gone are the skinny, waif-like bodies and knowing glances of under-age models encountered in his works of 1910–11. Only later did he occasionally revert to that kind of subject-matter, and then the children in question were usually chaperoned and also depicted in a far more 'innocent' fashion. This change in his art may also reflect a change in attitude, given that he was now growing up and also starting to think seriously about marriage. Certainly, his drawings and paintings of 1913–14 are increasingly populated by what look like mature, adult women. On the other hand, the topic of sexuality generally still occupies much of his work, including themes such as self-exposure and female masturbation, and also Schiele's obsessive interest in genitalia, evident in the present drawing. At the same time, this highly unusual rendering of the naked figure is clearly driven by other imperatives, which have more to do with the structure and visual coherence of the composition itself, almost regardless of its subject-matter.

As in so many of his figure studies, Schiele here omits everything he finds unnecessary, which in this case includes not only the head but also the hands and feet of the standing figure. But he also subjects the human body to a degree of distortion that strains the bounds of anatomical plausibility, especially in his treatment of the preternaturally long thighs and what little we can see of the girl's calves. The muscles of the left calf, in particular, look impossibly swollen. One can only conclude that the artist has drawn these exaggerated lines not in order to depict accurately the way the model looked as she stood and posed, but rather as a way of anchoring the savagely truncated lower body more securely to the bottom edge of the sheet of paper.

The model has some kind of blouse or jacket draped around her shoulders, but the sleeves are empty and the garment itself appears somewhat tattered, rather like the ragged shirt that does little to cover the nakedness of the male figure in cat. 26. One curious feature is the dense area of black that occupies the space between the woman's left arm and her waist, echoed by just a glimpse of a much smaller area of the same colour slightly above the right hip. What it represents is unclear: it might be the darker lining of the blouse or jacket, since the empty left sleeve appears to have a similar lining, or perhaps part of another over- (or under-?) garment. Apart from these more densely painted areas, which also include the vivid red of the ends of the sleeves, the viewer's eyes are inescapably drawn to the centre of the composition, occupied by the woman's pubic hair and an unsparingly detailed delineation of her sexual organs, which seem to have been the main focus of the artist's attention.

1 Regarding the accusations that led to the artist's arrest and imprisonment see above, p. 23.

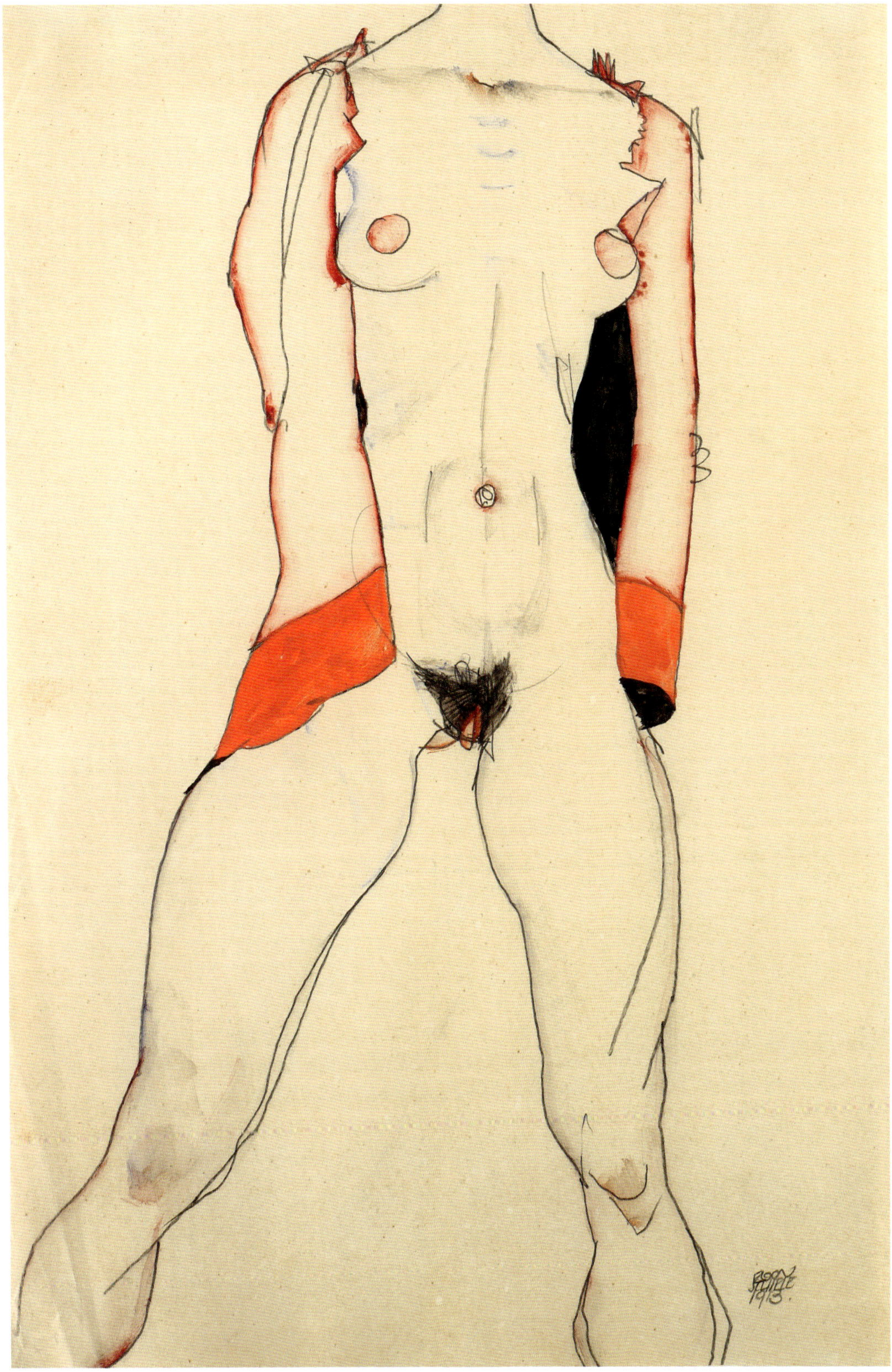

25

GIRL KNEELING ON RED CUSHION

1913
Pencil and gouache, 47.4 x 32 cm
Leopold Museum – Privatstiftung, Vienna (Kallir D. 1285)

This drawing provides further evidence of the new-found interests apparent in Schiele's works of 1913, in several important respects a transitional year as regards the development of his art. In figure studies such as this, not only is he preoccupied with depicting the human body; now equally important to him is the skeletal structure of the drawings themselves, regarded as quasi-abstract linear compositions in their own right.[1] In representational terms, much of what we see here is anatomically incorrect – for example, the left arm above the elbow or the fan-like succession of lines representing the rib-cage, which are in completely the wrong place. The kneeling figure also makes an awkward impression, its head bent forward as if compressed by some unseen force from above, while the head itself is sliced through by the upper edge of the sheet of paper. It must have been an uncomfortable pose to hold, and the expression on the face is also suggestive of discomfort or even distress. This impression is heightened by the smudges of red around the left eye, which make it look as if the girl has been crying or had recently been the victim of some physical assault.

Although used sparingly, colour plays an important role in this drawing. The vivid red of the cushion on which the girl is kneeling attracts the eye like a glowing beacon, while further touches of the same colour serve to emphasise the contours of the body, the left heel as it extends away from the viewer and the obviously made-up red lips. Somewhat puzzling is the occurrence of what in other, more traditional figure studies would be called *pentimenti* – additional lines, unexplained and inexplicable in terms of any ambition to render accurately the appearance of the physical object, which seem to reflect second thoughts or perhaps deliberate modifications made to the drawing in the course of its evolution. In his account of Schiele's drawing practice, based on repeated visits to his studio to watch him at work, Heinrich Benesch claimed that the artist never used an eraser nor attempted to make corrections. If a model happened to shift position in the course of a sitting or if he was dissatisfied with the first result, he would either throw the sheet of paper away or simply inscribe new lines and contours alongside the old ones.[2] This is one of a relatively small number of surviving drawings that support Benesch's claim. Especially striking is the tangle of criss-cross lines that partially obscure the fingers of the girl's left hand and the small but curious geometric pattern that occupies the space between her lips and her shoulder, a pattern which, while it does not disturb our view of the drawing, is hard to relate to anything the artist might have observed in the world of natural appearances.

1 As Rudolf Leopold notes in connection with other drawings of this period, the geometrisation of the human figure became an increasingly evident preoccupation in many of Schiele's works from 1913 onwards; see Leopold 2009, p. 160.
2 'Egon Schiele', in Benesch 1973, pp. 185ff.

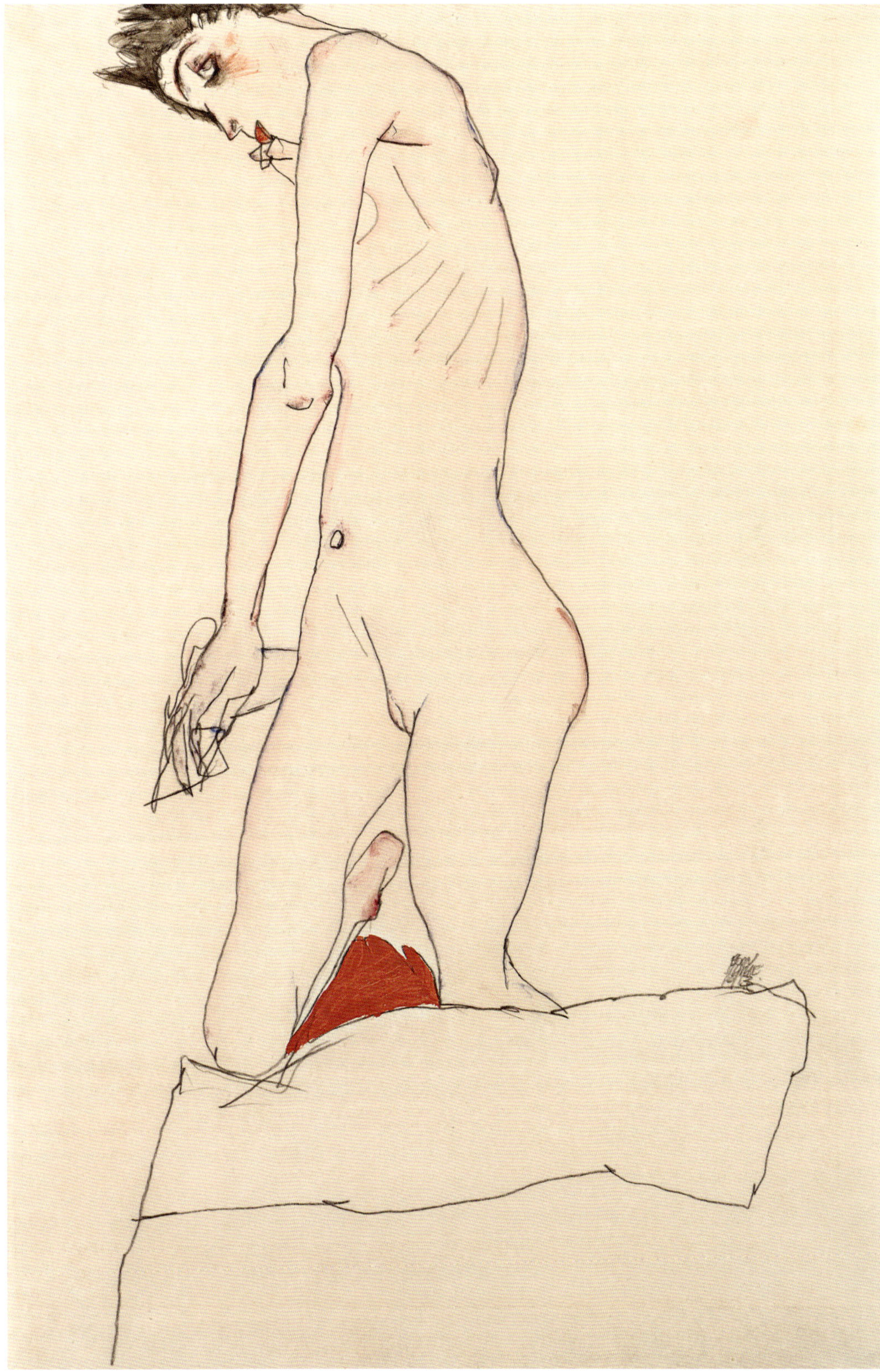

26

STANDING MAN

1913
Gouache, watercolour and pencil, 48.1 x 31.8 cm
Private collection (Kallir D. 1415)
Inscribed *Stehender Mann* at lower right

During 1912–13, Schiele became increasingly preoccupied with allegorical and religious subject-matter, nurturing ideas for narrative paintings which sometimes took the form of complex multi-figure compositions conceived on a monumental (and occasionally quite impractical) scale.[1] Some of the larger works were never competed; other pictures were destroyed or are now lost. Among those known to have survived, we sometimes find images of Egon and Wally appearing as actors in these painted dramas, as in the paired paintings *Holy Family* and *The Blind I*, also of 1913.[2] Others are pervaded by a kind of religious iconography that was highly personal to Schiele, as part of which he would depict himself in a variety of roles – as a monk, for example, or as a hermit or martyr. Usually, he would work out his ideas for the disposition of the figures in the form of pencil annotations committed to the pages of a small sketchbook. By contrast, his more elaborate or highly finished drawings were mostly viewed not as adjuncts to paintings but as quasi-independent works of art in their own right. However, we occasionally find ourselves confronted with fully worked-out drawings, many of them thinly disguised self-portraits which, though not obviously conceived as composition studies in any strict sense, nevertheless betray a certain affinity with certain of the large-scale narrative compositions.

It is to this rather special category that both the present drawing and cat. 27, *The Dancer*, belong. In the case of *Standing Man*, although it is clearly not a composition study as such, there is a striking resemblance between this half-naked figure seen from the back, wearing some kind of shirt or brief jerkin so short that it fails to conceal either his buttocks or his genitals, and the principal figure in Schiele's painting of the same year, *Begegnung*

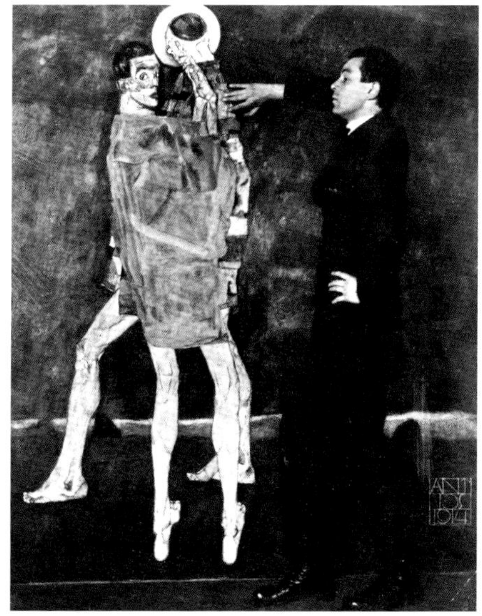

34
ANTON TRČKA
Egon Schiele next to his Painting Encounter *of 1913* (now lost), 1914
Photograph
Leopold Museum – Privatstiftung, Vienna

(Encounter).[3] In that now-lost (and probably never completed) picture, the encounter in question appears to be taking place between the artist himself, likewise seen from the back and wearing only a short smock with bare legs protruding beneath it, and a saint, identifiable as such by his halo. That it is, once again, Schiele himself who plays one of the two main roles in that painted drama is underlined by a photograph taken by Anton Trčka (fig. 34), which shows the artist, neatly suited, standing in front of the painting, striking an affected pose and gesturing theatrically.[4] Perhaps

1 See note 3 below.
2 Kallir P. 248 and 249.
3 When exhibited at Vienna's Kunstsalon Pisko in January 1914, *Encounter* was described as a "design for a mural painting". At that point, the unfinished picture measured approximately 2 m², according to Kallir 1998, p. 318. However, a note in the Kunstsalon Pisko catalogue explained that the artist envisaged adding a succession of figures representing blind people on the right-hand side of the composition, thereby extending it by some 5 or 6 m; see Nebehay 1979, p. 298, doc. 623.
4 Trčka's photograph is, in fact, the only surviving image of the painting, visible in the background propped up against the wall of Schiele's studio.

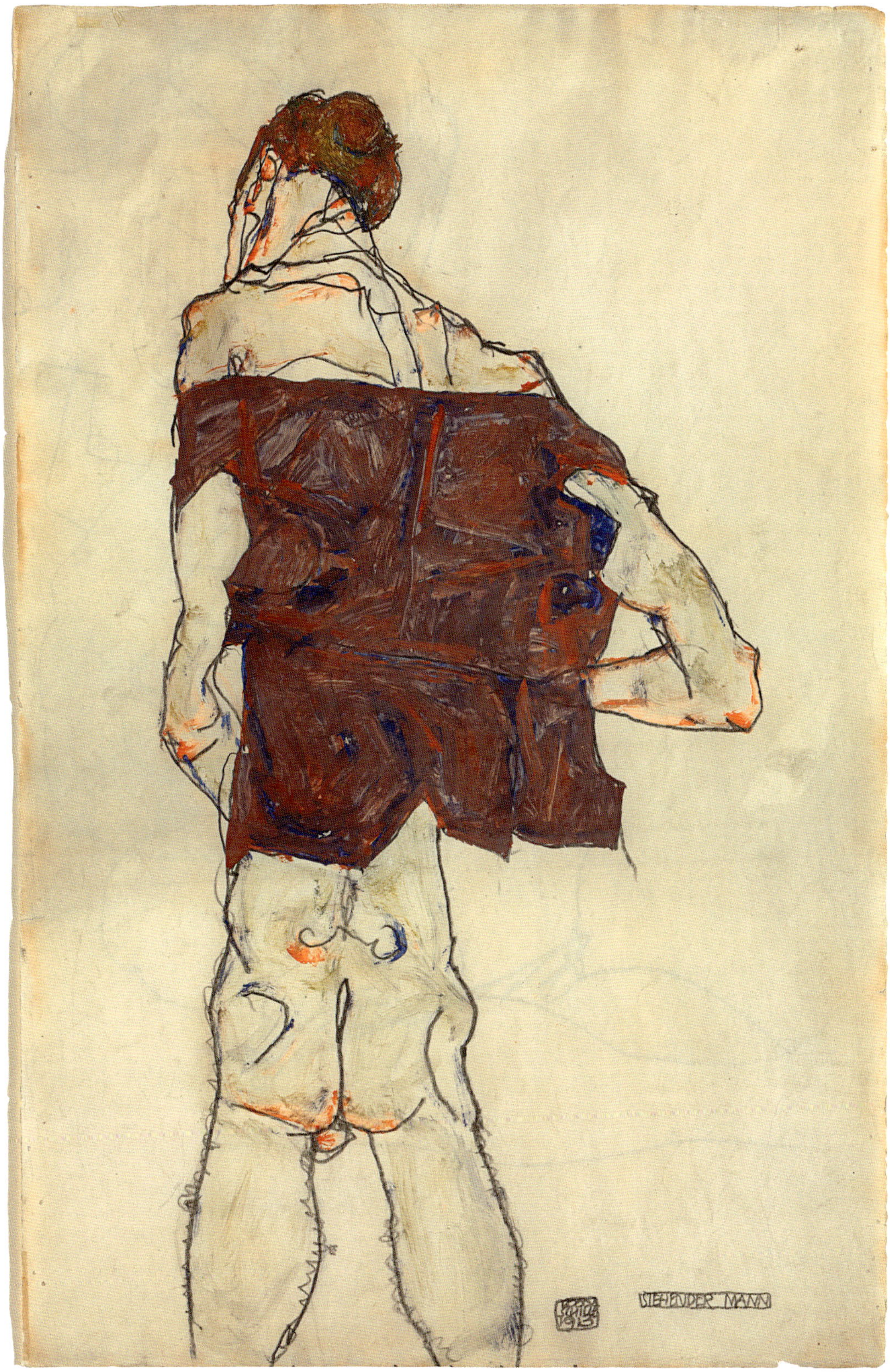
1913
STEHENDER MANN

on account of the evident similarity between the two works, it has been generally accepted that *Standing Man* likewise depicts Schiele's own half-naked and seemingly half-starved body, already familiar to us from so many of his earlier self-portraits. For example, the entry in the catalogue of an auction in which the work was offered for sale proposed that the drawing "evokes the artist, still struggling financially, the victim of persecution, wearing nothing but coloured rags", an interpretation that fits well with the role of martyr or hermit that Schiele assigned to himself in other narrative or allegorical paintings and drawings.[5]

Stylistically, *Standing Man* looks both forwards and backwards. In some respects, it recalls earlier drawings by Schiele in which expressive line and contour perform a crucial function in capturing the essentials of the human figure. Here, the nervous, sometimes jagged outlines, reinforced in places by small areas of hatching, are every bit as important as in those earlier drawings. But there is also a new interest in the body's three-dimensionality and in carefully executed internal modelling that anticipates Schiele's figure drawings from 1914 onwards, as seen, for example, in cat. 30 and 31. In some places, the musculature of the bony figure is captured by light touches of grey and brown; in others, details are highlighted in blue or a somewhat startling red, as in the dimples at the base of the spine, the curve of the lower buttocks and the distinctly sore-looking elbows. The most densely worked area of colour is, however, the half-length jerkin, a complex weave of blues, reds and a deep maroon, giving an air of solidity to the garment at odds with the apparent frailty of its awkward, seemingly insubstantial wearer.

This drawing is one of several examples of a sheet of paper which has been used by the artist on both sides; on the verso is a pencil study, known as *Liebespaar* (Loving Couple).[6]

5 Christie's (London), *Impressionist and Modern Art*, Evening Sale (Sale 7562), 4 February 2008, entry for lot 61.

6 Kallir D. 1452.

27

THE DANCER

1913
Gouache and pencil, 48 x 32.2 cm
Leopold Museum – Privatstiftung, Vienna (Kallir D. 1414)
Inscribed lower centre, in cartouche *Der Tänzer*

Visually, this is one of the most remarkable of all Schiele's works on paper. Extraordinarily free in its execution, it is marked by a high degree of animation, the artist apparently carried away by the sheer pleasure of drawing. While some lines serve to delineate the principal contours of the figure, others seem little more than a kind of frantic scribbling which, in rendering the limbs and musculature of this tilted, gyrating figure, helps none the less to create an impression of solidity and density. At the same time, there is a nervous intensity about the apparent rapidity of execution, matched by an evident fascination with the variegated colours and textures of flesh and skin. The pose appears highly precarious, as if the dancer had been interrupted in the midst of a rapid sequence of movements and might easily fall over at any moment. Only by bracing his left elbow against the right-hand edge of the page does he prevent himself from tipping backwards into the void created by the otherwise blank sheet of off-white paper.

Not only does this drawing bear an obvious resemblance to cat. 26, *Standing Man*, it is also clearly related to a succession of further drawings from 1913, all of them inscribed by the artist, which include *Fighter* (fig. 35) and *The Preacher*.[1] Only in a small number of instances did Schiele himself add specific titles such as these; by far the greater number of his works on paper are untitled – or, rather, the titles by which they are known were invented by dealers, curators or compilers of catalogues. When he added a title, in almost every case he framed it within a rectangular cartouche. Quite apart from any other purpose, this element of the drawing was clearly a carefully considered graphic component in its own right, one that contributes to the visual effect produced by the composition as a whole.

This practice, as well as the meaning of the titles themselves, has given rise to a good deal of debate among art historians and connoisseurs of Schiele's art. One hypothesis is that he simply wanted to

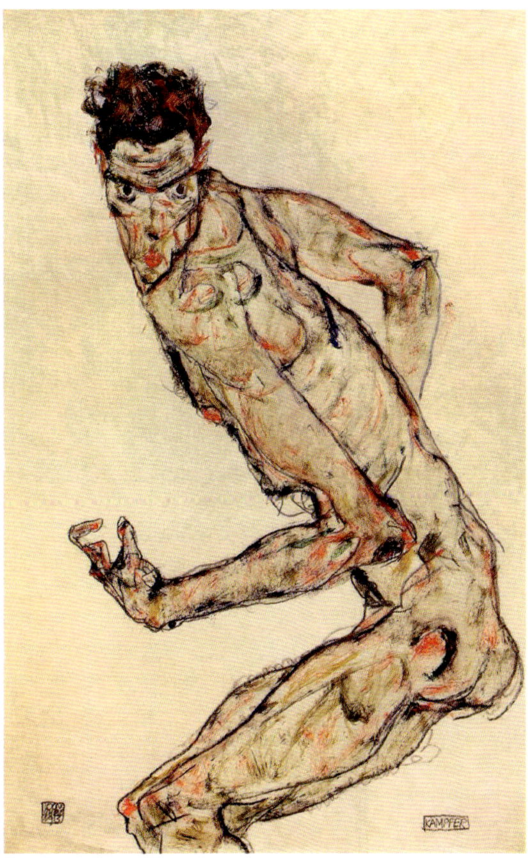

35
EGON SCHIELE
Fighter, 1913
Gouache and pencil, 48.8 x 32.2 cm
Private collection (Kallir D. 1438)

1 Kallir D. 1441.

keep track of his drawings – which ones he had sold, which had been exhibited and so on.[2] But, if so, why only these drawings, and why only at this particular moment in his career? If he could no longer remember which drawing was which, why did he soon abandon the practice of giving them titles? Why not compile his own catalogue or a hand-list of some kind? More convincing is the idea that at least some (although by no means all) of these works are, yet again, a barely disguised form of self-portraiture which, however, now takes on a more overtly allegorical or even theatrical aspect, reflected in these titles.[3] In some of his earlier self-portraits, even when he is gesturing or grimacing or clearly acting out a role, one of his aims was still to capture some form of physical likeness. In his later drawings, by contrast, that no longer seems part of his agenda; instead, it is more a matter of expressing in each case the character of the various roles he assigned to himself and the movements and body language peculiar to each.

Even so, the significance of some of Schiele's titles remains obscure. In some cases, they bear little obvious relation to the figure as actually depicted; in others (for example, 'The Truth Unveiled') it is far from clear what meaning should be attached to them.[4] Perhaps this should not surprise us unduly. According to Rudolf Leopold, Erich Lederer, who as a young boy knew Schiele well and who later became one of his most avid collectors, recalled that the artist "generally gave very little thought to the inscriptions that commonly appear on his drawings from 1913, inventing them only after the works had been completed".[5]

On the verso of this sheet is a pencil drawing of a female nude.

2 See Kallir 2003, pp. 224-25.
3 Pereña Sáez 2010, pp. 28ff.
4 Kallir D. 1443.
5 Leopold 2009, p. 166.

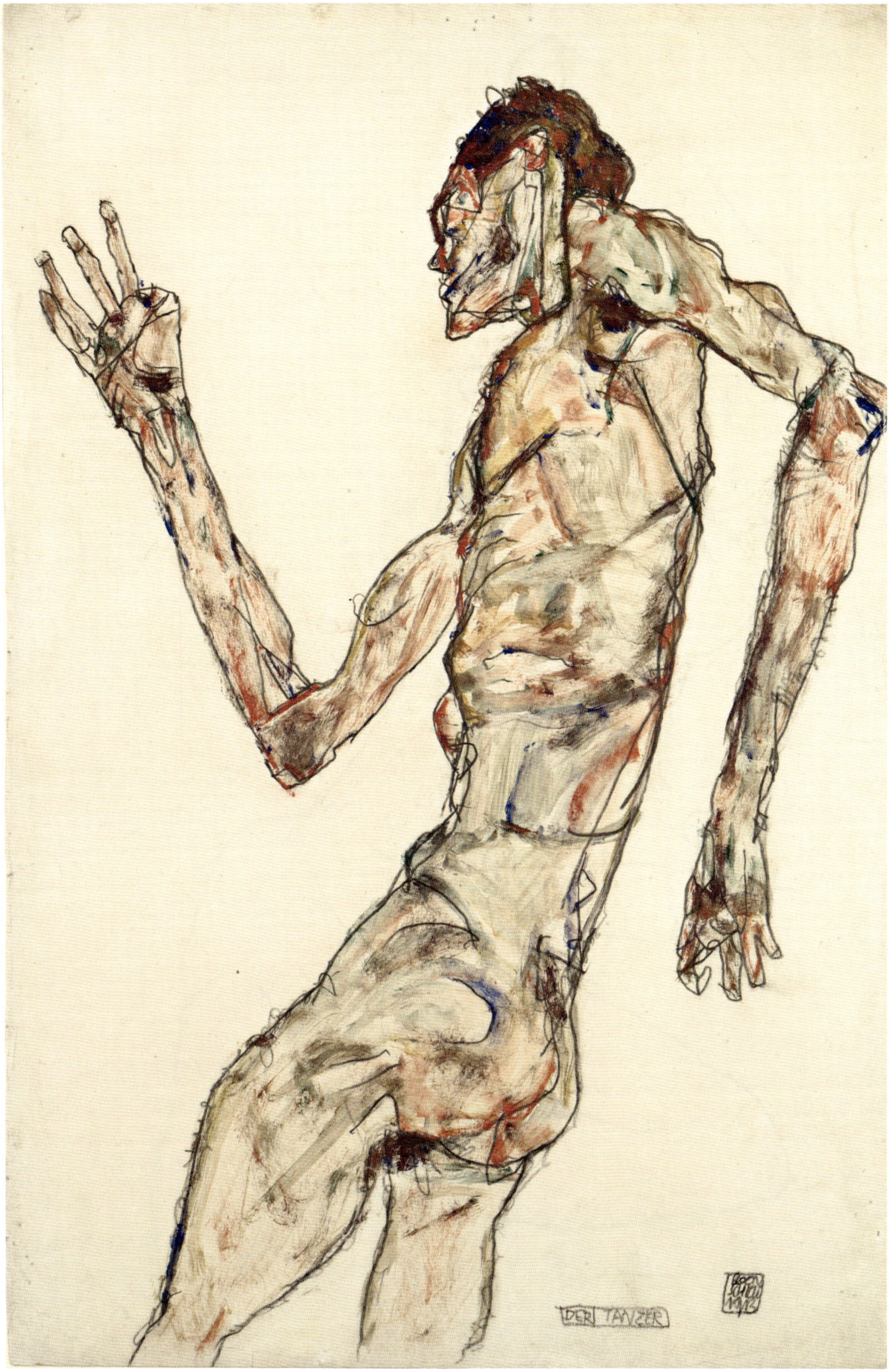
DER TANZER

28

BEFORE THE MIRROR

1913
Gouache and pencil, 48.3 x 32.1 cm
Leopold Museum – Privatstiftung, Vienna (Kallir D. 1362)
Inscribed lower right, in cartouche *Vor dem Spiegel*

This is another case in which the title Schiele inscribed on his drawing, 'Before the Mirror', poses something of a conundrum.[1] We know that he relied heavily on the large mirror visible in several photographs of his studio, which seems to have been an indispensable adjunct to his study of the nude figure, both his own and other people's. In one famous drawing of 1910 (see fig. 16), he even included his own reflection as he sat sketching the standing female model, who is thus seen both from the front (her reflection in the mirror) and from the back (as seen both by the artist and by ourselves, implicated not only as the intended audience for the drawing itself but also as potential voyeurs). In other nude studies and especially in some of his nude self-portraits, it would scarcely have been possible to capture the pose depicted without the aid of a mirror – that is, assuming that Schiele drew only from life rather than from the imagination, as several of his contemporaries insisted. The *Male Nude* included in the present exhibition (compare cat. 2) affords an example of just such a drawing.

Even so, it is far from clear what, if anything, the present work has to do with mirrors. Immediately striking is the decidedly awkward pose of this seemingly deformed figure, with dislocated pelvis and, if we are to believe the drawing, one withered leg. However, deformed or not, it would scarcely have been necessary to stand in front of a mirror in order to hold such a pose, which, as so often in Schiele's art, seems to have more to do with the repertoire of theatrical gestures used by mime artists or perhaps with modern dance than with the naturalistic representation of the human form. The odd position of hands and head may even recall the awkward, disjointed movements of those Oriental puppets which made such a deep impression on the artist when he saw several of them in Roessler's collection, as well as the crudely carved wooden figurines that he himself collected.[2] Indeed, the rather pathetic doll-like figure depicted here looks almost as if dangling from wires held by some unseen puppeteer. This impression is reinforced by the curious pencil lines that occur for no apparent reason in the region of the woman's elbows, which perform no obvious function either compositionally or as regards the delineation of her figure.

Stylistically, *Before the Mirror* is very much of a piece with other works of 1913–14 such as cat. 32, *Crouching Woman with Green Headscarf*. One distinguishing feature of these gouaches is the clearly deliberate contrast between the delicate and, for the most part, lightly worked flesh tones and the more intense areas of vivid colour, usually reserved for clothing or drapery. In the case of cat. 28, the visually most arresting element is the bright, luminous green of the woman's shirt, which immediately draws the eye to the upper part of the sheet. Some of this green even looks as if it has 'escaped' from the area of the shirt and invaded the woman's upraised right hand, while further touches of the same colour are used to model the face, hips and navel and to accentuate the contours of the thighs, contrasting with an equally non-naturalistic, vivid red. Most of the remaining body parts are merely implied by the blank surface of the buff-coloured paper, with the addition of only a few light pencil strokes, just enough to ensure that we 'read' these areas as flesh and not as part of the empty space that forms the background to the figure. Apart from these, it is the blank paper, heightened with just these few light touches of colour, that has to do the job of suggesting the reality of skin and flesh, muscle and bone.

1 The title added to the drawing may, however, have been one of the inconsequential afterthoughts described by Erich Lederer, son of Schiele's (and Klimt's) patron August Lederer: see above, pp. 129-30.
2 See below, p. 142.

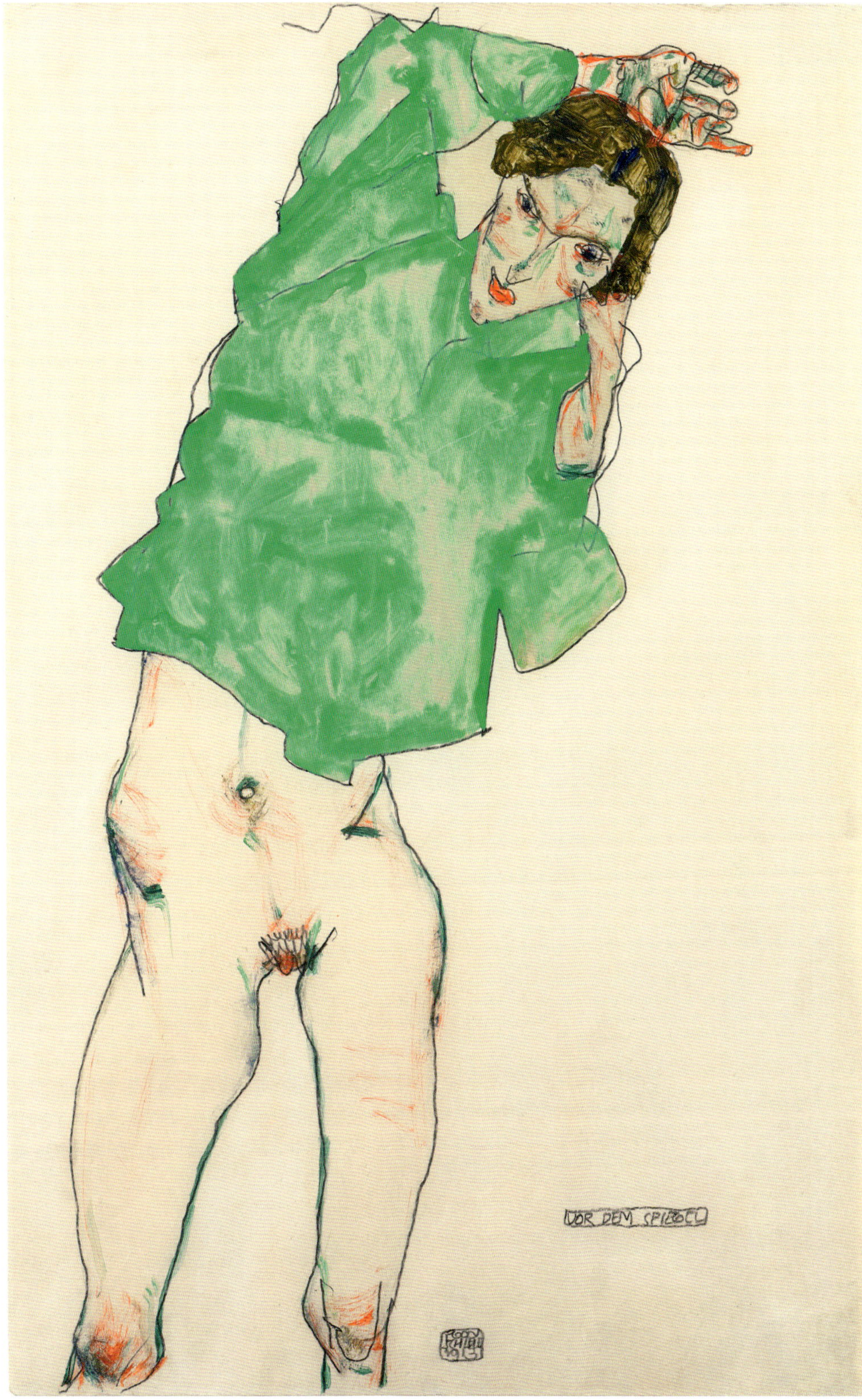
VOR DEM SPIEGEL

29

STANDING NUDE WITH STOCKINGS

1914
Gouache and black chalk, 48.5 x 32.1 cm
Germanisches Nationalmuseum, Nuremberg (Kallir D. 1489)

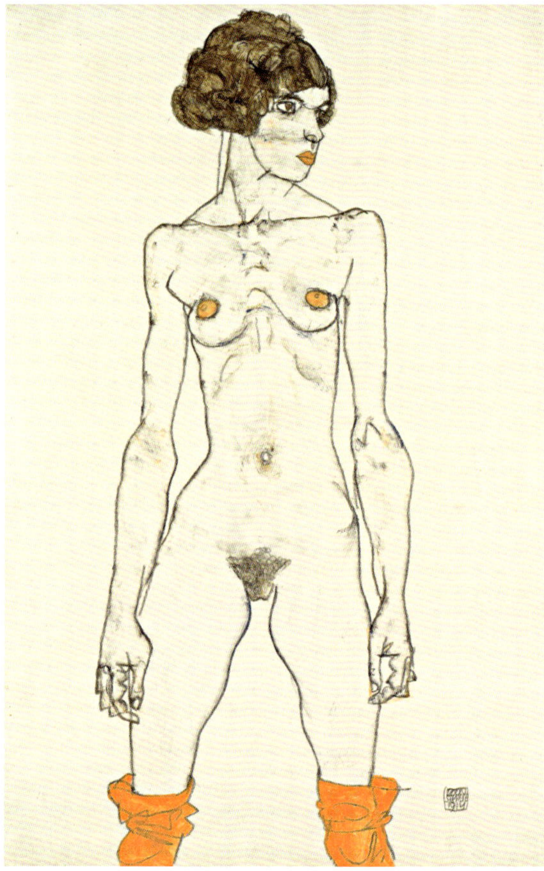

36
EGON SCHIELE
Standing Nude with Orange Stockings, 1914
Gouache and black chalk, 48.5 x 32.1 cm
Leopold Museum – Privatstiftung, Vienna (Kallir D. 1488)

The model who appears in this drawing, with her sensuous face and well-developed physique, can be recognised in several other works by Schiele dating from this period, for example in the Leopold Museum's *Standing Nude with Orange Stockings*, also of 1914 (fig. 36).[1] In that closely related drawing, the woman is depicted in an uncompromisingly frontal pose, standing facing us (or perhaps facing a mirror) with legs wide apart as if she were about to undertake some callisthenic routine. Schiele's new-found interests of the years 1913–14 are clearly apparent in the succession of geometric shapes, predominantly arcs and triangles, which give balance and structure both to the figure itself and to the overall structure of the drawing. Only the turn of the head and slight twist of the upper body in the opposite direction prevent this from becoming an almost entirely symmetrical composition. By contrast, in the present work the nude figure is shown in a more obviously asymmetrical pose, with one shoulder much lower than the other and most of the weight being taken by the right foot. As a consequence, deliberate measures are needed in order to restore balance, for example the jutting left elbow and the pronounced contour of the right arm, reinforcing that of the bulging upper thigh. In both drawings, the legs are seemingly cut off at the knee by the lower edge of the sheet of paper; here, yet again, the artist simply dispenses with those parts of the body that are irrelevant to the composition.

1 Kallir D. 1488.

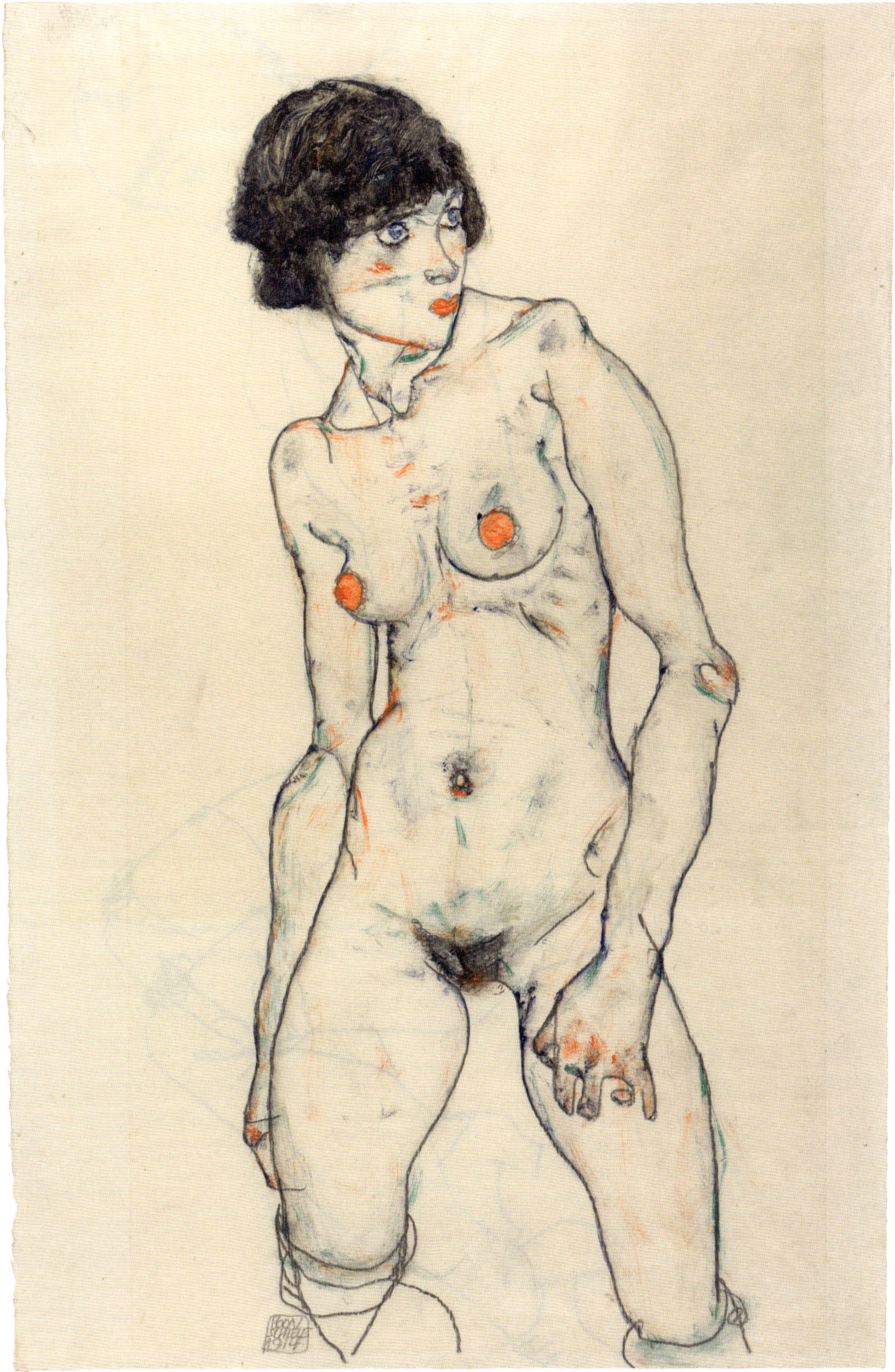

30

FRIENDS

1914
Gouache and pencil, 48.5 x 32.5 cm
Private collection (Kallir D. 1605)

Like masturbation, lesbianism was one of the 'taboo' subjects frequently treated in Schiele's drawings and watercolours. In some of his late works on paper, mostly dating from 1917–18, he repeatedly depicted female couples locked in an erotic embrace, seemingly oblivious to any observer who might catch them in the act of gratifying themselves or each other. But if the drawing exhibited here, which merely shows two naked figures standing with their arms around one another, was intended as some form of comment on the topic of female homosexuality, in this instance the commentary is of a far more discreet kind. The women seem passive, pensive, perhaps even wistful; they certainly do not appear to be engaged in or even contemplating any kind of sexual activity. Nor does the pose adopted look very spontaneous; rather, the models may have been merely following instructions given them by the artist. If that is so, this may be yet another example of Schiele's sitters being called upon to assume fictive identities or act out a particular role. Such a hypothesis appears more likely than any notion that this drawing was intended to communicate important truths about the personalities of the two women or the nature of their relationship.

Whereas 1913 might plausibly be considered a transitional year in the development of Schiele's art, during which he tried out a number of divergent approaches to the depiction of the human figure, by 1914 he seems to have established a drawing style quite different from that of his earlier figure studies. In his pencil drawings, line (as opposed to shading or modelling) was still his principal means of expression and the outlines of the body were often conveyed with some delicacy. By contrast, in his gouaches and watercolours heavier and more definite contour lines, sometimes reinforced by repeated pencil strokes, were coupled with an obviously greater interest in the internal modelling of the figure and in rendering details of muscle, flesh and bone. In the case of the present work, this is achieved by means of carefully sculpted washes and glazes consisting predominantly of browns and ochres, with accents in red, green and other more vivid colours laid down on top.

The contrast between these fully mature, statuesque, heavily muscled figures and the fragile-looking waifs and strays encountered in many of Schiele's earlier drawings could scarcely be greater. His attitude to the women portrayed is also noticeably different, being marked by an obvious lack of personal involvement or even any great interest in his models other than as starting points for what appear largely formal exercises in life drawing. If what had excited the twenty-year-old artist had been skinny, pre-pubescent bodies, the hefty figures depicted here with their bulging biceps and massive thighs seem to have held less immediate appeal. We do not know who these women were; given their exceptionally well-developed physique, they may have been acrobats or circus artists doubling as models. But that they were professional models appears beyond doubt; as Kallir remarks, at this juncture the artist's relationship with his models seems likewise to have been a purely professional one.[1] How he could afford them remains unclear, given that, for much of 1914, his financial situation remained as precarious as ever.

1 Kallir 2003, p. 277.

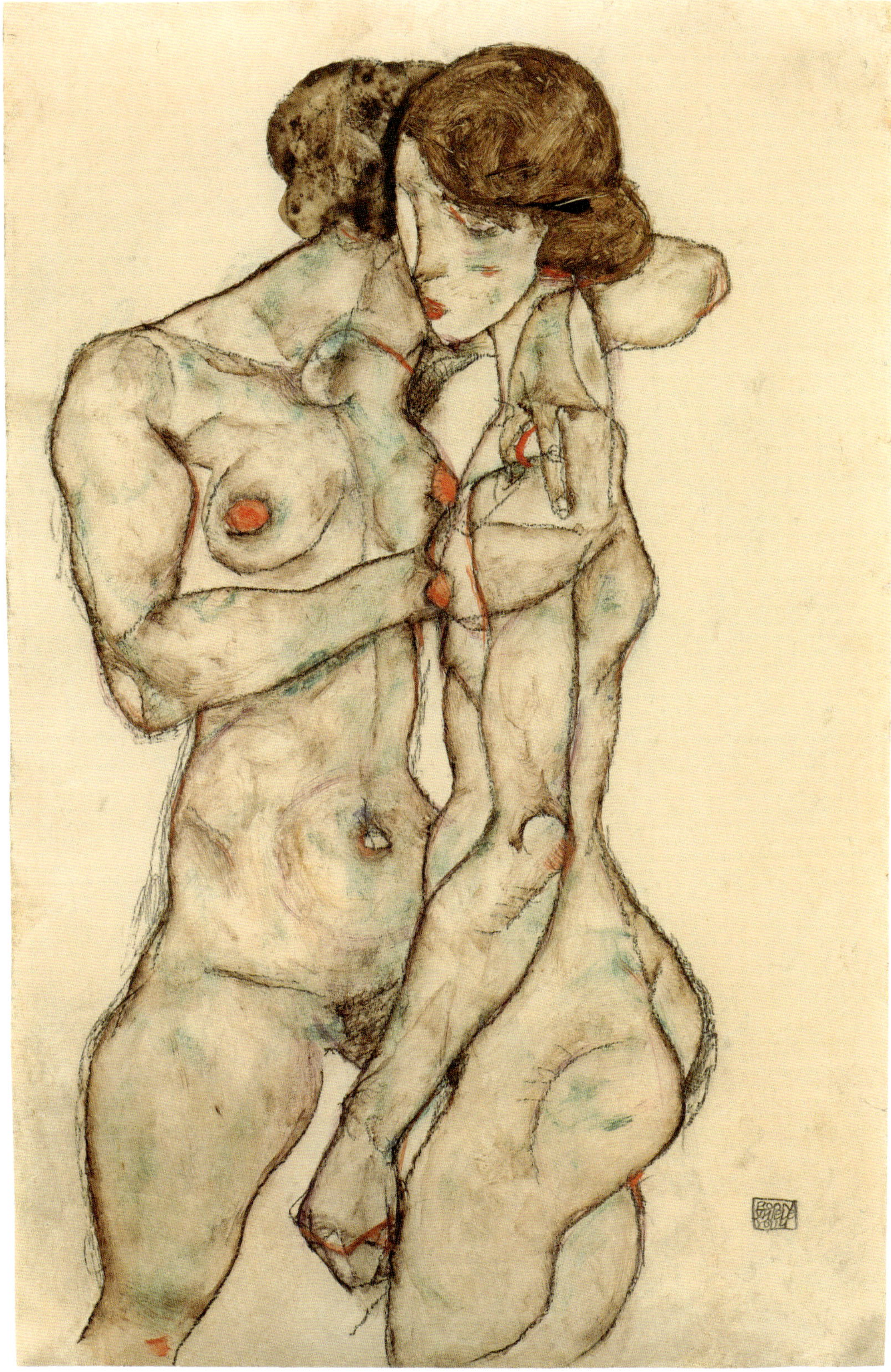

31

SIDE VIEW OF A SEMI-NUDE

1914
Watercolour and pencil, 48 x 38.1 cm
Private collection (Kallir D. 1541)

This is one of the most abstract of all Schiele's drawings. Here, his growing preoccupation with creating what is an essentially geometrical composition, also evident in his studies of a standing female nude with stockings (see cat. 29), is at its most obvious. Compared with his evident delight in creating a seemingly autonomous play of spiralling, curving lines, the careful delineation of elements of the human figure appears to be of only secondary interest. In the lower half of the sheet, the woman's thighs and the half-turn of her hindquarters are depicted in a relatively naturalistic manner, consistent with the style of painting in watercolour or gouache the artist had been seeking to perfect for the past year or more. Here, the flesh is largely modelled with glazes or washes mainly composed of ochres and greyish browns, on which are superimposed smaller touches of more vivid colours. But from the waist up, the figure becomes increasingly difficult to read, being largely concealed beneath a complex mass of clothing or drapery that dominates the upper part of the composition. In the top quarter of the drawing, even the drapery itself has become largely indecipherable, making it difficult to judge whether these are discarded clothes or possibly cushions on which the figure is lying, or whether the artist intended to suggest the presence of an otherwise unseen second figure.

Our task is made all the harder, not only because the figure depicted is not set in any spatial context, being left floating in an apparent void, but also because, in the upper part of the drawing, the overlay of repeated lines seems to obey nothing other than a formal logic all its own. Schiele's interest in the expressive possibilities afforded by a primarily linear composition may have been fuelled by his short-lived experiments with printmaking techniques – in particular, the medium of drypoint, which relies for its effect on meticulously incised lines, at which he tried his hand during the early part of 1914. However, his biographer Roessler was at pains to point out that his protegé harboured no desire to abandon representation, nor did he allow himself to be swayed by the latest trends such as Cubism or the rise of abstract painting. The content of his art, Roessler insisted, was timeless; all that was new was the visual expression he gave to traditional forms and the unfamiliar rhythms by which they were impelled.[1]

1 Roessler 1921, pp. 98-99.

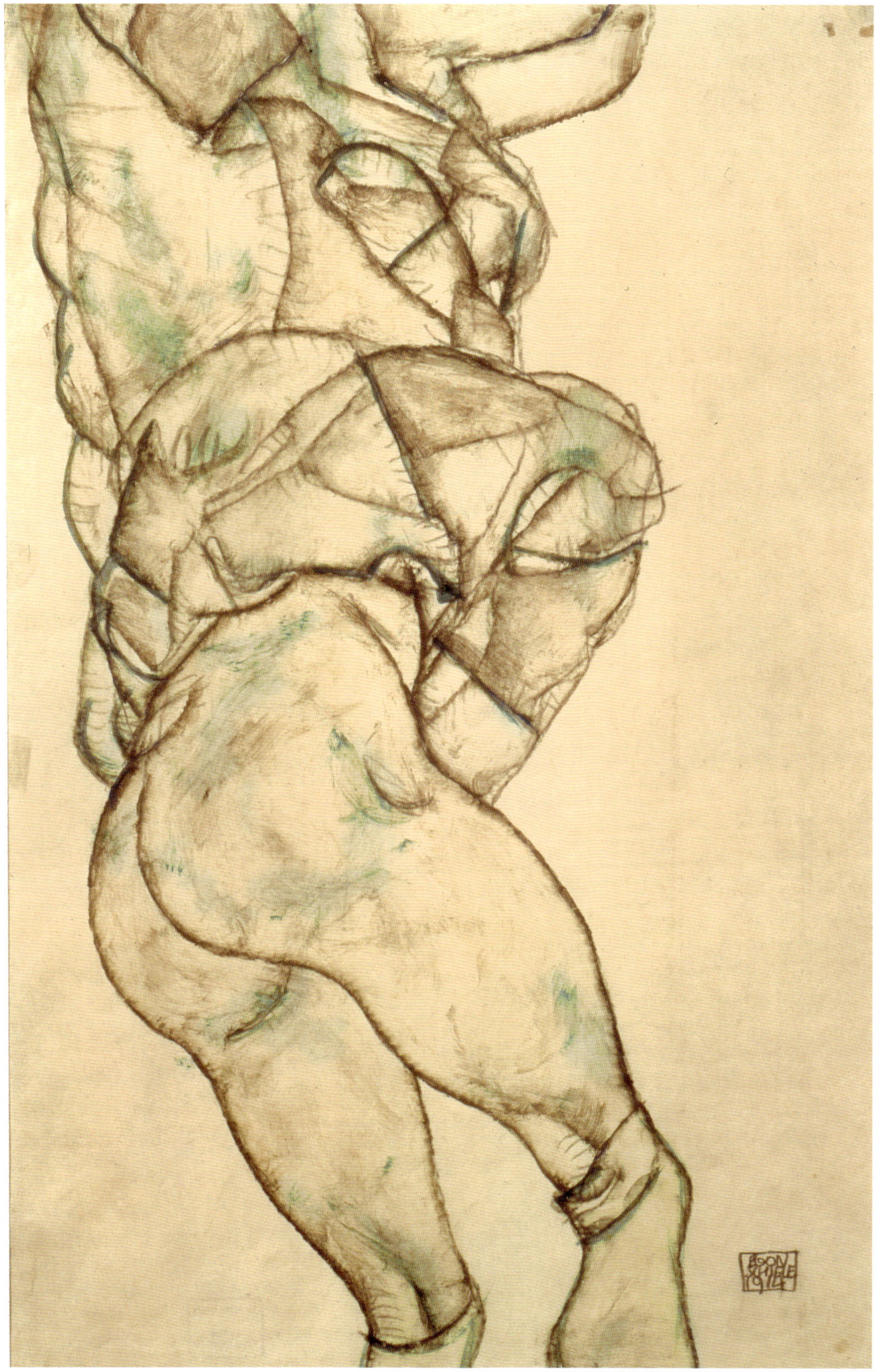
EGON
SCHIELE
1914

32

CROUCHING WOMAN WITH GREEN HEADSCARF

1914
Gouache and pencil, 47 x 31 cm
Leopold Museum – Privatstiftung, Vienna (Kallir D. 1500)

During 1914–15, Schiele embarked on a further series of pictures, some in oil, others in gouache, on a theme he would revisit at intervals throughout his career – that of motherhood. This topic was clearly of considerable importance to him psychologically, perhaps in part because of his strained relationship with his own mother, but also because of the highly personal association he seems to have made between fecundity and artistic creativity on the one hand and blindness, sterility and impotence (both physical and psychological) on the other. Paintings including *The Birth of Genius* (also known as *Dead Mother II*: see fig. 19), *Young Mother* and *Blind Mother* all testify to his concern with subject-matter of this kind. The last two, painted in 1914, may also have been a form of pictorial soliloquy provoked by the impending marriage of his friend Anton Peschka to Schiele's younger sister Gerti. This was a match that evidently caused him a good deal of soul searching, perhaps on account of the earlier intimate relationship between brother and sister (see cat. 3).

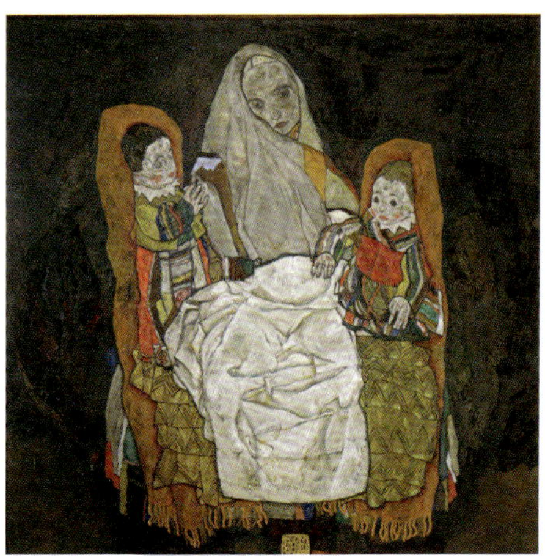

37
EGON SCHIELE
Mother with Two Children III, 1915–17
Oil on canvas, 150 x 158.7 cm
Belvedere Museum, Vienna
(Kallir P. 303)

Although the present work makes no explicit reference to any maternal theme, in its compositional structure, the pose of the figure and the inclusion of a headscarf or shawl *Crouching Woman with Green Headscarf* bears a distant resemblance to the final version of Schiele's later painting *Mother with Two Children III* (fig. 37). However, it displays a somewhat closer affinity with an earlier version of the same composition, painted in 1915, which likewise shows a female figure with a scarf pulled across the upper part of her head, seated in an equally uncomfortable-looking, wide-legged posture.
There is also a degree of kinship with *Blind Mother* of 1914, which, like *Mother with Two Children III*, depicts an awkwardly seated young woman nursing two infants. In that earlier (and darker) painting, the young mother again wears a green headscarf or turban, while the blue swaddling clothes in which one of the infants is wrapped create a distinctive colour accent comparable to the intense blue of the cloth that occupies the lower part of *Crouching Woman with Green Headscarf*. That this work, too, has to do with sexuality and fecundity is implied by the further colour accents created by the bright orange lips, nipples and navel as well as by the small area of pubic hair glimpsed between the girl's forearm and upper thigh. But the shrouded head and especially the boots worn by this otherwise naked figure also suggest that, as in many other instances, there may be a significant relationship between this unusual image and some of the fetishistic visual pornography circulating in Vienna at this time.[1]

1 For a more detailed account of this topic see the essay by Gemma Blackshaw in this catalogue, esp. pp. 40ff.

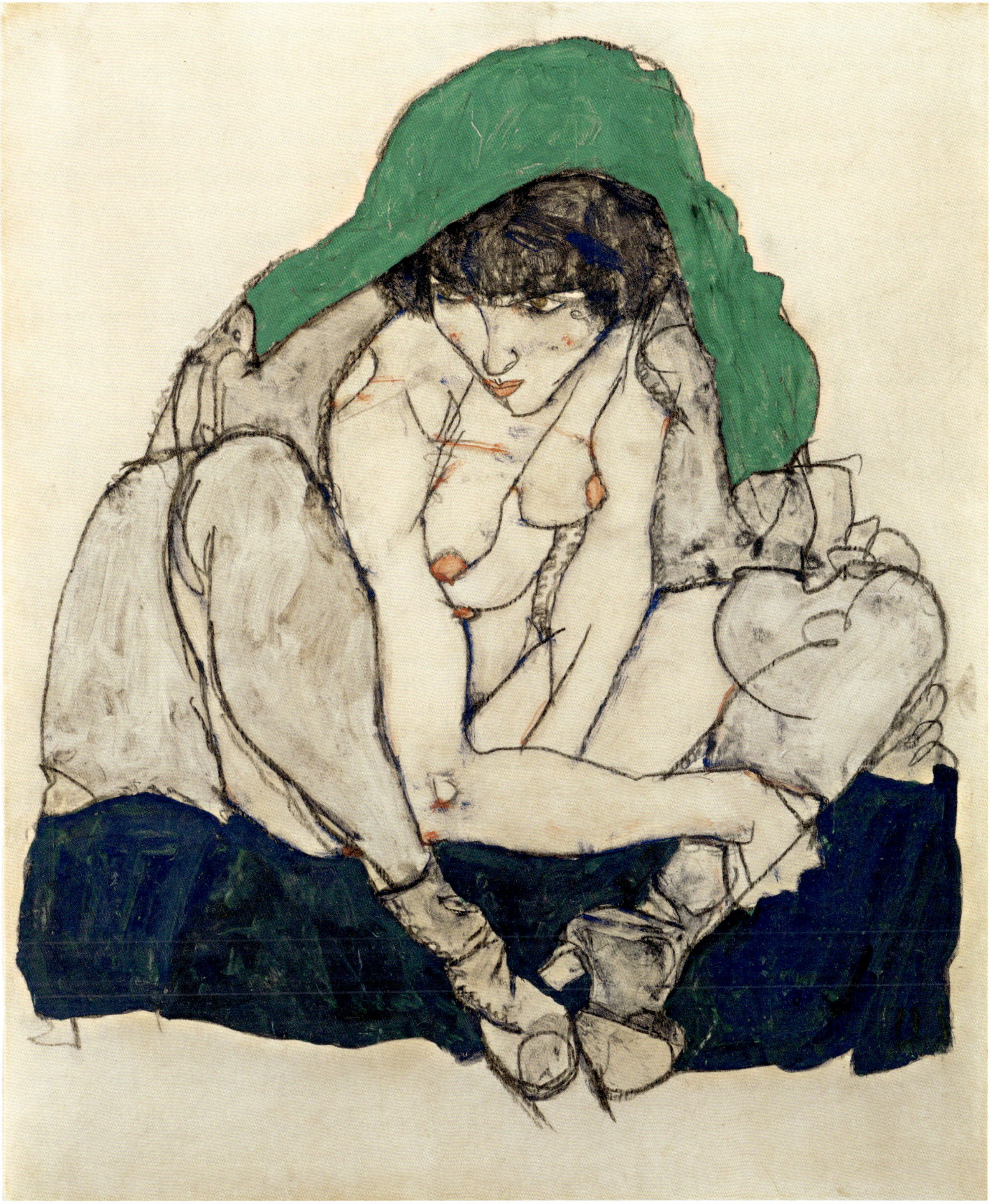

33

TWO GIRLS EMBRACING (TWO FRIENDS)

1915
Gouache, watercolour and pencil, 48 x 32 cm
Szépművészeti Múzeum, Budapest (Kallir D. 1742)

Schiele's figure studies from 1914 onwards exhibit several characteristics not seen in his earlier drawings. At first sporadically, then more frequently, faces become increasingly difficult to identify, often mask-like with pinprick eyes and a blank expression, seemingly devoid of interest or passion. As Jane Kallir remarks, by the middle of that year the artist had begun "deliberately and almost malevolently to 'put out the eyes' in his nudes", not only in his portrayal of female models but even, on occasion, in his depictions of himself.[1] At the same time, the figures often appear doll-like, resembling puppets or articulated figurines.

We may hazard a guess as to the reasons for this change. We know the artist was fascinated by the Indonesian theatrical puppets he first encountered in the home of his champion Arthur Roessler. Such was his enthusiasm that he persuaded Roessler to give him one of his extensive collection of Javanese 'shadow figures' (*Schattenspielfiguren*). From time to time, Schiele traded pictures for 'exotic' objects from Roessler's collection; an old photograph shows two such puppets hanging on the wall of the writer's apartment alongside paintings by Schiele.[2]

Another source of inspiration were crudely carved (and equally crudely articulated) wooden dolls, several of which, as Roessler tells us, the artist carried around with him even on his travels. Not only the featureless faces but also the jerky, rectilinear movements which were all that such dolls were capable of may have influenced his angular, 'unbeautiful' treatment of the human figure in many of his later paintings and drawings.[3] However, if we are to account for the change in style evident in the present drawing, psychological factors are likely to have been just as important as any visual antecedent. A certain emotional distancing from his subject, coupled with the not unreasonable demands of Edith, his bride-to-be, as regards his use of studio models, probably combined to produce an attitude to the subject of the female nude that was more complicated, more subtle and more nuanced than was the case in many of his figure studies of the years c. 1910–12.

In all these respects, this famous watercolour occupies an exceptionally important position within Schiele's oeuvre. It also presents us with an image that is singularly difficult to interpret. It appears to depict two women locked in a lesbian embrace, yet it seems unlikely that these were real models or, indeed, real lesbians: Edith's strictures would probably have precluded any such involvement with live models. Although several of Schiele's contemporaries insisted that he drew only from life, in this instance it seems more likely that the figures depicted were created either from memory or from the imagination. Moreover, the obvious contrast between the two protagonists – one to all appearances a passionate, sensual woman of flesh and blood, the other a limp, doll-like figure – has caused several commentators to question exactly what this pointed juxtaposition of two such contrasting figures might imply about the artist's attitude to the represented subject or, indeed, his mental state at this time.

One suggestion put forward by Jane Kallir in her account of Schiele's drawings and watercolours is that what the artist had in mind was some kind of 'good girl/bad girl' scenario, the sensual woman evoking memories of his former lover and favourite model Wally Neuzil, the 'good girl' being, of course, the more socially acceptable and more proper (although, in reality, anything but frigid) Edith.[4] Does the drawing therefore allude to the artist being torn between past memories and

1 Kallir 2012, p. 194.
2 See Tobias G. Natter, '"Nichts und niemand half mir!" Egon Schiele und sein Promoter Arthur Roessler', in Natter and Storch 2004, p. 12; the photograph of Roessler's apartment is reproduced on p. 64 of the same publication.
3 The importance both of the wooden puppets and of the Indonesian *Schattenspielfiguren* has been explored by Katharina Sykora in her essay 'Performative Selbstinszenierung und Geschlechterirritation bei Egon Schiele', in Müller-Tamm 1995, esp. pp. 48ff.

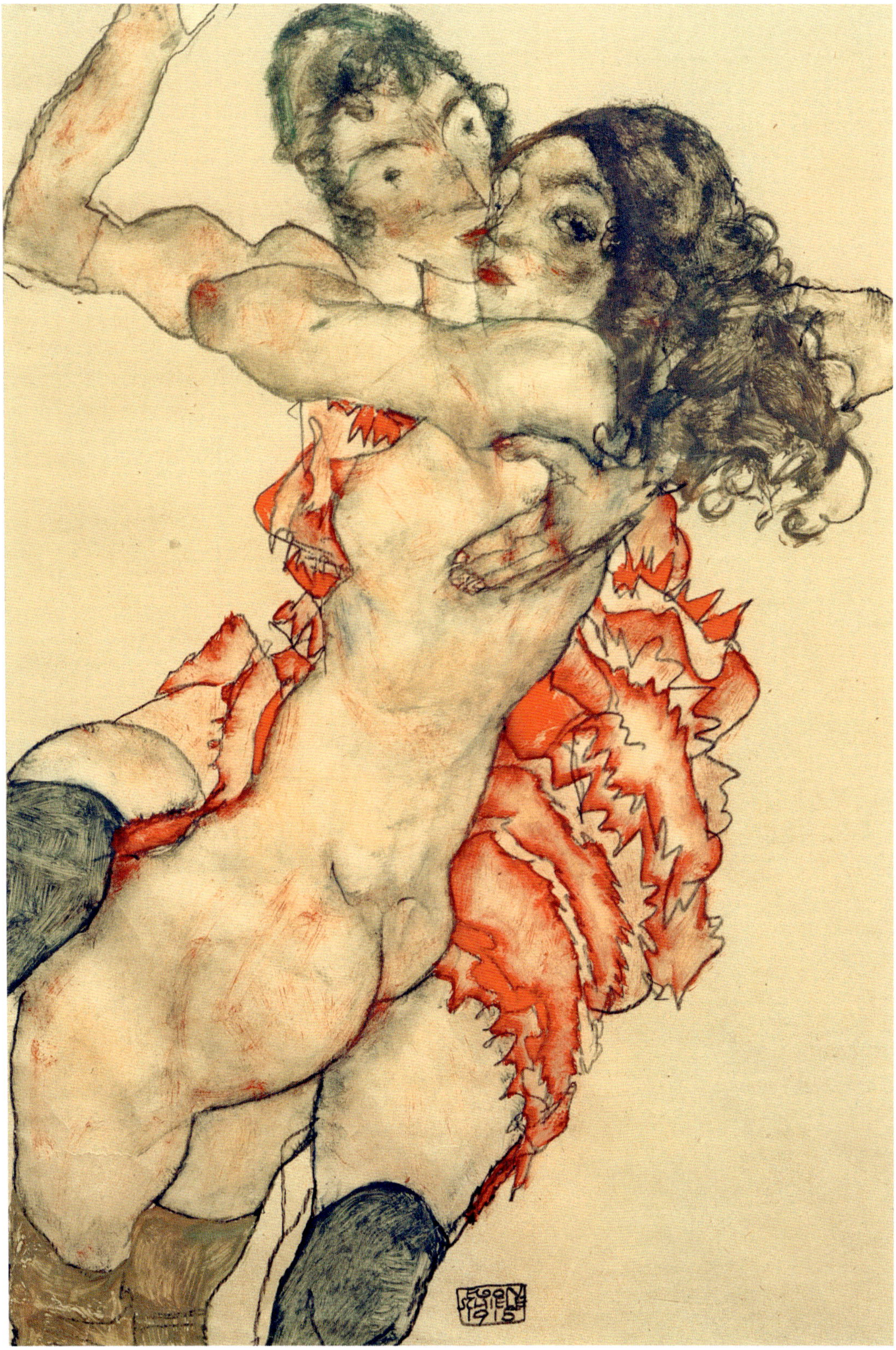
EGON
SCHIELE
1915

the prospect of married bliss? If so, which does the artist seem to prefer? Unflattering though it might be to Edith, the drawing itself provides few clues, if any, that might help to answer this awkward question. In her more recent study *Egon Schiele's Women*, however, Kallir appears to have abandoned this hypothesis, merely describing the one partner as looking like a "full-fledged human being", the other as a "button-eyed, soulless cipher".[5] This more cautious interpretation appears preferable, especially given that the 'bad girl' depicted in this drawing bears absolutely no resemblance to Wally, whose distinctive features – in particular, her auburn hair and pale blue eyes – are instantly recognisable in numerous earlier paintings and watercolours by Schiele (see fig. 33, for example).

4 Kallir 2003, p. 323; on Edith and Egon's active if somewhat sporadic love life, see p. 326.

5 Kallir 2012, p. 187.

34

RECLINING SEMI-NUDE WITH LEGS SPREAD

1916
Gouache and pencil, 30.9 x 44.4 cm
Leopold Museum – Privatstiftung, Vienna (Kallir D. 1833)

This drawing has been identified as a study for Schiele's later oil painting *Reclining Woman* (fig. 38), executed the following year.[1] The painting reproduces almost exactly the lower half of the woman's body as it appears in cat. 34 save for the shoes, which feature only in the earlier work. However, there are several obvious differences between the drawing and the painting. In the former, the upper part of the body is clothed, whereas in the latter the breasts are exposed. In the painting, the woman has her hands behind her head; in the drawing, she is propping herself up on one elbow. The faces, too, are quite different, as is the hair – loose and flowing in the painting, piled up in a complicated mass in the drawing.

According to Rudolf Leopold, Schiele's sister-in-law Adele Harms confirmed that the drawing depicted the artist's wife Edith, even though in neither the painting nor the drawing do the woman's features bear the slightest resemblance to what we know of Edith from portraits and photographs.[2] This may be because, following their marriage in early summer 1915, Schiele soon found himself obliged to accept that his wife did not like being identified as the subject of some of his more obviously 'erotic' pictures. Thus, on quite a number of occasions when he portrayed her in sexually explicit poses, he disguised her appearance in deference to her wishes.

It is also noticeable that the depiction of the genitals is far more explicit in the earlier study than in the finished oil, perhaps because drawing has often been considered a more private medium than painting. Works such as the present drawing would probably have been known, at least initially, only to a small and relatively select circle of male buyers who, after 1915, were an increasingly important source of income. However, following the artist's

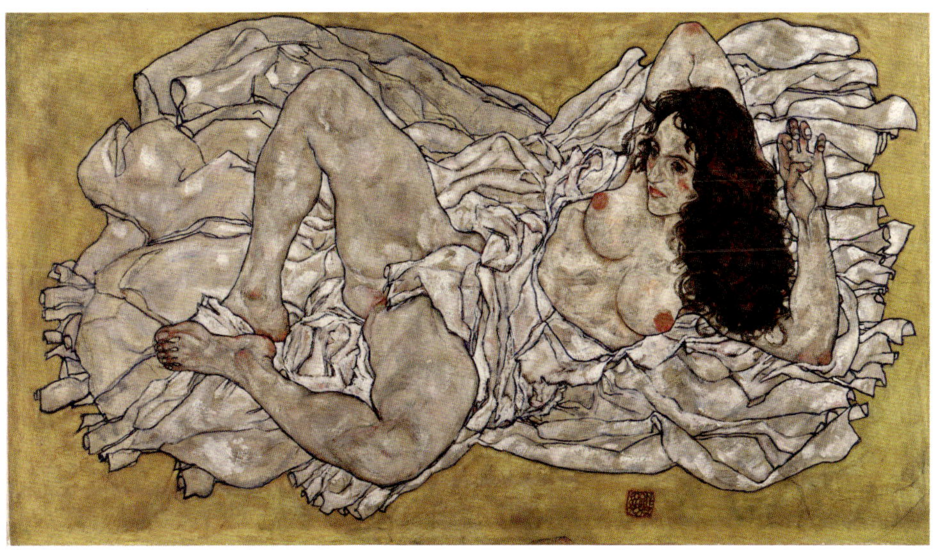

38
EGON SCHIELE
Reclining Woman, 1917
Oil on canvas, 95.5 x 171 cm
Leopold Museum – Privatstiftung, Vienna (Kallir P. 306)

1 Kallir 1990, P. 306.
2 Leopold 2009, p. 228.

death in 1918, both the present work and another equally explicit drawing of Edith, again with altered features, were included in a posthumous portfolio of five erotic drawings by Schiele in lithographic reproduction, presumably intended for wider distribution; on the tangled but intriguing history of that now rare portfolio see the essay by Gemma Blackshaw in this catalogue.[3]

Whether this disconcertingly explicit depiction of the woman's genitals means that the drawing – or, for that matter, its reproduction – should rightly be termed 'erotic' or even 'pornographic' is a different matter. Anatomically detailed representations of those body parts usually regarded as private do not necessarily equate with erotic interest or sexual arousal. As remarked in connection with cat. 35, one distinguishing feature of Schiele's later nude studies is what seems to be a more dispassionate attitude towards the depiction of the naked female body, apparent both in the present drawing and in the related painting.

It has sometimes been claimed that, when Schiele first painted the oil version, he left 'Edith's' genitals fully exposed and only covered them up later – again, perhaps in order to spare his wife's blushes.[4] But, if true, that 'covering up' was only partial. Although one might not wish to be found peering too intently at that part of the painting, closer inspection reveals that at least part of the woman's vulva is still visible. Rather than being motivated by modesty, this 'now you see it, now you don't' approach might equally have been impelled by a desire to tantalise and provoke, in contrast to the seemingly disinterested and even somewhat clinical rendering of the sexual organs that characterises the drawing.

A further riddle, familiar by now to anyone well acquainted with Schiele's work, concerns the orientation of the signature. As in several other instances, the artist has signed and dated this sheet as if it were meant to be viewed vertically.[5] If that was really his intention, such a re-orientation would have the effect of disguising still further the relationship between the drawing and the painting, since the latter can, of course, only be viewed horizontally. In the drawing, both the pose of the obviously recumbent figure and the way she supports herself on her elbow are only truly convincing if the sheet is likewise displayed horizontally, at least to the eye of the present author.

3 See above, pp. 31ff. The second drawing of Edith, now in a private collection, is Kallir D. 1834; it is reproduced in colour in Hollein and Natter 2005, p. 228.
4 This claim is based on information given in an interview between Rudolf Leopold and Alessandra Comini which took place in August 1963: see Comini 1974, p. 245, note 55.
5 Compare cat. 26 and 37.

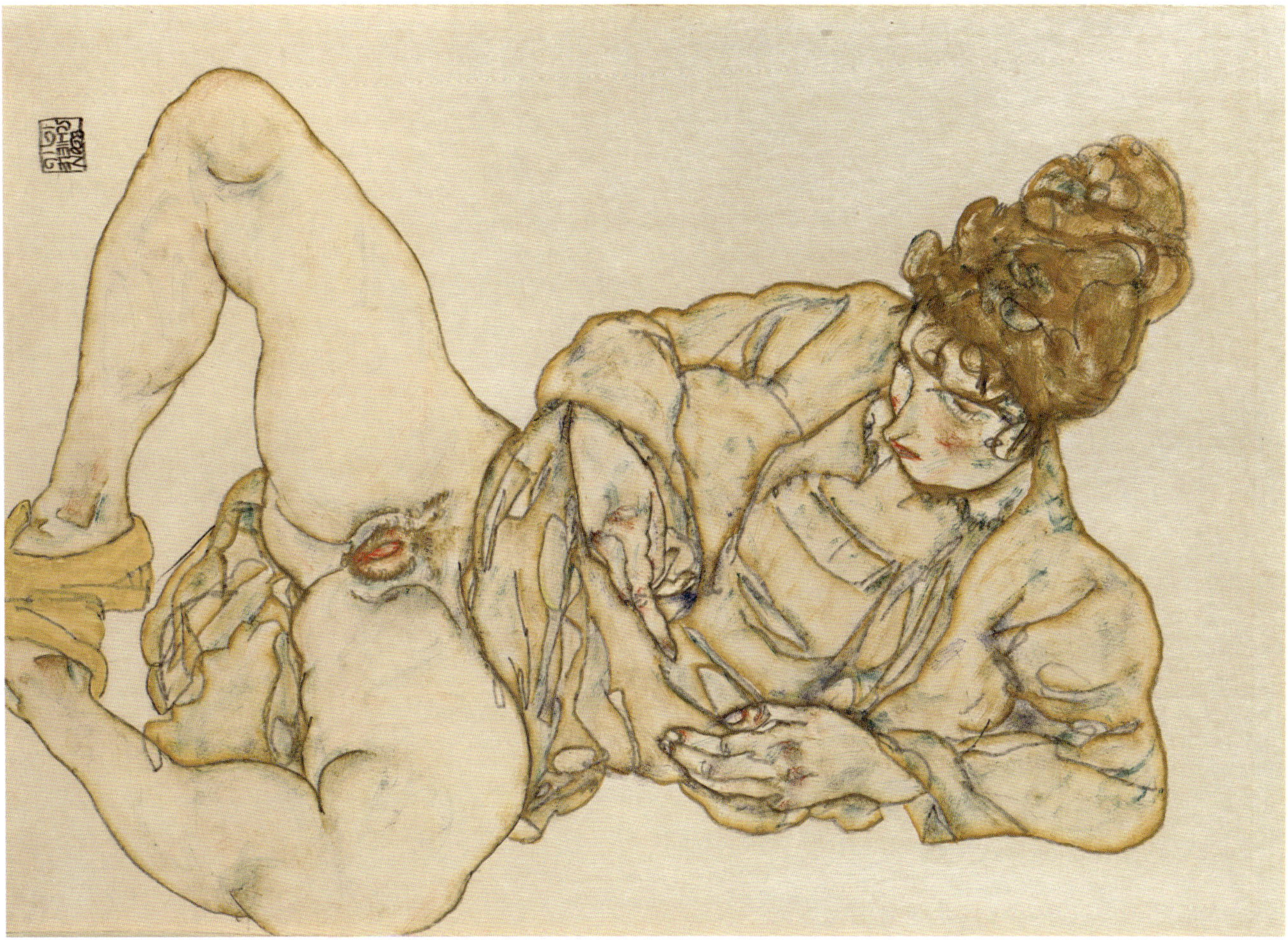
EGON
SCHIELE
1916

35

SQUATTING GIRL

1917
Gouache and black crayon, 46 x 28.8 cm
Staatliche Graphische Sammlung, Munich (Kallir D. 1941)

36

FEMALE NUDE, BACK VIEW

1917
Gouache and black crayon, 46 x 29.5 cm
Staatliche Graphische Sammlung, Munich (Kallir D. 1966)

Arguably, 1916 had been the least productive year of Schiele's brief career – the consequence of his military duties, repeated re-deployments and the resulting disruption to his normal routine. But once he had been seconded to the Imperial and Royal Military Supply Department at the beginning of 1917, his more settled circumstances allowed him to start thinking once more about a further series of allegorical paintings, although not on the same grandiose scale as his projected but only partially completed works of 1913.[1] He also devoted much of his spare time to drawing portrait studies (many of them commissioned) and nudes, which together accounted for by far the greater proportion of his works on paper. Ironically, the almost complete hiatus of 1916 now serves merely to underline the distance he had travelled, given his previous attitude towards the nude figure.

Schiele's improving financial situation meant that, from 1917 onwards, he could increasingly afford to employ a whole succession of studio models, which is precisely what we see depicted in these two drawings. These are professional models, hired to provide a professional service, whom the artist now regards dispassionately, showing little or no interest in them personally nor any real desire to capture anything of their moods, their character or personality. Gone, too, are the alarmingly truncated limbs and dramatic cropping of the figure that characterise many of his earlier nude studies, along with his penchant for histrionics and role play and the theatrical gestures that were the result of previous attempts to involve his sitters as actors in some fantasy drama. Nor does he seem to be aroused by the naked bodies of his female models or at all interested in them sexually. Rather, a tendency towards ever greater realism in his drawings and watercolours from 1914 onwards means that most of his efforts are now directed towards capturing the plasticity of the human form, the density of flesh and the solidity of muscle. To this end, he continues to employ black crayon, which produces a denser and more palpable contour, and a more restricted palette, consisting mainly of subtly varied flesh tones, with more vivid colours reserved for the depiction of drapery, outer garments and other routine appurtenances such as stockings and shoes or boots.

In *Squatting Girl*, the model's face is averted. To judge by the position of her body and her head propped up on her hand, she seems oblivious to her surroundings and quite disengaged from anything to do with the whole business of posing nude. She might even be asleep. That she is made to appear unconscious of the fact that she is exposing herself suggests a certain voyeuristic intent; even so, this drawing has a noticeably lower erotic charge than the majority of Schiele's earlier nudes. In *Female Nude, Back View*, the erotic temperature is even lower. The model cannot engage visually with the viewer since her face is hidden from view, and the absence of even so much as a wisp of pubic hair seen from behind suggests that the artist's otherwise obsessive interest in genitalia has temporarily deserted him. Only the inclusion of stockings, pulled up to just above the knee, and the merest suggestion of boots link this sexually rather less than provocative nude study to the world of conventional erotica.

As with so many of Schiele's works on paper, it is highly likely that both of these nude studies were quite rapidly drawn. Unsurpassed as products of his maturity as a draughtsman, they testify to his astonishing mastery in composing with a minimum of means. Now, he takes little trouble to locate his figures in relation to the edges of the sheet

1 See above, p. 126.

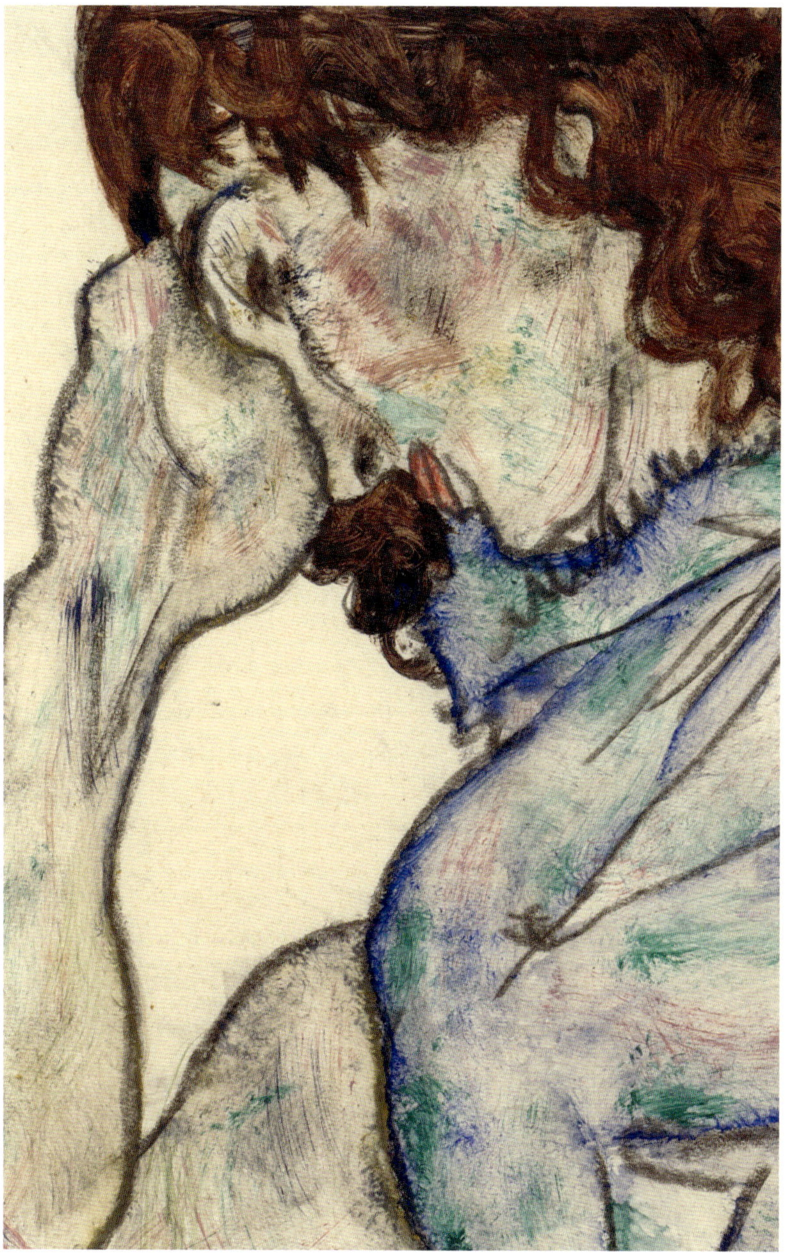

of paper. Instead, he simply sets them down on the page with such unerring confidence that they appear solid and compositionally secure, even though still placed against the same featureless void that, by this date, had become part of the artist's 'signature style'. We have little difficulty in accepting these studies as convincing images of real flesh and blood, at the same time marvelling at the visually satisfying structure, which scarcely betrays any hint of having been carefully calculated or studied in advance, but gives the impression of having been wholly intuitive.

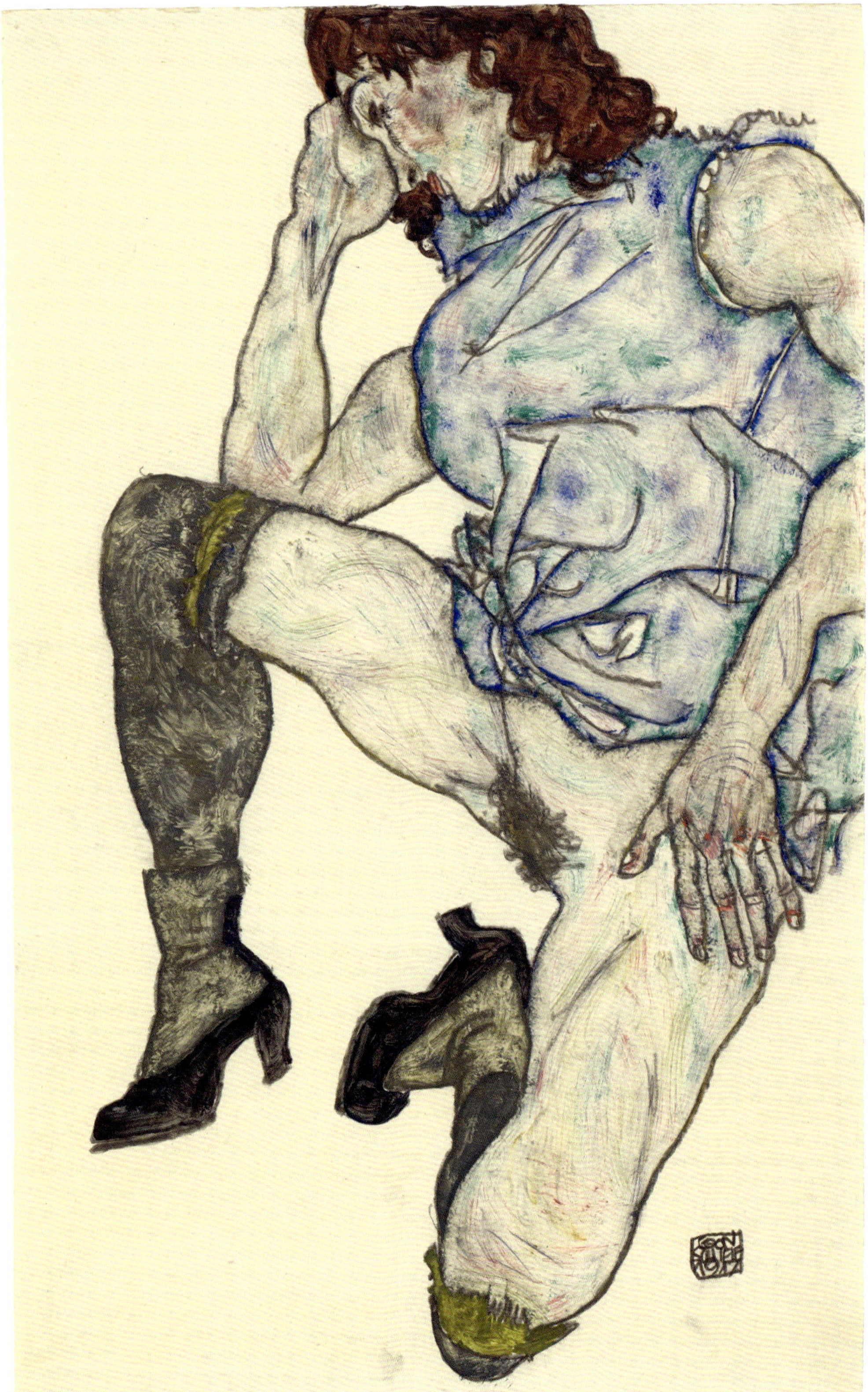

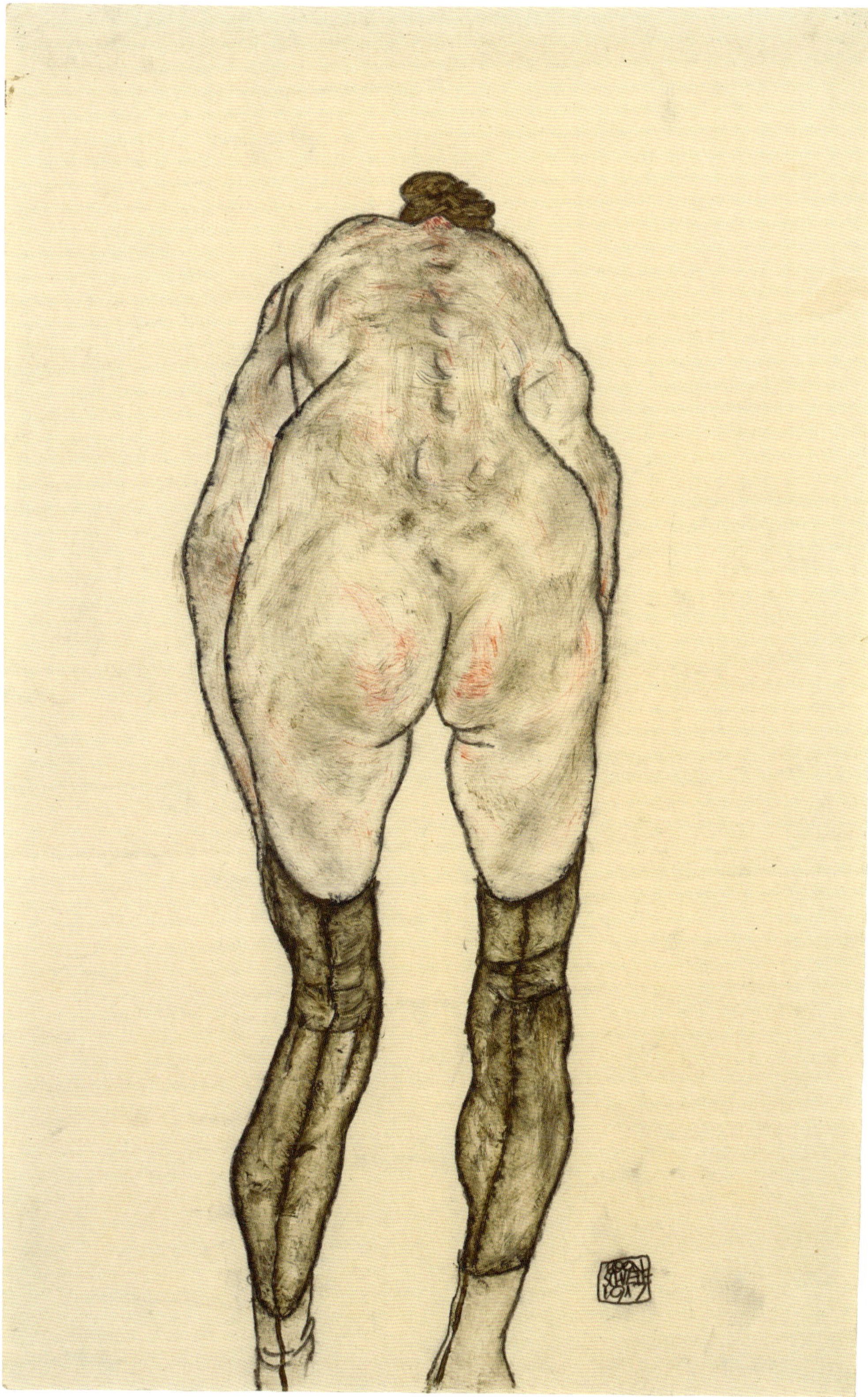

37

NUDE GIRL WITH LOWERED HEAD

1918
Watercolour, gouache and black chalk, 29.7 x 46.2 cm
Leopold Museum – Privatstiftung, Vienna (Kallir D. 2204)

In the spring of 1918, Schiele worked closely with the well-known Viennese printer Alfred Berger to produce the lithographic poster advertising the 49th exhibition of the Vienna Secession – the exhibition that witnessed the artist's long awaited critical and commercial success and for whose organisation he had been largely responsible. Shortly afterwards, he turned again to Berger for help and advice, this time in response to an invitation from Vienna's Gesellschaft für vervielfältigende Kunst (Society for Graphic Art) to submit designs for a colour lithograph to be published in the association's annual print portfolio. Up until this point, Schiele had acquired relatively little experience in the art of printmaking, apart from the small number of drypoints he executed in 1914 at Roessler's instigation and a couple of woodcuts published by Franz Pfemfert's Berlin periodical *Die Aktion*. His only venture into lithography had so far consisted of just two prints submitted for inclusion in the portfolio issued by the Munich artists' association 'Sema' in 1912.

But despite Berger's assistance, it seems that, from the very beginning, Schiele got off on the wrong foot, paying almost no attention to the stipulations laid down in the invitation sent to him on behalf of the Society by the artist Dr Arpad Weixlgärtner.[1] Weixlgärtner made it clear that he and his colleagues wanted a coloured design and suggested that Schiele submit either a nude study or a landscape or both; what they actually got was a black-and-white portrait of Schiele's painter friend Albert Paris von Gütersloh.[2] In a tactfully worded letter dated 27 April 1918, Weixlgärtner emphasised how important it was that Schiele should be represented in the forthcoming portfolio alongside well-known artists including Lovis Corinth, Karl Sterrer, Wilhelm Laage and Ludwig Heinrich Jungnickel. He ventured the opinion that the design they had received did not really do justice to the "strength and originality" of Schiele's art, and suggested he should submit another.[3]

It seems that, second time round, the Society did receive a nude study, although apparently still only in black and white. In a further letter, Weixlgärtner expressed concern over the excessively detailed depiction of the genitals, which he thought likely to offend his fellow committee members; he also insisted on Schiele providing a coloured drawing, as originally requested.[4] The present study in watercolour and gouache may have been the drawing in question, in which case it can be dated with relative precision, that is, to the latter part of June 1918. It reproduces almost exactly, although in reverse, the print as finally pulled by Berger, which was not published in the artist's lifetime, since the Society finally decided that both this and its predecessor (the portrait of Gütersloh) were unsuitable and withdrew its offer.

One odd feature of the drawing is that Schiele has signed it as if the composition were meant to be read vertically, even though it is clear that the model can only have posed lying down. As noted earlier, this is a phenomenon we encounter in quite a number of his other works on paper including two in this exhibition.[5] Over time, various hypotheses have been advanced by way of explanation, some more plausible than others. These have included pointing out parallels with contemporary theories of perception – for example, those put forward by the Viennese physicist and philosopher Ernst Mach, who, stressing the essentially subjective nature of our perceptions, had called in question what was claimed to be the objective nature of both time and space. In her thought-provoking study *Egon Schiele: Wahrnehmung, Identität und Weltbild*, art

1 Letter dated 6 March 1918: Egon Schiele-Archiv, inv. no. 970; Nebehay 1979, p. 456, doc. 1411.
2 Kallir G.16; compare also D. 2447 and 2448.
3 Egon Schiele-Archiv, inv. no. 1036; Nebehay 1979, p. 466, doc. 1519.
4 "*Hoffentlich wird das etwas auffällige Genitale des Mädchens keinen Anstoß erregen*"; letter dated 19 June 1918; Egon-Schiele Archiv, inv. no. 1038; Nebehay 1979, p. 472, doc. 1601.
5 Compare, for example, cat. 4 and 34.

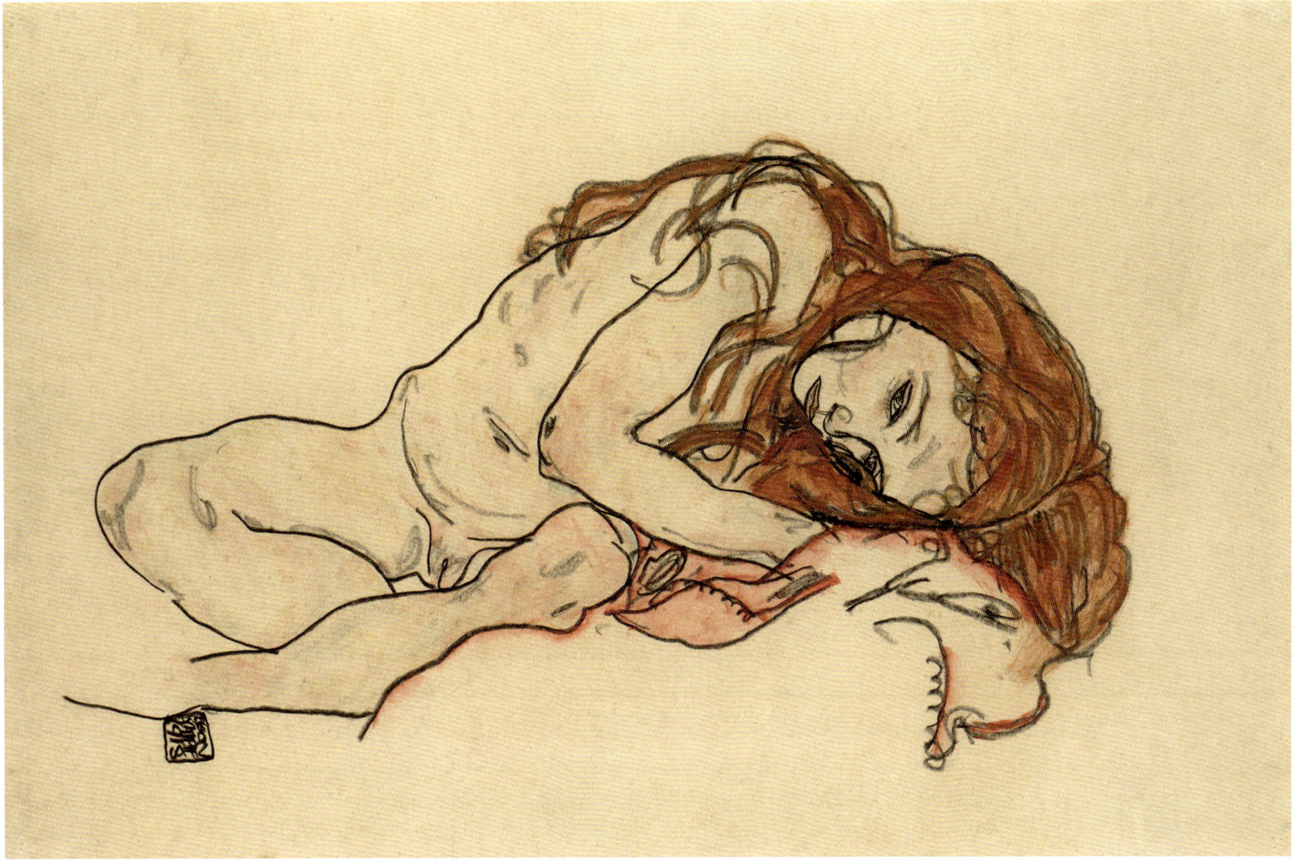

historian Helena Pereña Sáez claims that Schiele was "certainly familiar" with Mach's ideas from discussions that took place in Vienna's coffee houses, insisting that an "intense preoccupation with the problem of perception" was reflected in his work and that it "decisively influenced his conception of space".[6] She is also clearly of the view that the placing of the signature, even if it contradicts the pose of the figure, should invariably determine the way in which works are displayed, pointing to the example of the 2005 Schiele exhibition mounted by Vienna's Albertina, where, in every case, the drawings were hung according to the orientation not of the subject-matter but of the signature.[7]

However, in the case of *Nude Girl with Lowered Head*, any suggestion that the artist might have wanted to offer the spectator an alternative way of viewing the image strains the bounds of credulity. Try exhibiting the sheet vertically and it becomes obvious that the composition simply does not work that way, not least because of the evident weight of the figure upon the supporting cloth or cushion, which, if the drawing is turned through 90°, ends up hanging meaninglessly in mid air. The psychological effect, too, alters drastically depending on the way the sheet is displayed. If viewed in the same orientation as the drawing was originally created – that is, horizontally – this 'crouching nude girl', as she has often been called, appears to be not so much crouching as cowering, as if averting her gaze from some perceived (or imagined?) threat and raising her arm to protect herself.[8] Similarly, her flowing red locks are so arranged that they shield her head in what looks like a form of protective covering. Thus there seems to be a subtle but nonetheless real undertone of menace about the way in which the naked figure is depicted. Apart from the blatant display of her genitalia, this may have been another reason why the Society for Graphic Art finally decided that it would not be including Schiele's print in its portfolio; a further letter sent on behalf of the committee informing the artist of their decision described it as "more suitable for a small circle of collectors and devotees than for the majority of our members".[9]

6 Pereña Sáez 2010, pp. 94-96.
7 Pereña Sáez 2010, p. 107.
8 For example, the recent catalogue of the Leopold collection proposes the title *Kauerndes Nacktes Mädchen*, literally, 'crouching' or 'squatting'; see Leopold 2009, p. 244. Kallir's oeuvre catalogue of Schiele's works calls this drawing *Nude Girl with Lowered Head*, the title we have used here.
9 Letter dated 28 June 1918: Egon Schiele-Archiv, inv. no. 237; Nebehay 1979, pp. 472-73, doc. 1614.

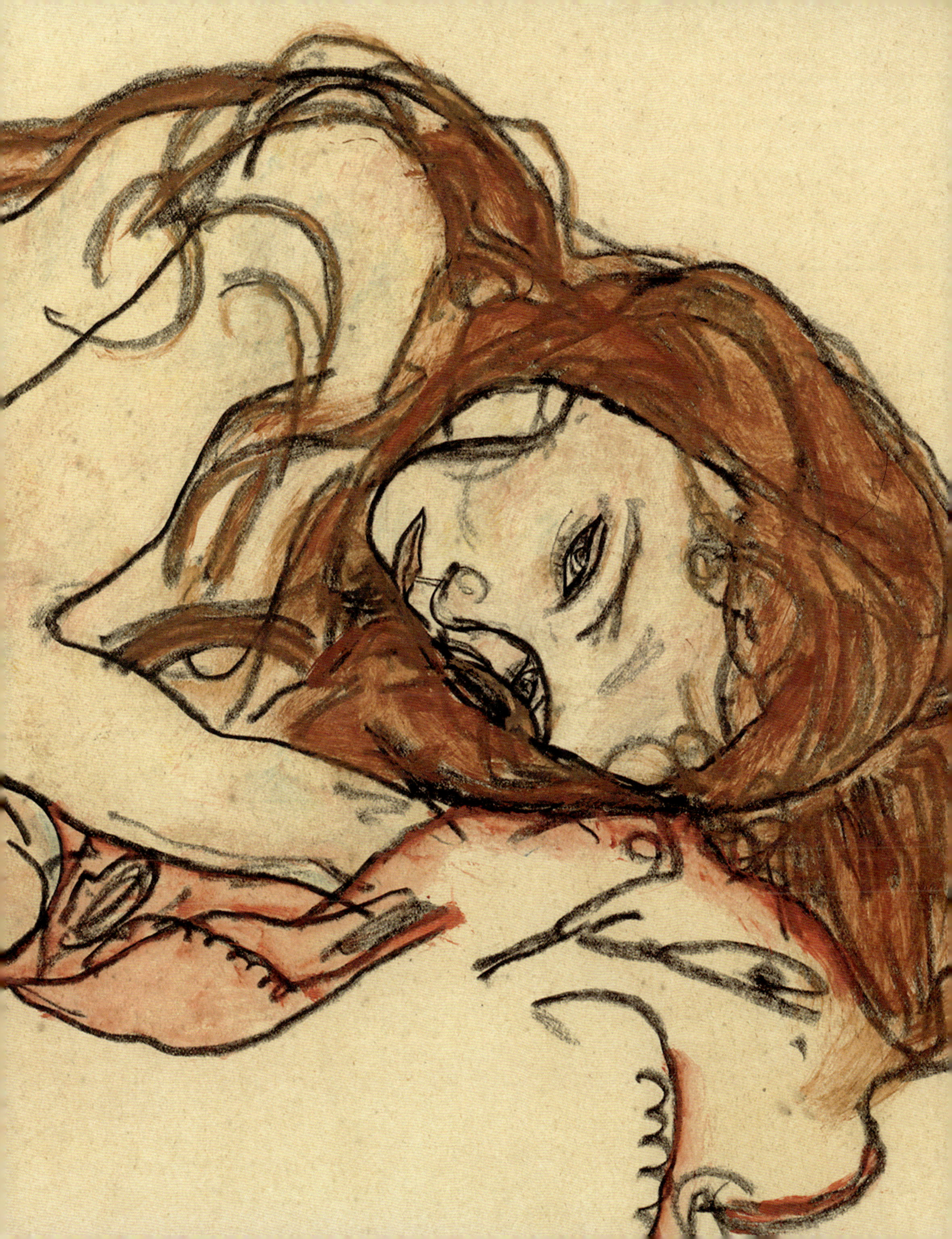

38

WOMAN IN BOOTS WITH RAISED SKIRT

1918
Black crayon, 43.5 x 28 cm
Private collection, courtesy of Richard Nagy Ltd, London (Kallir D. 2418)

Boots feature yet again in this drawing dating from the last months of Schiele's life. This time, they are of the button-and-laces variety still favoured today by more traditional Austrian waitresses. They were also part of the stock-in-trade of the routine and easily available photographic pornography which, during the latter part of the artist's career, clearly influenced his treatment of erotic subjects. Now, however, his attitude to this kind of subject-matter is more obviously detached than in his earlier works, many of which seem driven by an obsessive interest in the sexuality of his female models. As Kallir remarks, most of Schiele's late drawings tell us little about his own mental state or, indeed, his private or emotional life.[1] At this point in his career, with financial success already secured, he seems rather to be pandering to the interests of his ever-growing circle of predominantly male clients. Given its clearly voyeuristic agenda, with the model's skirt raised just far enough to reveal the fact that she is wearing nothing underneath, *Woman in Boots* may well have been created with that same clientele in mind.

Despite the artist's own increasing remoteness from any emotional involvement with his models, this remains a somewhat uncomfortable image to contemplate. Her face partly obscured by her exuberant mass of hair, the woman's single staring eye may appear to modern audiences just as disconcerting as her exposed sex, here represented in what seems a somewhat perfunctory fashion, at least by the standards of some of Schiele's earlier nude studies (compare, for example, cat. 23). Equally disconcerting is the way in which her one eye and her sex seem somehow in competition with one another to be the main focus of the viewer's attention.

As in most of his drawings of this period, Schiele here employed black crayon to create a softer, at times even slightly smudgy effect compared with the precise and occasionally brittle lines produced by the hard pencil used in many of his earlier works on paper. Relatively few of these late drawings are coloured (and some that are may well have been 'completed' by another hand).[2] Instead, the artist relies principally on contour to convey everything he wishes to communicate. His mastery of his chosen medium is remarkable, as is the manner in which he captures the essentials of the figure using only a small number of unbroken lines. It is as if, once he had put crayon to paper, a few quick flourishes were enough to create an outline that is both economical and expressive at the same time. Schiele was inclined to boast about his fluency as a draughtsman and about the number of works on paper he could create in a short space of time. Confronted with a drawing like this, it is easy to believe such claims and imagine that it took him no more than a couple of minutes to complete this undeniably accomplished study of the half-naked figure, even allowing for the complexities of her crumpled sleeve and mass of curls.

1 Kallir 2003, pp. 445-46.
2 On the "posthumous colouring" of Schiele's late drawings see Kallir 1998, p. 602.

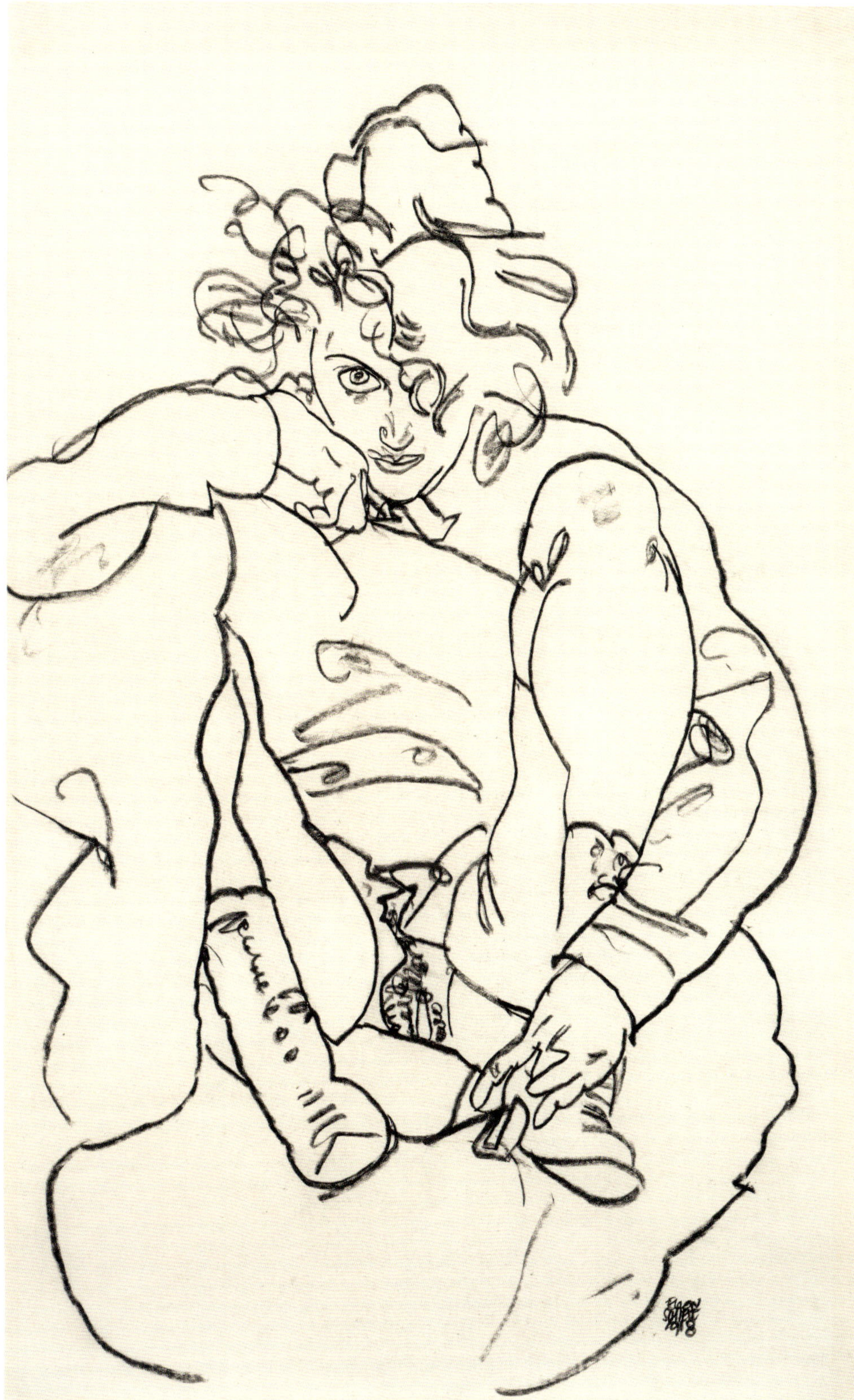

BIBLIOGRAPHY

Bahr 2007
Hermann Bahr, *Die bildenden Künste: 1910–34*, Vienna (Akademie der bildenden Künste) 2007

Bauer 2013
Christian Bauer, *Egon Schiele: Der Anfang/The Beginning*, exh. cat., Munich (Hirmer) 2013

Beller 2001
Steven Beller (ed.), *Rethinking Vienna 1900*, New York and Oxford (Berghahn Books) 2001

Benesch 1965
Heinrich Benesch, *Mein Weg mit Egon Schiele*, New York (Verlag der Johannespresse) 1965

Benesch 1973
Eva Benesch (ed.), *Otto Benesch. Collected Writings*, vol. IV, London (Phaidon) 1973

Bisanz-Prakken 1980
Marian Bisanz-Prakken, *Gustav Klimt, der Beethovenfries: Geschichte, Funktion und Bedeutung*, Munich (Deutscher Taschenbuch Verlag) 1980

Blackshaw 2007
Gemma Blackshaw 'The Pathological Body: Modernist Strategising in Egon Schiele's Self-Portraiture', *Oxford Art Journal*, vol. 30 (2007), no. 3, pp. 377-401

Blackshaw 2013
Gemma Blackshaw, *Facing the Modern: The Portrait in Vienna 1900*, exh. cat., London (National Gallery/ Yale U. P.) 2013

Blackshaw and Topp 2009
Gemma Blackshaw and Leslie Topp, *Madness and Modernity Mental Illness and the Visual Arts in Vienna 1900*, London (Lund Humphries) 2009

Cernuschi 2002
Claude Cernuschi, *Re/Casting Kokoschka: Ethics and Aesthetics, Epistemology and Politics in Fin-de-Siècle Vienna*, Madison, NJ (Fairleigh Dickinson U.P.)/London (Associated University Presses) 2002

Comini 1973
Alessandra Comini, *Schiele in Prison*, New York (New York Graphic Society) 1973

Comini 1974
Alessandra Comini, *Egon Schiele's Portraits*, Berkeley (California U. P.) 1974

Dennis 2009
Kelly Dennis, *Art/Porn: A History of Seeing and Touching*, Oxford/New York (Berg) 2009

Faistauer 1923
Anton Faistauer, *Neue Malerei in Österreich*, Vienna (Amalthea Verlag) 1923

Foucault 1990
Michel Foucault, *The Will to Knowledge, The History of Sexuality: Volume One*, London (Penguin) 1990 (first published 1976)

Friedman 1967
Paul Friedman, *On Suicide: With Particular Reference to Suicide among Young Students. Discussions of the Vienna Psychoanalytic Society, 1910*, New York (International Universities Press) 1967

Gordon 2009
Rae Beth Gordon, *Dances with Darwin, 1875–1910: Vernacular Modernity in France*, Farnham (Ashgate) 2009

Gütersloh [1911]
Paris von Gütersloh, *Egon Schiele: Versuch einer Vorrede*, Vienna (Verlag Brüder Rosenbaum) n.d. [1911]

Hofmannsthal 1979
Hugo von Hofmannsthal, *Reden und Aufsätze I, 1891–1913*, Frankfurt am Main (S. Fischer) 1979

Hollein and Natter 2005
Max Hollein and Tobias G. Natter (eds.), *The Naked Truth: Klimt, Schiele and Other Scandals*, exh. cat., Schirn Kunsthalle, Frankfurt, and Leopold Museum, Vienna (Prestel) 2005

Husslein-Arco and Kallir 2011
Agnes Husslein-Arco and Jane Kallir (eds.), *Egon Schiele: Self-Portraits and Portraits*, Munich/London/ New York (Prestel) 2011

Hutter 1987
Heribert Hutter (ed.), *A.P. Gütersloh: Zum 100 Geburtstag*, Vienna (Österreichischer Kunst und Kulturverlag) 1987

Jensen 2001
Robert Jensen, 'A Matter of Professionalism: Marketing Identity in Fin-de-Siècle Vienna', in Beller 2001, pp. 195-219

Kallir 1998
Jane Kallir, *Egon Schiele. The Complete Works*, London (Thames & Hudson) 1998 (first published 1990)

Kallir 2003
Jane Kallir, ed. Ivan Vartanian, *Egon Schiele, Drawings and Watercolours*, London (Thames & Hudson) 2003

Kallir 2012
Jane Kallir, *Egon Schiele's Women*, Munich/London/ New York (Prestel) 2012

Karpfen 1921
Fritz Karpfen (ed.), *Das Egon Schiele Buch*, Vienna (Verlag der Wiener Graphischen Werkstätte) 1921

Knafo 1993
Danielle Knafo, *Egon Schiele: A Self in Creation: A Psychoanalytic Study of the Artist's Self-Portraits*, London (Associated University Presses) 1993

Leopold 1973
Rudolf Leopold, *Egon Schiele. Paintings, Watercolours, Drawings*, London (Phaidon) 1973

Leopold and Tretter 2008
Rudolf Leopold and Sandra Tretter (eds.), *Egon Schiele: Letters and Poems 1910–1912 from the Leopold Collection*, Munich (Prestel) 2008

Loos 1931
Adolf Loos, *Trotzdem*, Innsbruck (Brenner Verlag) 1931

McGrath 1974
William J. McGrath, *Dionysian Art and Populist Politics in Austria*, New Haven and London (Yale University Press) 1974

Müller and Tatzkow 2010
Melissa Müller and Monika Tatzkow (eds.), *Lost Lives, Lost Art: Jewish Collectors, Nazi Art Theft and the Quest for Justice*, London (Frontline Books) 2010

Müller-Tamm 1995
Pia Müller-Tamm (ed.), *Egon Schiele: Inszenierung und Identität*, Cologne (DuMont) 1995

Natter 2003
Tobias G. Natter, *Die Galerie Miethke: Eine Kunsthandlung im Zentrum der Moderne*, exh. cat., Jüdisches Museum der Stadt Wien, Vienna, 2003

Natter 2005
Tobias G. Natter, 'On the Limits of the Exhibitable: The Naked Body and Public Space in Viennese Art around 1900' in Hollein and Natter, pp. 17–42

Natter and Storch 2004
Tobias G. Natter and Ursula Storch (eds.), *Egon Schiele & Arthur Roessler. Der Künstler und sein Förderer: Kunst und Networking im frühen 20. Jahrhundert*, exh. cat., Vienna/Ostfildern-Ruit (Wien Museum/Hatje Cantz) 2004

Nead 1990
Lynda Nead, 'The Female Nude: Pornography, Art and Sexuality', *Signs*, vol. 15, no. 2 (Winter 1990), pp. 323-35

Nebehay 1979
Christian M. Nebehay, *Egon Schiele 1890–1918. Leben, Briefe, Gedichte*, Salzburg (Residenz Verlag) 1979

Nebel 1988
Cecile Nebel, *The Dark Side of Creativity: Blocks, Unfinished Works and the Urge to Destroy*, Troy (Whitston Publishing) 1988

Nickl and Schnitzler 1971
Therese Nickl und Heinrich Schnitzler (eds.), *Arthur Schnitzler: Jugend in Wien, Eine Autobiographie*, Munich (Deutscher Taschenbuch Verlag) 1971

Nietzsche 1954
Friedrich Nietzsche, *The Portable Nietzsche*, New York (Penguin) 1954

Nietzsche 1967
Friedrich Nietzsche, *The Will to Power*, New York (Vintage) 1967

Nietzsche 1973
Friedrich Nietzsche, *Beyond Good and Evil*, translated with an introduction and commentary by R.J. Hollingdale, London (Penguin) 1973

Nietzsche 1974
Friedrich Nietzsche, *The Gay Science*, translated by Walter Kaufmann, New York (Vintage Books) 1974

Nietzsche 1990
Friedrich Nietzsche, *Twilight of the Idols / The Anti-Christ*, translated by R.J. Hollingdale, introduction by Michael Tanner, London (Penguin) 1990

Nietzsche 2005
Friedrich Nietzsche, *The Anti-Christ, Ecce Homo, Twilight of the Idols, and Other Writings*, ed. Aaron Ridley and Judith Norman, translated by Judith Norman, New York (Cambridge U. P.) 2005

Pereña Sáez 2010
Helena Pereña Sáez, *Egon Schiele: Wahrnehmung, Indentität und Weltbild*, Marburg (Tectum) 2010

Ponstingl 2013
Michael Ponstingl, '"Die grosse Abwechslung der gebotenen Stellungen und Modelle ... wird jeden Künstler befriedigen": Die Geschäfte des Wiener Berufsfotografen Otto Schmidt mit dem Nackten', in *Die nackte Wahrheit und anderes: Aktfotografie um 1900*, exh. cat., Museum für Fotografie, Berlin, 2013, pp. 43–51

Price 2005
Renée Price (ed.), *Egon Schiele. The Ronald S. Lauder and Serge Sabarsky Collections*, exh. cat., Neue Galerie, Museum for German and Austrian Art, New York (Prestel) 2005

Roberts 1964
Keith Roberts [review of Schiele exhibition at Marlborough Fine Art, London, 1964], *The Burlington Magazine*, vol. 106, no. 741 (December 1964), p. 584

Roessler 1921
Arthur Roessler, *In Memoriam Egon Schiele*, Vienna (Richard Lanyi) 1921

Roessler 1922
Arthur Roessler, *Egon Schiele im Gefängnis: Aufzeichnungen und Zeichnungen*, Vienna/Leipzig (Carl Konegen) 1922

Schröder 1995
Klaus Albrecht Schröder, *Egon Schiele: Eros and Passion*, Munich/New York (Prestel) 1995

Schwartz 2012
Schwartz, 'Architecture and Crime: Adolf Loos and the Culture of the "Case"', *Art Bulletin*, vol. 94, no. 3 (September 2012), pp. 437-57

Solomon-Godeau 1986
Abigail Soloman-Godeau, 'The Legs of the Countess', *October*, vol. 39 (Winter 1986), pp. 65-108

Stark 1981
Gary D. Stark, 'Pornography, Society and the Law in Imperial Germany', *Peer Reviewed Articles*, Paper 12, 1981, pp. 200–29, retrieved 2 January 2014 from http://scholarworks.gvsu.edu/hst_articles/12

Steiner 2000
Reinhard Steiner, *Egon Schiele: The Midnight Soul of the Artist*, Cologne (Benedikt Taschen Verlag) 2000

Timms and Robertson 1990
Edward Timms and Ritchie Robertson (eds.), *Vienna 1900 from Altenberg to Wittgenstein* (*Austrian Studies*, vol. 1), Edinburgh (Edinburgh U. P.) 1990

Updike 1997
John Updike, 'Can Genitals Be Beautiful?', *New York Review of Books*, vol. 44, no. 19 (1997), pp. 10-12

Vergo 1993
Peter Vergo, *Art in Vienna 1898–1918: Klimt, Kokoschka, Schiele and their contemporaries*, London (Phaidon), 3rd rev. edn ,1993

Werkner 1994
Patrick Werkner (ed.), *Egon Schiele: Art, Sexuality, and Viennese Modernism*, Palo Alto, CA (Society for the Promotion of Science and Scholarship) 1994

Willsdon 1996
Clare A.P. Willsdon, 'Klimt's Beethoven Frieze: Goethe, Tempelkunst and the Fulfilment of Wishes', *Art History*, vol. 19, no. 1 (March 1996), pp. 44-73

Wischin 1994
Franz E. Wischin, *Die Stadt am blauen Fluß: Egon Schiele und Krumau*, Vienna (Wirtschaftstrend Zeitschriftenverlag) 1994

Wischin 1998
Franz Wischin, *'Ich Gefangener, schuldlos gestraft, gereinigt!': Kunst oder Kinderpornographie: die Affäre von Neulengbach 1912*, Vienna (Christian Brandstätter) 1998

Zweig 1970
Stefan Zweig, *Die Welt von Gestern*, Frankfurt (S. Fischer) 1970

PHOTOGRAPHIC CREDITS

BUDAPEST
© akg-images / Imagno: cat. 33

CAMBRIDGE, MASS
Photo: Imaging Department © President and Fellows of Harvard College, fig. 7

LINZ
© Photo Austrian Archives/Scala Florence: fig. 8

LONDON
© Christie's Images / The Bridgeman Art Library: cat. 26
© The Courtauld Gallery (Samuel Courtauld Trust, Princes Gate Bequest, 1978): fig. 31

MUNICH
© Staatliche Graphische Sammlung: cat. 35, 36

NUREMBERG
© Germanisches Nationalmuseum, Nuremberg. Foto: M. Runge: cat. 29

NEW YORK
© 2014. Digital image, The Museum of Modern Art, New York/Scala, Florence: cat. 11
© Galerie St. Etienne: cat. 31; figs. 11-15, 19

TULLN
© Gradisch collection, Egon Schiele Museum: fig. 4

VIENNA
© akg-images / Imagno: fig. 3,5
© Albertina, Vienna: p. 6, 11; figs. 1, 9, 20, 21, 28-30
© Photo Austrian Archives/Scala Florence: cat. 3, figs. 2, 25, 32, 37
© Photo Fine Art Images/Heritage Images/Scala Florence: figs. 16, 26
© Leopold Museum: cat. 1, 5, 8, 10, 13-14, 16, 17, 18, 19, 25, 27, 28, 32, 34, 37; figs. 6, 23, 24, 27, 33, 34, 36, 38
© OeNB: fig. 10
© Wien Museum: cat. 15

PRIVATE COLLECTION
© Christie's Images Ltd - ARTOTHEK: cat. 4
© 2014. Photo Austrian Archives/Scala Florence: cat. 22
© akg-images / Erich Lessing: fig. 22
© Private collection / The Bridgeman Art Library: fig. 35
© Private collection: cat. 2, 6, 7, 9, 12, 20, 21, 23, 24, 30, 38